THE AFRO-AMERICAN
AND THE
SECOND WORLD WAR

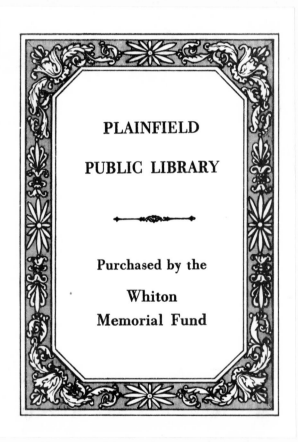

THE AFRO-AMERICAN
AND THE
SECOND WORLD WAR

Revised Edition

Neil A. Wynn

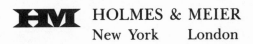

HOLMES & MEIER
New York   London

Second edition published 1993 by
Holmes & Meier Publishers, Inc.
30 Irving Place
New York, New York 10003

First edition published in the United States of America 1976 by Holmes & Meier

Library of Congress Cataloging in Publication Data

Wynn, Neil.
   The Afro-American and the Second World War.
   Revised Edition

   Bibliography: p.
   Includes index.
   1. World War, 1939–1945—Afro-Americans.
2. United States—Armed Forces—Afro-Americans.
3. United States—Race question.   4. Afro-
Americans—Civil rights.   I. Title.
D810.N4W93   1993   940.58'1503'96073
ISBN 0-8419-1333-1 (pbk.: alk. paper)

Manufactured in the United States of America

For Kate Westoby,
Jeff and Robin
who taught me so much

Contents

Acknowledgements

'Draftees' Prayer' from *Baltimore Afro-American*, January 16, 1943, is quoted by courtesy of Afro-American Newspapers; Witter Bynner's 'Defeat' from *Take Away The Darkness*, New York 1947, by permission of Alfred A. Knopf, Inc.; Langston Hughes' 'The Ballad of Margie Polite' and 'Roland Hayes Beaten' from *One Way Ticket*, and 'Peace' from *The Panther and the Lash*, by permission of Harold Ober Associates Inc. and Alfred A. Knopf, Inc., © 1949 and © 1948 by Langston Hughes. Acknowledgement is due to the US Department of Labor, Bureau of Labor Statistics, for permission to quote tables from *Negroes in the United States: Their Employment and Economic Status*; and to the US Public Health Service for statistics from *Public Health Reports*.

Preface to the Revised Edition

When I first began work on this subject in 1968, there was surprisingly little material available in print. Filling the apparent gap led to the production of a PhD and ultimately to the first publication of this book. Even in those days a reader of the manuscript queried my use of 'Afro-American', claiming never to have heard the term. Today much has changed: 'African-American' is in general use and a student beginning research in this area would find not only my work, but books and journal articles by Richard Dalfiume, Russell Buchanan, Lee Finkle, Harvard Sitkoff, and others, not to mention the many chapters on the subject in general studies of American society in wartime. The publication of a new edition of my book enables me to take account of this extensive scholarship and provides an opportunity to reconsider some of my earlier conclusions. Fifty years after the event we are perhaps now better placed to arrive at an overall assessment of World War II's significance for black Americans.

The search for 'turning points' in history is a dangerous business. Writing in the 1960s and 1970s, when civil rights action and reform seemed to promise so much, it was easy to see the 1940s as the moment when positive change was set in motion. Now, when views of the sixties are more pessimistic and when the limits of reform are more apparent, it may seem necessary to qualify judgements on the importance of World War II. I have tried to do this in the Epilogue in which I summarise some of the more recent findings with updated bibliographic information in the footnotes.

The use of oral history must rank as one of the most important developments which have had an influence on the subject since 1973, and I have tried to incorporate some of the views of the participants in my summary. Overall, these expressions reinforce my original conclusion that the contribution by blacks to the war effort was considerable and that the war had an equally significant effect on African-Americans, at both a personal and a general level. Wartime social and economic changes certainly helped to shape the growing black consciousness and white awareness of the racial issue. But as John Hope Franklin recalled in 'The Living and Reliving of World War II' (*Journal of American History,* 77, 2, September 1990), it was, and continues to be, an ongoing struggle.

Neil A. Wynn
University of Glamorgan
1993

Preface to the First Edition

This book is the product of a study of black American history over a number of years and a parallel interest in the effects of war on society. In combining the two subjects and in concentrating on Afro-Americans during World War II, I do not intend that the war be seen as more important than any other one event; rather, I want to fill in the gap between the Depression years and the 1950s which has long existed in black history. It is essential that the sense of historical continuity and the interconnectedness of events be maintained, for just as the 'Negro revolt' of the 1960s cannot be understood unless seen from the perspective of wartime change, neither can the full impact of the war be appreciated unless seen against the background of the Depression or even earlier developments.

Throughout the book I use the terms 'Afro-American' and 'black' interchangeably and in preference to 'Negro.' This was, and still is, a matter of debate, but for me 'Afro-American' sums up the situation of the black man in America. It indicates his African origins, heritage and culture; it also recognizes his American-ness. 'Black' is more accurate in the sense that it is the opposite of white, but it also took on an emotional significance during the 1960s which is still valid today.

My work on this subject has been enormously influenced by my involvement in the preparation and teaching of the Open University history course 'War and Society.' My former colleagues on that course, Clive Emsley, Chris Harvie and John Golby, provided many insights from their own subjects. Richard Middleton of the Music Department gave me a great deal of help and guidance on the section relating to jazz and the blues. A number of other people at other institutions gave advice and encouragement, and suggested areas of study. They include Dr Don Bain, Professor Thomas Cripps, Professor Richard M. Dalfiume, Professor John Hope Franklin, Professor John Milligan, Dr Sean Murray, Professor L. D. Reddick, Mr Bayard Rustin, Professor George Shepperson, Mr Ralph Watkins and Mrs Walter White. My former supervisor and professor,

Arthur Marwick, has been a constant source of help and encouragement.

Research posts and financial assistance from the Open University and the History Department of the State University of New York at Buffalo, and research time at the Polytechnic of Wales, made it possible for me to write this book. But my research would not have been possible without the assistance and tolerance of many librarians including those at the Open University, SUNY at Buffalo and the Polytechnic of Wales.

Special thanks must go to Mr Bernard Chertok of the Sherman Grinberg Film Library, Mrs Eileen Bowser of the Museum of Modern Art, Mr James Moore and Mr Bill Murphy of the Audiovisual Section of the National Archives, and Mr Ted Troll of Hearst Metrotone News Inc. Mr Delli Donne, Mr Hohman, Mr Taylor and Mr James Walker all gave me the benefit of their expertise in the National Archives. Mr Ernest Kaiser of the Schomburg Collection, Mrs Dorothy B. Porter of the Moorland-Spingarn Collection, and Mr Donald Gallup of the Yale University Collection of American Literature gave me a free hand in their libraries. Mrs Ann Allen Shockley allowed me to use material in the Charles S. Johnson Collection at Fisk University and Mrs Jean Y. Webber of the AFL-CIO Library sent me information on blacks and the unions.

Finally, grateful thanks to Mrs Sue Boss, Mrs Sue Power and Mrs Lynn Shott for typing various versions and parts of the book. Margaret Wynn proofread, checked notes, and provided moral and even financial support over a long period of years.

Neil A. Wynn
Polytechnic of Wales

THE AFRO-AMERICAN
AND THE
SECOND WORLD WAR

1

War, Society and the Afro-American

Attitudes toward war and the study of war change with the times. Until very recently the social history of America during the 1940s was ignored: attention was concentrated instead on either the Depression and New Deal or the foreign policy implications of World War II and the subsequent Cold War. The same gap existed in Afro-American history as the student jumped from the Harlem renaissance to the 1954 Supreme Court decision and the civil rights movements of the 1960s. Now, perhaps in response to the domestic repercussions of the war in Vietnam, there are a number of studies of the American home front during World War II. Richard Lingeman, Richard Polenberg and Geoffrey Perrett have dealt specifically with the war years while other historians, including K. L. Nelson, Ralph de Bedts and R. S. Kirkendall have treated the same period but in wider contexts.[1] Several writers have also recognized the significance of the war as a force for change in the lives of black Americans. Most have followed Richard Dalfiume in seeing the war years as 'the "forgotten years" of the Negro revolution' and have concentrated primarily on the attitudes of blacks, their rising militance and increased expectations.[2] Little detailed treatment has been given to the underlying and fundamental alterations which occurred in the economic, social, political and cultural life of Afro-Americans during the war. Moveover, questions about the nature of war and the manner in which it can bring about social change have been left unanswered. In this respect an examination of some theories of war and social change, and their relevance to black Americans in wars prior to World War II, can provide some insights.

One approach to the interrelationship between war and social change has been suggested by Arthur Marwick.[3] In his 'four tier model' Marwick argued that war brings *destruction* and *disruption*, *tests* existing institutions and leads on occasion to their transformation or collapse, necessitates *participation* of underprivileged groups, and is a colossal *psychological* experience. All four tiers or dimensions can be applied to American and

Afro-American history, but in respect of the latter, two tiers seem particularly relevant. First, the idea that war is the supreme test of a country's military, economic, political and social institutions. These institutions either prove able to meet the challenge of war or adapt to do so: alternatively, as in Russia in 1917, they disintegrate. Segregation and discrimination have always been part of America's institutions and as such were subject to the test of war. As we shall see, however, the extent of such tests varied from one war to another.

More obviously relevant to black history is the second idea, that war involves the participation of underprivileged groups and therefore leads to the possibility of social gains. This is a simplified statement of the Military Participation Ratio theory first posited by the sociologist Stanislas Andreski in *Military Organization and Society* (1954). Andreski stated, in quite mathematical terms, that as the proportion of the total population in the armed forces, i.e. the military participation ratio, increased so did the extent of social welfare. While the problems of quantification and measurement involved in such a theory are enormous, the view that participation in a country's war effort, whether military or industrial, can lead to economic and social gains and increased selfconsciousness and political awareness is little more than common sense. As Marwick expressed it, war, especially total war, 'needs someone to do the fighting, and someone to furnish the weapons and food: those who participate in the war effort have to be rewarded . . . '[4] The rewards can be not only the result of direct or 'guided' government actions (such as perhaps was the case with the extension of the franchise to women in Britain and America after World War I), but also as a result of 'unguided' change resulting from participation itself, such as increased purchasing power and improved standards of living resulting from work in war industries.

Underlying both ideas is the relationship between citizenship and the defense of the state. In modern democracies it is taken for granted that it is the duty of the citizen to defend his (and in more recent times, her) country. Nowhere has this been more clearly demonstrated than in the United States where law and tradition require that citizens or intending citizens serve in the armed forces. In 1863, during the Civil War, US officials stipulated that any alien who had formally declared his intention of becoming a citizen and had exercised political rights under state law was subject to conscription. Those who claimed exemption as foreigners had to leave the country within 65 days. In 1941 no resident alien was excluded, and although exemption could be requested, to do so meant forswearing American citizenship.

In return for armed service, the individual is guaranteed certain rights: a say in government, protection of the laws, and so on. This type of reasoning was one of the justifications for the lowering of the voting age to eighteen in America and Britain, and just as the argument can be applied to those under the age of twenty-one, or to women, so too to Afro-Americans. However, while it follows that members of a minority group called to serve their country in times of war can ask to be recognized as first-class citizens, it also follows that the state's refusal to permit armed service, or restrictions upon such service, can provide a rationale for denying equal rights. This issue arose in every war which America fought (apart from the Mexican war of 1848) as blacks sought to serve in the armed forces and secure the rewards which they expected.

During the war for independence, the question of armed service by blacks was further complicated by the contradiction between the revolutionary philosophies of the time and the existence of slavery. The position of the colonists as oppressed subjects *and* as slave-owners created a dilemma. While some argued that the 'inalienable rights of man' applied equally to blacks and whites, others denied it or avoided the issue, preferring to blame King George III for slavery. To allow blacks to participate in the struggle against Britain would have implied equality of the races. More important, the idea of arming blacks, whether slave or free, raised the specter of slave revolts. The question was solved by Washington when he took command of the Continental Army in 1775: ignoring the active part played by blacks at Lexington, Concord and Bunker Hill, he forbade the enlistment of black soldiers.

The situation would probably have remained unchanged but for the proclamation issued by the deposed governor of Virginia, Lord Dunmore. In November 1775 he offered freedom to 'all indentured servants, Negroes or others'[5] who took up arms with the loyalists. Here was an invitation for slaves to rise against their masters, the very thing the colonists feared. To counter this offer, the Americans liberalized their own policies to allow both free blacks and slaves to enlist in the Continental Army; in return, slaves who served were promised their freedom. This change in attitude was further encouraged by the necessities of war.

As the conflict dragged on whites became increasingly reluctant to serve outside their states, or to serve at all in a war which seemed endless. The disastrous winter spent in Valley Forge was followed by large scale desertion, and as a result of the general manpower shortage black enlistments were increased. Only Georgia and South Carolina refused to use black soldiers, and of the 300,000 men who fought the British approximately 5000 were black.

Several thousand slaves were freed as a reward for their services. However, those that secured their liberty were fortunate, for despite the general loyalty of blacks and the pleas of antislavery campaigners, slavery remained firmly entrenched in the South and was recognized in the Constitution. Any ruling on the slave trade was to be delayed until after 1808. Although the war, the theories of the rights of man, and economic circumstances led to the end of slavery in the North, even there participation did not win equality for blacks. Once the emergency was over, blacks were not only excluded from the militias, but also gradually separated from the white community by law and custom. The troublesome contradiction between the revolutionary philosophies and the actual subordination of those of African descent was solved by the commonly accepted view that the black was less than a man.

Not until the Civil War did the question of black participation in the armed forces again reach any serious proportions. During the second war with Britain in 1812 both sides once more offered freedom to slaves who served in the forces, and many fought in both armies and navies. However, most were returned to their masters once the war had ended, and the Treaty of Ghent provided for the mutual restoration of properties, including slaves. The active part played by Afro-Americans in the defense of the republic did nothing to deter the growth of slavery, and as the nineteenth century progressed it became a continual source of conflict between North and South. Although the Civil War was fought to prevent the disintegration of the Union, slavery and the position of the Afro-American was a central issue.

President Lincoln attempted from the first to prevent slavery from becoming *the* issue between North and South, and he continued to do so even after war broke out in 1861. Black volunteers for armed service were turned away for fear of jeopardizing the loyalty of the slave-holding border states of Delaware, Maryland, Kentucky and Missouri. Many white Northerners, including military officers, felt that Afro-Americans would make poor soldiers, and like Lincoln they thought that arming blacks would turn the war into a struggle over slavery, a commitment few were prepared to make. For exactly that reason the federal government refused to take a stand on the issue of fugitive slaves from the South. Until early 1862 those who crossed the Union lines were returned to their owners and any attempt by Federal officers to arm runaways was quickly nullified by the President.

The Confederacy actually recognized the military value of Afro-Americans before the North. Faced with manpower shortages from the start, the South was quick to use slaves in noncombatant roles in order to free able-bodied whites for military service. Thousands of slaves provided the muscle and backbone of the Confederate Army, building forts, repairing bridges and railroads, and working as cooks and general laborers. By 1864 the Confederacy was even prepared to consider arming slaves and such a move was authorized in 1865. It was then too late: the war was over and the South defeated.

A change in policy only came in the North after a series of defeats, heavy casualties, and a campaign by black and white abolitionists for the use of black troops. In July 1862 Congress authorized the President to employ black soldiers and in 1863, 'as a fit and necessary war measure,' Lincoln issued the Emancipation Proclamation and called for black volunteers. By the end of the war almost 200,000 had fought in the Union Army while another 300,000 had acted as servants and laborers; almost 29,000 served in the Union Navy. But while blacks were finally allowed to serve, they were not regarded as equals.

Segregated in all-black regiments, Afro-Americans were, until 1864, paid under half the amount received by white soldiers. While discrimination limited the number of black officers to less than a hundred, whites who commanded black regiments, such as Thomas 'Wentworth Higginson, were looked down upon or ostracized by their former West Point colleagues. Even in combat there was no equality, and the mortality rate among blacks was almost 40 per cent higher than among white soldiers. This was partially due to inferior equipment, conditions and medical attention, but it was also due to the attitudes of some Confederates to black soldiers. In April 1864 black soldiers, civilians, women and children were massacred at Fort Pillow, Tennessee; in the same month wounded prisoners of the First Kansas Colored Volunteers were killed by rebel troops at Poison Springs, Arkansas.[6]

Despite these limitations on their service, the Civil War did bring gains for the Afro-Americans. Future participation in the military was guaranteed under the Army Reorganization Act of 1866 which established four segregated, black, regular Army units—the 9th and 10th Cavalry and the 24th and 25th Infantry. More immediately important was the end of slavery and the pledge of voting and citizenship rights under the Thirteenth, Fourteenth and Fifteenth Amendments to the Constitution. Although the result of radical Republican dominance in Congress, these measures were also the logical outcome of wartime emancipation and the use of blacks in the forces. However, the gains of the 1860s proved shortlived, and service in the Indian and Spanish American wars notwithstanding, by the end of the nineteenth century blacks in the South (90 per cent of the total black population) were subject to physical discrimination, disenfranchisement and economic deprivation.

After the end of Reconstruction in the 1870s both the American government and people lost interest in the plight of the Afro-American and became more concerned with industrial growth, westward expansion and imperialism. Racial prejudice increased during the latter part of the nineteenth century, encouraged by imperialism with its justification of the white man's burden, and by the pseudoscientific writings of the period which confirmed the superiority of the Aryan race. In the 1890s Southern states began to pass the Jim Crow laws which first restricted black voting rights and later introduced segregation into most aspects of life: transport, work, recreation, education and health facilities. As C. Vann Woodward pointed out in *The Strange Career of Jim Crow* (1955), this trend continued in the years immediately preceding World War I. Progressivism, when it came, did little for blacks, and under Woodrow Wilson's 'New Freedom' the Afro-American actually suffered setbacks.

Wilson was himself a Southerner who believed in the separation of the races. As president of Princeton he had barred blacks from attending the university; as President of the United States he delighted in telling 'darky' stories to his Cabinet—five of whom were also from the South. More serious was the introduction of segregation to government departments in the national capital and the refusal to make traditional black diplomatic appointments. But even if he had been concerned with the situation of black Americans, with the outbreak of war in Europe Wilson's attention was increasingly diverted from domestic matters. As Kelly Miller, Dean of Howard University, was later to observe, Wilson reversed the old motto: for him 'charity began abroad rather than at home.'[7]

Blacks themselves were in no position to demand change in the pre-war years. With a predominantly rural and ill-educated black population there was not the basis for a strong civil rights organization. The pre-eminence of Booker T. Washington, with his public emphasis, at least, on racial separation, evolutionary change and vocational training for his race, encouraged acceptance of existing patterns between blacks and whites. Although his views were increasingly challenged by men like the Boston journalist William Monroe Trotter and the writer and historian W. E. B. DuBois, Washington's counsels still held sway, even after his death in 1915. New bodies like the National Association for the Advancement of Colored People (NAACP), formed in 1909, or the National Urban League, set up in 1911, were still in their infancy, trying to formulate policies and establish themselves when America entered World War I in 1917.

The preconditions for change were not promising, and given the weakness of the black population and the dominant attitudes among whites, it is not surprising that Afro-Americans met opposition to their requests for equal treatment in the war effort. Black volunteers were accepted only as long as places remained in the four black Army regiments; once those places were filled, they were turned away. Despite the past records of blacks in military service, many whites still felt that they made poor soldiers, that equal service would degrade white troops, or that blacks might use their military training and weapons at home. Senator Vardaman of Mississippi, for example, opposed universal conscription because 'millions of Negroes who will come under the measure will be armed [and] I know of no greater menace to the South than this.'[8] However, the Selective Service Act of May 1917 did not exclude blacks and almost three million were registered under the Act. Because of discrimination by certain draft boards on deferment, nearly 31 per cent (some 370,000) were drafted compared to 26 per cent of white registrants. This practice continued in military life and the range of service open to blacks remained limited.

In the Navy, black men could work only as messmen, cooks, or coal-heavers; they were barred entirely from the Marine Corps, Coastguard and the Army Aviation Corps. Although in theory all branches of the Army were open to them, in practice some 380,000 of the 400,000 black soldiers were members of Services of Supply regiments, acting as stevedores, drivers, engineers and laborers. Only a small number saw combat duty, and then beside French troops who had had experience of dealing with colonial forces of their own.

Even in such limited roles, blacks were subjected to indignity and insult. At Camp Hill in Virginia during the bitter winter of 1917–18, black soldiers lived in tents without blankets or stoves, and with few facilities for medical attention the death rate among the trainees was high. Many training camps were located in the South where soldiers had to accept local Jim Crow laws and suffer harassment from white civilians. Within the camps they were often maligned by their own officers, many of whom were white Southerners chosen because they 'would understand the Negro temperament.'[9] (Only after protests from civil rights bodies was a segregated black officer training camp established, but there were still only 1200 black officers at the end of the war.) In Houston, Texas in November 1917, following a number of clashes between whites and black soldiers, members of the all-black 24th Infantry were involved in a race riot in which seventeen whites died. Sixty-four black soldiers were accused of murder and after a one-day trial thirteen were sentenced to death and the rest to life imprisonment.

Even overseas, added to the hazards of the trenches, blacks found discrimination. While the French population was often prepared to treat the black soldier as a social equal, such attitudes were discouraged by the Americans. In August 1918, in a secret memorandum, the French liaison officer attached to the American HQ warned his compatriots against dealing with blacks 'on the same plane as with the white American.' He also suggested that blacks should not be commended too highly in front of white Americans. Such was the American irritation at fraternizing between the races that in Britain white troops were reported to have reacted violently towards interracial couples.[10]

Despite the many barriers in their way, black troops did serve with some valor and distinction. Three regiments of the black 93rd Infantry were awarded the Croix de Guerre, as were more than a hundred individual black soldiers. Such records, however, tended to be forgotten in American military circles. Instead, the collapse and disintegration of a regiment of blacks from the 92nd Division was remembered and emphasized, even though a subsequent investigation blamed inexperience, poor leadership and lack of artillery cover. Similarly, rumours of inefficiency, of numerous incidents of rape and disorder, persisted long after the war—again despite evidence to the contrary. While blacks were given few opportunities to demonstrate their equality, real or supposed cases of poor performance confirmed the prejudices of many whites.

If there was little change within the armed forces, there was much more on the domestic front—but more as a consequence of spontaneous and 'unguided' change than of any official action. The most important and dramatic of these was the 'great migration' of blacks from the South to the North. The demand for labor to meet the expansion of industry during the war, coupled with the almost complete stop in European immigration, added a pull to the already existing pressure of poverty and discrimination in the South. The slow but steady movement of blacks from the South in the twenty years preceding the war now turned into a flood. Estimates of the numbers involved vary from 150,000 to over two million, but a more likely figure lies somewhere between 400,000 and 600,000. Some of the wartime migrants returned home following the peace, but even so the black population in the North rose from 1,036,000 in 1910 to 1,551,000 in 1920. Over 61,000 blacks entered Chicago alone, and it was to major cities that most of them went.[11] While the migration became one of the major social issues of the day, destroying the idea of race as a purely Southern problem, some 77 per cent of the black population still lived in the South in 1940, and as we shall see, a more diverse movement occurred during World War II.

Although not organized in any official way, the migration during World War I was encouraged by letters from earlier migrants, by appeals in the black newspaper the *Chicago Defender*, and by labor agents from Northern industries. While many of the new arrivals found that they had been misled by the labor agents or exaggerated advertisements, there was a considerable demand for workers and it was not too difficult to find emplovment. Both the *Chicago Defender* and the National Urban League acted as clearing houses for job information, and with or without such guidance 'some 255,000 blacks found new jobs in the wake of the war emergency.'[12] The conditions of employment were, letters from migrants suggested, much better than those in the South. Blacks spoke of daily wages of six to eight dollars a day, often the equivalent of a week's wages in the South; in Chicago the average rate of pay was 50 cents an hour compared to 75 cents *a day* in the South. The type of job available to Afro-American workers was also better than before as they secured their first foothold in industry. As semi-skilled and clerical jobs opened up there was a shift away from traditional types of employment: in 1910 in Chicago 51 per cent of black men worked in service industries; by 1920 this had dropped to 28 per cent. Black women also made some progress, replacing white women (themselves replacing white men) in the textile, clothing, food and tobacco industries. Between 1910 and 1920 the number of black women in manufacturing and mechanized production rose from 67,937 to 104,983. Little wonder that the *Chicago Defender* could say 'The opportunity we have longed for is here. . . . The war has given us a place upon which to stand.'[13]

The gains for both sexes were not, however, without their limits. For men, the majority of jobs were in the unskilled sectors of industry and concentrated in a few fields such as iron and steel, meat packing, shipbuilding and the automobile industry. For black women restrictions still applied, and the chief source of employment, even for those with an education, was domestic service. Moreover, gains made in industry during the war proved to be tenuous. During the recession of 1919–20 there were massive layoffs and the wholesale displacement of black workers, and although some jobs were regained later in the twenties, their vulnerability persisted and was demonstrated again during the Depression.

The alteration in population and employment patterns among Afro-Americans caused some reaction from their white countrymen. During the war there were many indications that the American people wished to prevent change, particularly in racial affairs. The psychological impact of the war led to a heightened sense of national unity, but with an intensification of in-group feelings reflected in hostility and intolerance towards foreigners or racially 'un-American' groups. The Ku Klux Klan, revived in 1915, grew in strength during the war and was only a part of the widespread attack on minority ethnic and racial communities. Blacks specifically were the victims of increasing violence throughout the war years as whites fought to prevent changes in the status quo.

The migration of blacks from the South, at first welcomed as a possible cure for that region's racial problems, soon attracted mounting opposition from all parts of the country. In some areas of the South whites, concerned about the loss of their labor supply, attempted to prevent blacks from leaving, outlawed labor agents, and tried to discourage the sale and distribution of the *Chicago Defender*. In the North, too, the arrival of large numbers of black migrants was viewed with increasing alarm. While members of the middle classes were concerned about the effects on their cities, labor organizations feared that blacks would be used as strikebreakers or that employers were deliberately creating a surplus in manpower in order to undermine existing conditions. Conflict over jobs and housing led to a riot in East St Louis in 1917 in which at least forty blacks were killed, and other smaller clashes occurred in New York and Philadelphia. In Chicago, the city which received the largest influx of Afro-Americans, there were more than twenty-four bomb attacks on homes occupied by blacks, or on real estate agents who sold to blacks, between 1917 and 1919.[14]

This violence continued in the immediate post-war years and during the 'red summer' of 1919 there were more than twenty race riots in different cities across the country. The worst took place in Chicago where 38 people were killed and over 500 injured in a riot which lasted six days. Lynchings, which had risen in number from 38 in 1917 to 64 in 1918, reached a height of 83 in 1919. Among the victims of such attacks were a number of black soldiers, some of whom were still in uniform.

By and large, the federal government remained unresponsive to this deteriorating situation. Despite repeated requests from blacks for some action on race relations, President Wilson did not speak out against mob violence until July 1918—and then without mentioning the racial context. Yet the government could not completely ignore the Afro-Americans during the war. In October 1917, following the East St Louis riot, Secretary of War Newton D. Baker appointed Emmett J. Scott as Special Assistant to advise on racial matters. Scott, former secretary to Booker T. Washington, did initiate action against discriminatory draft boards, but his chief function was to provide liaison between the government and black leaders, tour training camps and investigate complaints. His main duty was to handle public relations, as was also the case with the second black appointment, that of George E. Haynes, a professor at Fisk University, as Director of Negro Economics within the Department of Labor. Like Scott, Haynes concentrated on organizing meetings and committees to discuss racial problems. In some cases such bodies did help to place black workers in employment, and Haynes himself arranged several black appointments within Labor Department bureaus. However, he attempted little reform, and even within federal offices discrimination continued. Both posts were a considerable departure from the Wilson administration's previous lily-white policy, but they were entirely war-oriented morale-boosting exercises designed to increase contributions to the war effort rather than bring long-term changes in race relations.

Given the prevailing racial attitudes of whites in the years before and during the war (and given that slavery had only ceased to exist some fifty years earlier), it is not remarkable that so little change should occur during the war. Even sympathetic whites tended to speak of Afro-Americans in the stereotyped terms of 'uncle,' 'Hottentot,' 'pickaninny' and as 'boys who do not grow up even under shellfire.' An Army Signal Corps film *Training of Colored Troops*, presumably made for recruiting purposes, is full of such images.[15] The dramatized story of a black soldier from induction to training, the film concentrates on comic aspects and includes shots of a watermelon eating competition and, more frequently, blacks dancing to their band. The soldier concerned is, of course, joining the Engineers. More encouraging were the attempts of some Southerners to counteract racial tensions by forming interracial committees. During the violence of 1919 some of these committees came together under the Commission on Interracial Co-operation headed by a white Southerner, Will Alexander. Although attacking only discrimination and not segregation, the Commission was, until World War II, the chief voice of Southern moderation. Sadly, it was struggling against the tide in the 1920s and could only reach a small number of people. For the majority of white Americans black participation in the war effort was a fact to be ignored or resented. Rather significantly, the major study of the impact of the war on America, Frederic Paxson's three volume *American Democracy and the World War* (1936, 1939, 1948), has the very barest mention of blacks with no reference at all to their role in the armed forces or industry, nor any comment on wartime racial violence.

Afro-Americans had hoped for much more than this, and they had been only too willing to support the war effort and demonstrate their loyalty. While the *Chicago Defender* could demand 'let us, too, make America safe for democracy,' it could also, the following week, say that the black man's duty was 'to keep a stiff upper lip and make the most out of the situation.' Refusing to 'rock the boat,' the *Defender* urged blacks to set aside their grievances until the war was over, for 'If we again demonstrate our loyalty in the face of injustices . . . those injustices will disappear.'[16] This view was shared by W. E. B. DuBois, the editor of the NAACP's magazine *The Crisis*. As the *Defender* had done, DuBois suggested that country should come before rights in the Afro-American's order of priorities. Liberation would come from participation: 'Out of this war will rise, too, an American Negro with the right to vote and the right to work and the right to live without insult.' It was this belief which led him to call 'close ranks' in July 1918, and to ask blacks to forget their complaints while the war was on—racial prejudice would then disappear naturally as a result of their service beside whites.[17]

Some black leaders, including Emmett Scott and Booker T. Washington's successor at Tuskegee, Robert Russa Moton, were even less critical of racial policies during the war than DuBois, but the difference between the 'accommodationist' stance and that of other blacks was in reality only slight. Basically both camps maintained, implicitly or otherwise, that wholehearted support for the war effort would bring rewards. Most blacks accepted this view—a fact demonstrated by their willingness to volunteer and their contribution of more than $250,000 in war loans. Among the very few to oppose participation were A. Philip Randolph and Chandler Owen, editors of the socialist journal *Messenger*. They argued that the war was a capitalist venture from which only capitalists would benefit, and they repeatedly pointed out the discrimination and segregation faced by blacks in the war effort. 'Since when,' they asked, 'has the subject race come out of a war with its rights and privileges accorded for such participation?'[18]

In the minority during the war, Randolph and Owen were more in line with the general black mood once the war had ended as other Afro-Americans saw that their hopes of recognition were not to be fulfilled. The disillusion which set in following the post-war racial violence was best summed up by a young black war veteran (who had been chased by a mob in Chicago) when he asked,

Had the ten months I spent in France been all in vain? Were those white crosses over the dead bodies of those dark-skinned boys lying in Flanders fields for naught? Was democracy merely a hollow sentiment? What had I done to deserve such treatment?[19]

In February 1919 the *Chicago Defender* found it hard to believe that men who had fought in Europe would 'tamely and meekly submit to a program of lynching, burning and social ostracism'; and following the Chicago riot, in which 15 whites were among the 38 dead, the paper commented that blacks were 'no longer content to turn the left cheek when smitten upon the right.'[20] DuBois was equally bitter. His slogan for the post-war period was 'We *return*, we *return from fighting*, we *return fighting*,' and privately he remarked that he had not realized war's 'wide impotence as a method of social reform.'[21]

But the war had brought some change: the black man was not prepared now to stand idly by, the passive victim of racialism. The 'new Negro' had arrived, and during the riots in Chicago, Washington, D.C. and other cities there were many instances of blacks retaliating against white attacks. This mixture of despair and militancy was best captured by the ebullient and arrogant Marcus Garvey whose Universal Negro Improvement Association, with its stress on black pride, the African heritage *and* racial separation seized the imagination of many among the mass of ordinary blacks. Financial ineptitude, corruption among his supporters, opposition from more elitist black leaders, and harassment from the government led to Garvey's downfall in 1925 and subsequent deportation in 1927. Without him the UNIA broke up into a number of splinter organizations. Like the UNIA the 'new Negro' was not in evidence for long, and for most Afro-Americans 'normalcy' meant a return to the pre-war situation.

If World War I, the first 'total' war, brought little reward for black participation, World War II was to have a much more decisive impact. Indeed, it had a much greater influence on American society generally than any previous conflict—including, perhaps, the Civil War. Certainly one recent writer has argued that the war 'radically altered the character of American society and challenged its most durable values.'[22] While this view may still be subject to debate, it is now clear that it was one of the major forces in shaping mid-twentieth century America.

World War II touched on the lives of nearly every American citizen even though the country was not subject to direct attack, invasion or bombing. Lasting twice as long as World War I, it cost 330 billion dollars, involved over 14 million men and women in the armed forces, and led to the addition of another 10 million people to the labor force. The necessity for efficient organization, mobilization and production *tested* the adaptability of American institutions and attitudes, challenging old ideas in a way which exceeded even the New Deal. Using his authority as Commander-in-

Chief, Roosevelt extended the power of the presidency in foreign affairs and domestic matters to unprecedented limits. Under the War Powers Acts of 1941 and 1942 the President was given complete power to allocate priorities and resources and to create new agencies with executive functions as he thought fit. Using this power, he formed numerous committees and agencies, involving the federal government in almost every aspect of civilian life.

While the War Production Board supervised the conversion of industry, allocation of materials and production quotas, the War Manpower Commission handled the distribution of manpower to industry and the armed forces. The National War Labor Board adjudicated in labor disputes and to some extent controlled wages; price and rationing controls were dealt with by the Office of Price Administration; transport was directed by the Office of Defense Transportation; and the Office of Scientific Research and Development initiated and co-ordinated research in universities, colleges, private laboratories and industry. It was not just capitalism that was state-managed—the ordinary citizen found that government control extended beyond the economic and military necessities of waging war and into the press, radio, movies and the mails. Nearly 10 million civilians were themselves involved in the Office of Civilian Defense, preparing for attacks which never came but nonetheless participating in the war effort.

With this rapid growth of new government bodies and the overall concentration on the war effort, the importance of the New Deal agencies waned. The Civilian Conservation Corps, the Works Progress Administration and the National Youth Administration all ceased to exist, while other agencies were either run down or swallowed up by wartime committees. In at least one sense, much of the New Deal was no longer needed—the growth of industry and the armed forces during the war meant that the problem was no longer to find jobs for men, but to find the men for all the jobs. By 1943 unemployment was down to a mere 800,000 and by 1945 the number of people employed had reached 64 million. Although attempts to introduce some form of conscription of labor under a National Service Act failed, such measures were hardly necessary. The war not only revealed an abundance of economic resources, which enabled the United States to produce as much in 1944 as the Axis and other Allied powers put together, it also demonstrated that such an effort could be mounted without serious civilian sacrifice.[23]

Even rationing, when it came, did not impose great hardship. Gasoline rationing began in 1942 and was soon followed by controls on sugar, coffee, meat, butter and canned foods. There were shortages of consumer goods—whiskey had almost completely disappeared by 1944—but these were more of an inconvenience than a cause of suffering. Americans were still better fed and better clothed than any of their European counterparts, and if anything the war resulted in an improved overall standard of living.

Participation in the war effort brought a number of rewards, the most obvious being full employment. With increased employment and a tightening labor situation, salaries and wages also increased. In 1939 the average weekly wage was $23.86; by 1945 it was $44.39. Even allowing for the rise in the cost of living, average earnings increased by about 50 per cent. There were still many people with poverty level incomes, but the number declined significantly during the war. There was also a degree of social levelling: the incomes of the lowest paid groups rose by 68 per cent while those of the highest rose by 20 per cent.[24] Overall, Americans were much better off than they had been for some time, and that new affluence was to continue in the postwar years.

Organized labor benefited from the war effort. Manpower shortages strengthened bargaining positions, and the increase in employment led to an expansion in union membership. By 1945 the number of people in unions had risen by 6 million to almost 15 million. The importance of labor during the war led to the inclusion of union representatives on government boards and their involvement in local management-labor committees. In an attempt to limit industrial strife the War Labor Board introduced a 'maintenance of membership' scheme in 1942 which virtually granted unions the right to closed shops. But on the other hand, labor had to make some sacrifices to the war effort. Restrictions on the number of hours worked were set aside, and while workers in defense industries worked a minimum of 48 hours as of February 1943, average weekly hours rose to 45. For some employees 50 or even 60 hours became the weekly norm.

More serious for labor than the increase in the length of the working week were the restrictions placed on collective bargaining. As early as December 1941 the unions agreed to hold their right to strike in abeyance and generally that pledge was kept. However, in 1942 the War Labor Board in the 'little steel formula' pegged wage rises to the cost of living in order to try to curtail inflation, and by 1943 a number of unions were attempting to secure more. Following a series of strikes in 1943, the most serious being that of the coal miners, various states passed laws restricting certain union activities. In June 1943 Congress followed suit and over Roosevelt's veto passed the War Labor Disputes Act (Smith-Connally Act) which made it illegal to encourage strikes in defense industries. Where strikes occurred the President was empowered to take over the running of the particular industry. Unions in non-defense industries had to observe a thirty day cooling-off period and have the support of the majority of their members before calling a strike. This Act provided the basis for the Taft-Hartley Act of 1947 which severely restricted later union activities.

As reaction to the strikes of 1943 indicated, the war appeared to encourage a move to the right in politics. Both Republicans and conservative Democrats grew in strength in Congress during the war and together they began to obstruct reform legislation. New social security programs were blocked, scheduled increases in payments were frozen, and restrictions on maximum earnings were successfully opposed. At the same time the concentration in government and by the President on winning the war led to regressive measures. Anti-trust prosecutions under the Sherman Act virtually ceased and increases in basic wages were prevented in order to control inflation. As 'Dr New Deal' was replaced by 'Dr Win-the-War,' many of the liberal reformers left Washington and were replaced by businessmen. However, the effects were not entirely negative: memories of the Depression remained vivid and many people suffered from what Davis Ross has aptly called 'depression psychosis'—the fear that the war would inevitably be followed by layoffs and mass unemployment.[25] Having seen the government spend huge amounts in order to wage war, they hoped that even a fraction of that amount would be spent to guarantee employment in peacetime.

Plans which offered security and comfort for the future were extremely popular, and even the British blueprint for the future, the Beveridge report, was widely read. In 1943 the National Resources Planning Board produced the American equivalent in its 'New Bill of Rights' which contained provisions for the maintenance of full employment, fair pay, medical care and improved social security for the old and sick. Although Congress rejected these proposals, Roosevelt's Economic Bill of Rights Message in 1944 at least recognized the federal government's responsibility for national employment levels. Some of the President's proposals were included in the Employment Act of 1946 which sanctioned deficit spending once and for all and established a Council of Economic Advisers to formulate national economic policies. After 1945 the political arguments were not over whether there should *be* a welfare state in America, but confined to the *extent* of the welfare state and federal programs.

If the Employment Act of 1946 can be seen as a reward for civilian participation and sacrifice in the war effort, a more obvious form of compensation was given to military participants under the Servicemen's Readjustment Act of 1944. The Act, popularly known as the GI Bill of Rights, provided returning veterans with a weekly readjustment allowance, loans to buy farms or businesses, and educational grants and subsistence allowances to enable them to return to college or school. By 1950 a third of the entire population had benefited from one aspect or another of the veterans' program and nearly 8 million veterans had taken advantage of the educational provisions alone.[26]

Of course the various benefits brought by the war have to be measured against its *disruptive* consequences. The most obvious cost was in lives lost in combat. Almost 400,000 men died, over three times the number in World War I, and another 675,000 were wounded. In addition there were the many thousands of deaths and injuries in war industries, where in fact the risks were higher than in the armed forces.[27] While these figures are small when compared with the 2–3 million Germans or the 7 million Russians who died, they are not insignificant. The effects of such losses at either a national or individual level are difficult to gauge; other consequences of the war lend themselves much more easily to measurement.

Encouraged by the needs of defense industries, the migration of people from the country to the cities, from the South to the North and West, greatly accelerated during the war. Between 1940 and 1945 some 15 million people moved from one community to another, either in search of new employment opportunities or to be near husbands and fathers in the forces. California, with almost half the nation's shipbuilding and aircraft industries, attracted 1·4 million migrants; another half million went to work in the converted automobile plants and aircraft factories around Detroit.[28] Few areas were prepared for the influx of newcomers and housing shortages and overcrowding resulted in many cities. Despite the creation of a National Housing Administration in 1942 to organize a war housing program, neither the federal nor local governments could cope with the problem. Families moved into already overcrowded homes or into the numerous trailer camps and shanty towns which sprang up around war production areas. In some areas the hot bed was a common feature: a day shift worker vacated his bed for a returning night shift worker.

Migrations and housing shortages added to the other strains of the war. The move from rural to urban areas brought problems of adjustment to new surroundings and unfamiliar living habits; there was often friction between newcomers and established residents. On top of this, there was the dislocation caused by the absence of fathers in the forces or working in distant defense plants. By 1945 3 million families were without a male head; in 1940 the number had been less than 800,000. With mothers also out at work, children often suffered from a lack of parental concern and control. An indication of this was the rise in juvenile delinquency, perhaps encouraged also by the sense of impermanence and excitement associated with the war. Other signs of the disruptive and *emotional* impact of the war can be seen in marriage, birth and divorce rates—all of which rose during the war years.[29]

While the war clearly had sweeping effects, it was especially significant for minority groups. The emphasis on national unity and cohesion and the need for 100 per cent participation in the war effort brought groups normally ignored or excluded into the mainstream of life. One such group was women, who had made substantial gains in industry during World War I. Their participation in the defense effort during that war persuaded political opponents of women's suffrage to reverse their views and to support the passage of the 19th Amendment in 1920. However, during the

subsequent Depression women faced a strong reaction against any change
in their traditional roles, and by 1940 'the percentage of females at work
was almost exactly what it had been in 1910.'[30]

World War II radically transformed the situation of women, providing
greater economic opportunities and a new sense of independence and
equality with the American male. Some 3 million women who would
normally have stayed at home went out to work during the war and the
total number of employed females rose from 12 million to well over
16 million; the percentage in the labor force rose from 25 per cent before
the war to 36 per cent in 1944. Jobs normally reserved for men opened up to
women: they worked as lumberjacks, lathe operators, crane drivers, arc
welders—even as taxi drivers in New York. By 1945 there were 2 million
women in heavy industries, steel mills, shipyards and aircraft plants.
Several thousand more joined women's branches of the armed forces where
they performed auxiliary, but still essential, services.[31]

The changes in employment patterns among women reflected a change
in public attitudes as 'Rosie the riveter' became a national heroine. Even
the reluctance to employ married women with children declined during
the war, and women over the age of forty were just as likely to find work as
younger ones. However, there was by no means complete acceptance of
women as equals: they were still excluded from most managerial jobs and
top policy-making bodies. Rather than include women in the War
Manpower Commission a separate body, the Women's Advisory
Commission, was formed. In salaries and wages differentials remained
despite an order from the War Labor Board *permitting* employers to pay
women the same as men. While some industries such as the automobile
companies immediately gave women a raise, many others ignored the
order or reclassified jobs as 'women's.' Even with the progress made
during the war, women's earnings lagged 40 per cent behind men's. There
was also a feeling that the changes in employment patterns were only
temporary and that they would, and should, end once the war was over. In
fact, 3 million women left work or were laid off in 1945–6, but as another
2·75 million were employed in the same period, the net decline was only of
600,000. At 29 per cent, the percentage of women in the labor force was
significantly higher after the war than it had been before, and several
taboos remained broken. Many married women continued to work and
female employment became an increasingly accepted part of middle class
life. Even for those women who did leave their wartime jobs, the temporary
emancipation could not be completely forgotten.[32]

Ethnic and racial groups experienced similar changes. The war actually
furthered the integration of some foreign-born groups into the rest of
society. There were not the hysterical attacks on Americans of German or
Italian extraction that there had been during World War I, and only 3000
German and 85 Italian aliens were considered dangerous enough to

warrant detention. While the war cut off foreign news and advertising, which led to a decline in foreign-language newspapers, German and Italian Americans demonstrated their loyalty by military service, and work in war industries brought financial security and middle class respectability.

Japanese-Americans were not so fortunate, and the military service of more than 12,000 brought little reward for their community. Fears of espionage and sabotage, encouraged by the Hearst press, the attorney general and governor of California and the military, were coupled with blatant racism and economic envy among the people of California, the state with the largest Japanese-American population. In February 1942 Roosevelt acceded to the demands of these various groups and authorized the removal of the Japanese. Over 110,000, most of them American born, were rounded up and shipped to barbed-wire-enclosed guarded camps in deserted regions of Arkansas, Colorado, Utah, Arizona and other states. They remained interned in the camps, even though subject to the draft from 1944, until January 1945 when the government lifted all restrictions replaced on Japanese-Americans. Restitution of the more than $400 million in property and possessions lost during the evacuation did not begin until some considerable time after the war.[33]

Only racial prejudice, inflamed by the attack on Pearl Harbor, can adequately explain the treatment of Japanese-Americans during the war. Prejudice also kept Mexican-Americans in an underprivileged position in society, like the Afro-Americans segregated, insulted and employed only in menial jobs. In 1941 not one single Mexican-American was employed in shipyards in Los Angeles. As the war progressed, however, the situation changed and by 1944 17,000 Mexicans worked in the shipyards and many more were employed in aircraft and other industries. An agreement between the United States and Mexico to allow the temporary importation of additional workers enabled the federal government to regulate their minimum wages and conditions and to help all Mexicans in America achieve the basic standards. Military service also secured some recognition from the government, but more important, it gave the Mexicans confidence and self-respect and made them less likely to accept discrimination at home. Several of the post-war Mexican leaders were not only veterans but also men who had benefited under the provisions of the GI Bill.[34]

Prejudice against Mexicans by no means disappeared during the war. The movement of people of Mexican origin into urban areas and industries often led to an increase in conflict. In 1943 Los Angeles was disrupted for four days by a riot which was almost entirely an attack by white servicemen and civilians on Mexican youths. Similar incidents on a smaller scale occurred in other cities on the West Coast and the attacks demonstrated that the war had only been marginal in effecting gains for Mexican-Americans.

The same was also true for American Indians, some 25,000 of whom served in the armed forces. Nearly twice as many were employed in war industries, but the effect of wartime incomes and military experience was to hasten the detribalization process and perhaps increase the sense of alienation and rootlessness among many Indians. At the same time, as defense spending increased there was a cutback in appropriations for the Indian Bureau and the programs established under the Wheeler-Howard Act of 1934. The rewards for Indian participation are hard to discern and the lasting image of the Indian during World War II, no doubt as a result of exaggerated and excessive media coverage, is of Ira Hayes, the Pima Indian war hero who died a chronic alcoholic.[35]

The war had a much greater impact on Afro-Americans than either Indians or Mexican-Americans because of differences in situation and stages of development. Afro-Americans comprised by far the largest of the non-European racial groups and the 13 million blacks represented 10 per cent of the US population—sufficient to guarantee that they could not be ignored for long in a war requiring such a total effort. Moreover, their situation had changed considerably since World War I. The urbanization and migration of 1917–18 continued in the inter-war years and led to a greater sophistication and self-consciousness, reflected in the literary movement of the Harlem Renaissance, rising circulation of the black press, and the increase in strength of civil rights organizations. By 1940 the combined circulation of more than 150 black newspapers totalled 1,276,600 and the *Chicago Defender*, a paper only established in 1905, had sales of over 82,000. By 1940 the NAACP had a membership approaching 90,000 and a budget of over $60,000.[36] During the 1930s it had fought and won several cases in the Supreme Court which were to help shape race relations in the coming decade.

In contrast to women, who had lost the political leadership and sense of unity and purpose of earlier years, blacks were just beginning to feel and exercise their economic and political power in the years before 1941. As well as the rise of black trade unionists such as A. Philip Randolph in the Brotherhood of Sleeping Car Porters, the 'jobs for Negroes' movement and the boycotts of stores in the 1930s were signs of growing self-awareness and an ability to mobilize at grassroots level. The swing of black voters away from the Republican Party and into the New Deal coalition also reflected an increased political concern and growing homogeneity.

At the same time, there is no doubt that the federal government was then much more sympathetic to blacks than the Wilson administration had been. Although Roosevelt's commitments to blacks in particular were few, his general humanitarian and liberal outlook affected Afro-Americans as part of the wider population. While his own dependence on Southern Democratic support made it impossible for him to identify with the black cause, Eleanor Roosevelt was able to speak and act on their behalf, providing both encouragement and moral leadership. Her activities were reinforced by the appointment of men sympathetic to blacks such as Harold Ickes, Will Alexander and Harry Hopkins, who could lay special emphasis on their needs within New Deal agencies. The unprecedented participation of a number of black advisers (including Robert C. Weaver, Mary McLeod Bethune and others) in government also helped to ensure that Afro-Americans received consideration in policy-making, if less in day-to-day administration.

The preconditions for change were, therefore, much more promising in 1940–1 than they had been in 1917. But there was still discrimination, even under the New Deal, and blacks did suffer disproportionately during the Depression. Prejudice still prevailed and when mobilization for war began in 1940 it appeared that they were again to be excluded from military and industrial preparations. However, on this occasion blacks immediately recognized that the war provided a crisis in which rights could be fought for and won. Unlike World War I, there was to be no restraint on protest: as the black author Chester Himes expressed it, 'Now is the Time! Here is the Place!'[37] The war unleashed and gave direction to a new black militancy; at the same time blacks were just as affected by the changes which the war brought to the rest of society. Together, black protest and the demands of the war brought greater advances than any preceding conflict.

2

The Test of War: Afro-Americans and the Armed Forces, 1940–45

The first priority for Afro-Americans on the eve of World War II was to ensure that they could participate fully and equally in the armed forces. Not only did they demand equal opportunities, but also an end to segregation and the explicit discrimination involved in the separation of the races. Racial restrictions on military service were opposed because they would impair claims to the same rights and privileges as other American citizens: but if they could fight as equals, then blacks could expect to be rewarded as equals. Military service thus became central to the whole campaign for civil rights, and the logic of the black argument was further strengthened by American and Allied propaganda which emphasized democratic principles and practices. Black protest and the need to live up to the ideals expressed in propaganda might themselves have produced changes in American military racial practices, but a more powerful and urgent force for change was the total nature of the war. As a post-war writer remarked, 'the lesson of total war, so belatedly learned, was that we must rigorously apply the principles of *economy of means* in the utilization of *all* resources for war—human as well as material.'[1]

Together, these three factors started the breakup of segregation and led in the immediate post-war period to the beginning of total integration in the American forces. This process, from segregation to integration, has been more than adequately dealt with by other historians.[2] It will only be necessary for me to outline the main developments and give new emphases. Especially important to this study is the attitude of blacks towards military participation, the effects of armed service on the attitudes of soldiers, and the implications of the wartime experience.

The fight for equal rights in the forces began with American mobilization even prior to Pearl Harbor. The situation of the black soldier had improved very little between 1918 and 1940, and although slight changes were made in military racial policy during the inter-war years, old misconceptions and prejudices prevented them from becoming practice. In line with general military policy, the four black regular Army units were run down in strength after World War I and Afro-Americans could only enter them as vacancies occurred. By 1939 there were only 3640 black regular soldiers and only five black officers, three of whom were chaplains. During the same period the Navy, which had limited black participation to work in the galleys, reduced the numbers employed in that capacity. On top of this, Afro-Americans were still excluded entirely from the Marine Corps and Army Air Corps, and involved only in limited numbers in the Coastguard.[3] With war imminent, they began to demand that greater opportunities in the military establishment be opened to them.

As early as May 1939 the voices of black protest were joined by the first organization created specifically to ensure black participation in the war effort, the Committee for the Participation of Negroes in National Defense. Founded in Washington, D.C., largely at the instigation of the influential black newspaper the *Pittsburgh Courier*, the committee was led by the historian and veteran of World War I, Rayford W. Logan. Under his leadership it immediately began to campaign for an end to discrimination in both industry and the armed forces. Military service was the more emotional and vital subject, however, as an appeal for the committee pointed out:

> The War Department and the Navy Department plans for the coming war DEGRADE you. They would make war without you if they could. *They would challenge your right to citizenship.* [italics mine][4]

Throughout 1939 and 1940 the committee co-ordinated the efforts of individuals and organizations in an effort to change military policies. Local branches were established, conferences and meetings held, and consultations were had with relevant government departments. In August 1940 Logan and spokesmen from the NAACP and the *Pittsburgh Courier* appeared before the House of Representatives Committee on Military Affairs to ask for an increase in the number of black military personnel and for full utilization of Afro-Americans in all branches of the armed forces. In order to achieve this, attempts were also made to secure the introduction of non-discrimination clauses in the Selective Services Bill then before Congress. Initial amendments, introduced by Senators Minton, Schwartz and Wagner, all Democrats, were rejected or altered in such a way as to negate their purpose. Finally Hamilton Fish, Republican Representative from New York, introduced an amendment, essentially that proposed by Logan, which was included in the Bill when it passed on September 14, 1940. Section 3(a) of the Act required that draftees be selected in an impartial manner, and section 4(a) stated that there should be no discrimination in either the selection or training of men.[5] In the course of the debate on selective service, however, Southern Congressmen made it clear that they did not expect this to mean the end of segregation—a view which was supported by a statement on military policy issued from the White House in October 1940.

The President's release was the result of a meeting held on September 27 with Walter White, executive secretary of the NAACP, A. Philip Randolph of the Brotherhood of Sleeping Car Porters and now a campaigner for black involvement in the war effort, and T. Arnold Hill, adviser on Negro affairs in the National Youth Administration and acting secretary of the National Urban League.[6] At the meeting the black spokesmen made their wishes clear in a seven point program. They asked that black officers and men be assigned duties according to their abilities; that provision be made for the training of black officers; that Afro-Americans be allowed full participation in all branches of the Army Air Corps; that blacks take part in the administration and operation of the selective service system; that black women be permitted to serve as nurses in the Army and Navy as well as in the Red Cross. Most important, that 'existing units of the Army and units to be established should be required to accept and select officers and enlisted personnel without regard to race.'[7]

President Roosevelt agreed to consider these points and to refer back to the black representatives at a later date, but without any subsequent discussion he signed the statement on military policy released to the press on October 9, 1940. Only a few of the blacks' proposals were incorporated and while the statement promised the use of Afro-Americans in the Army 'on the general basis of the proportion of the Negro population of the country' and in 'each major branch of the service, combatant as well as non-combatant,' it included important reservations. Increased opportunities were to be given to blacks to qualify for commissions, but such officers would only be assigned to all-black units. Moreover, the general policy of segregation was to be maintained as it had 'been proved satisfactory over a long period of years.' Changes 'would produce situations destructive to morale and detrimental to the preparation for national defense.'[8] Afro-Americans reacted angrily to the statement, the more so when they heard that White, Randolph and Hill had not, as was implied by the President's press secretary, Stephen Early, approved. The general response was summed up by the headline in *The Crisis*: 'White House Blesses Jim Crow.'[9]

Government embarrassment was increased by the Republicans, who made the most of the issue in an effort to capture black votes for the forthcoming presidential elections. A retraction by Early of his statement involving the black spokesmen was insufficient to repair the damage done, and on October 16 further concessions were made. Colonel Benjamin O. Davis, a soldier since the Spanish-American War, was promoted to the rank of general, the first black general in American history. Plans for the formation of black aviation units were announced and more black combat groups in the Army were promised. More significant was the appointment of William H. Hastie, Dean of Howard University Law School and a legal representative of the NAACP, as civilian aide to the Secretary of War. Colonel Campbell C. Johnson was made Negro Adviser to the Director of Selective Service. Roosevelt also wrote to White, Randolph and Hill and promised that 'further developments of policy will be forthcoming to insure that Negroes are given fair treatment on a non-discriminatory basis.'[10]

Some further progress did follow the furor of 1940: an Army Air Corps training base was established at Tuskegee Institute in Alabama in 1941 and the all-black 99th Pursuit Squadron flew its first combat mission in 1943. A considerable advance was made in 1942 when Afro-Americans were accepted for general service in both the Navy and the Marine Corps, if still on a segregated basis. This change in policy was carried out largely at the insistence of Roosevelt. Black Army officers were, from the start of the training program, taught with whites in fully integrated camps. In the Army generally, black strength rose rapidly from 97,725 in November 1941 to 467,883 in December 1942. However, that number did not bring the proportion of black soldiers up to that of blacks in the population, nor were they equally represented in all branches of the service.[11]

Despite these various improvements in the situation of the black serviceman, the White House press release remained the basis of wartime military policy and was regarded as presidential sanction of segregation. That little had really changed was revealed at a conference of black newspaper editors and publishers called for by Hastie and held in Washington, D.C. on December 8, 1941, the day after Pearl Harbor. Those present were told by Colonel Eugene Householder of the Adjutant General's Office that the Army could not take a stand on race relations that would antagonize the majority of American people. He went on to say that the Army was not a sociological laboratory and that,

> Experiments to meet the wishes and demands of the champions of every race and creed for the solution of their problems are a danger to efficiency, discipline and morale, and would result in ultimate defeat.[12]

This fear of jeopardizing white morale and of creating a white backlash during the war was often a greater force against change than the fear of black protest was for it.

Despite this argument, neither the black newspapermen nor their readers were impressed by Householder's justification of the maintenance of the status quo. Far from wishing to either hinder or impede America's war efforts, they only wanted 'the opportunity to serve their country to the full measure of their capacity and devotion.'[13] In this spirit, they would continue to fight for an equal opportunity to participate in the war and to oppose any abridgement of the constitutional guarantees which gave meaning and substance to their citizenship. In particular, the newspapers continued to oppose segregation, 'the root cause of all the ills the Negro suffers in this country.'[14]

While the black press kept up the verbal protest against discrimination, a number of young Afro-Americans refused to serve at all in the armed forces while segregation still persisted. The first case of this type arose in January 1941 when Ernest Calloway, the educational director of the Chicago local of the Transport Employees of America, wrote to his draft board, 'I cannot accept the responsibility of taking the oath upon induction into military service under the present anti-democratic structure of the United States Army and ask to be exempted from military training until such time that my contribution and participation in the defense of my country be made on a basis of complete equality.'[15] Calloway was a member of a group of blacks led by J. G. St Clair Drake, called Conscientious Objectors Against Jim Crow, which hoped to establish the right of Afro-Americans to claim exemption from service because of the segregation in the forces. But when Calloway failed to win his case and was sentenced to jail the movement evidently collapsed. However, he had won the support of the local NAACP and the black press. While the usually conservative black columnist George Schuyler urged other Afro-Americans to follow the young man's example, the *Chicago Defender* suggested that Calloway expressed the feeling 'of a substantial number of Negroes.'[16]

Lewis Jones of New York also won their approval. Like Calloway, Jones had objected to the racial practices of the armed forces. He was not a pacifist nor a conscientious objector, 'simply a colored American who insists on his constitutional rights to serve his country as a citizen unsegregated and unhumiliated in a Jim Crow Army.'[17] Jones was hopeful that his action would result in assignment to a mixed unit, but it was not to be. He refused to change his plea despite the arguments of the judge and of John P. Lewis, the sympathetic editor of *P.M.* The *Baltimore Afro-American* gave full coverage of the case in its issues of October and November 1942 and even reprinted Lewis's editorial from *P.M.* 'Why Colored Men Should Serve in the US Army,' which argued that the military front was more urgent than the fight for equality at home. Jones was still adamant and as a result was sentenced by a 'reluctant' court to three years' imprisonment, with the proviso that he could be released after three months if he would submit to the draft. He remained in prison until 1945.[18] As the November 14 editorial in the *Afro-American* pointed out, jailing Jones had not answered the questions he raised.

Equally firm in their stand, despite the powers of persuasion of the courts, were Donald W. Sullivan of New Jersey and George L. Haney of Chicago. Sullivan was sentenced, again by a 'reluctant' judge, to three years, and Haney to one year and a day.[19] Bayard Rustin, a Quaker and one

of the founding members of the Congress of Racial Equality, objected to
military service on both religious and racial grounds and he too received a
three year sentence which he completed in 1947.[20] (Information on other
blacks who objected to service on purely religious grounds is scarce; only
400 were classified as conscientious objectors and at least one black
Jehovah's Witness was jailed.) By far the most tragic method of escaping
the draft was that taken by Willie Harris, of Gary, Indiana. He committed
suicide in 1942 a few hours before he was due to appear for induction. In
the note he left his father, which was quoted in the *Chicago Defender* on
January 24, he said that he felt 'there was no future for Negro soldiers.' The
Director of Selective Service recognized the connection between Harris's
death and induction, and reported that there had been an attempted
suicide for the same reason.[21]

The most important and the longest legal battle against service in
segregated forces was put up by Winfred William Lynn, a thirty-six year old
vegetable gardener from New York. Lynn contended that his induction as
part of the black 'quota' was a violation of the Selective Service Act. In June
1942 the federal judge of the district court refused to hear the case until
Lynn submitted for induction, which he did, entering the Army in
December that year. His brother Conrad and Arthur Garfield Hays of the
American Civil Liberties Union, supported by A. Philip Randolph and the
NAACP, then applied for a writ of *habeas corpus* and named Lynn's
commanding officer as respondent. Their motion was denied in February
1944 by the US Circuit Court of Appeals in New York. In a two to one
verdict, the court ruled that section 4(a) of the Selective Service Act
prohibited discrimination but not necessarily segregation. Moreover, the
court pointed out that Lynn had in the end been inducted separately as a
delinquent and therefore not as part of the quota.[22]

The legal battle was kept up after this decision. A. Philip Randolph
continued to mobilize support for Lynn and was instrumental in the
formation of the National Committee for Winfred Lynn. The committee,
which referred to the Lynn case as the 'Twentieth Century Dred Scott Case,'
succeeded in securing moral and financial aid, and when the case went
before the Supreme Court in 1944 Lynn was defended by Hays with
NAACP lawyers Hastie, Marshall and Konvitz appearing as *amici curiae*.[23]
However, the Supreme Court ruled that 'since the soldier was serving in the
South Pacific, no one in the Eastern District of New York, where the case
arose, nor any War Department official, could produce him in court or
order his release.' The case was therefore declared moot and a later appeal
was also denied.[24] The whole process was seen by many blacks as a legal
trick to avoid ruling on military racial practices in a case which could have
proved embarrassing for the government. Certainly the case was not lightly
regarded by the federal government, and the opinion of members of the
selective service system and the Judge Advocate's Office was that if the
court had ruled, it would have been in Lynn's favour.[25]

Whatever the feelings among some military personnel about the legal weaknesses of segregation, separation of races remained intact other than in the training of officers, the WAVES and in most Army hospitals. Integration on a basis of one black to every nine whites was suggested by a planning group of the Army General Staff, but rejected on the usual grounds that it would cause disruption and lead to inefficiency. However, the failure of the Army's racial policy either to still black protest or to achieve the fullest use of manpower did lead to the formation of an Advisory Committee on Negro Troop Policies in August 1942. Chaired by Assistant Secretary of War John J. McCloy, the committee demonstrated a growing awareness of the injustice and inefficiency of segregation in the forces but initially saw little reason for change. Indeed, the attitudes of McCloy and the first actions of the committee contributed to the resignation of Hastie, the black civilian aide, in January 1943.[26]

Hastie had threatened to resign before 1943 but had always been persuaded to remain in office in the interests of morale. The fact that he had not been informed, prior to the event, of the formation of the McCloy committee and had then been excluded from its membership only added to his frustration. This was further increased by the disagreements he had with McCloy on the importance of the full, unsegregated use of black troops. The final straw for Hastie was the plan to establish a segregated black Air Officer Training School at Jefferson Barracks, contrary to the practices of all the other services. Again this plan had been drawn up without Hastie's knowledge and without any attempt to consult him.[27] His resignation and the attendant publicity did have some effect: the plan for the separate training school was dropped and the Air Corps generally relaxed its racial restrictions. Moreover, Truman Gibson, Hastie's successor, regularly attended meetings of the McCloy committee and appeared to be listened to with some respect.

Other crises in 1943 were also followed by some changes in Army policy. The most serious cause of alarm was the outbreak of racial violence in and around military camps in the North and South, involving members of all the services but especially soldiers. The cause of the friction was basically the segregation and discrimination which applied even to on-base facilities such as theatres, post exchanges and canteens. The situation was worsened by the prejudices of white soldiers, officers and military police. In the South, Afro-American troops also had to suffer the local Jim Crow laws and were subject to insult and attack from white civilians. Quite frequently the two elements, prejudice within the Army and among civilians, were combined in conflicts over bus services between Army camps and neighboring towns. The segregation of such services was strictly enforced by both military and civilian police forces and it was usual for blacks to give precedence to whites. Generally, this meant that they waited until all whites had boarded the vehicle; often they then had to stand because white passengers had taken all the seats; sometimes it even meant that they missed the bus altogether because it was filled by whites. To refuse to accept such local laws led at least to jail, often to a beating, and occasionally to death. This was in spite of the assurance given by Assistant Secretary of War Patterson that 'the War Department can and will maintain the dignity of the uniform and the personnel which wears it.'[28]

Given the extent of discrimination faced by Afro-Americans in the forces, it was not surprising that their morale was low. Black servicemen wrote to the President and to black organizations and newspapers complaining of their treatment. Not only did these letters deal with particular acts of discrimination, but a great many also discussed the underlying moral contradiction of segregation within the army of a democracy. In a letter to President Roosevelt, one black soldier remarked on the paradox that the 'very instrument which our government has organized and built, the United States Armed Forces, to fight for world democracy, is within itself undemocratic.'[29]

There was, of course, a natural tendency for Afro-Americans to see everything in a racial context and therefore to take offense on occasion at what was often no more than common military practice. To a certain extent their civilian life had conditioned them to expect the worst from white authority, but segregation encouraged these feelings because it prevented blacks from seeing that white soldiers suffered many of the same hardships. One black soldier, for instance, complained of being treated like a dog, 'laying in the hot sun' with water 'very scarce.' What he failed to point out was that he and his comrades were in a desert training center.[30]

Not all Afro-Americans did object to their treatment in the Army. For many black servicemen Army life, even with its racial restrictions, was better than life as a civilian. The uniform gave a measure of self-respect and a degree of authority. More important, black soldiers were taught skills and trades, given a certain amount of education, as well as being fed, clothed and paid regularly. For a good number it was 'the first semblance of economic security they had ever known.'[31]

A War Department survey found that only one fifth 'of all Negro soldiers' thought the Army unfair, three fifths had mixed attitudes, and the remaining fifth thought it fair. The same survey reported that not all Afro-Americans in the Army were opposed to segregation, either. As many as 40 per cent thought separate post exchanges were a good idea, 48 per cent thought them a poor idea, and 12 per cent were undecided. Thirty-eight per cent of those questioned favored racially separate units, 36 per cent wanted integrated ones, and 26 per cent were undecided.[32] It is impossible to decide how many of these soldiers were giving what they thought to be 'safe' answers, but to the authorities it seemed clear that black opinion was divided. Still, one could hardly agree with the view held by the majority of white soldiers, that their black comrades were satisfied with their lot [33]

As commentators pointed out at the time, the attitude of the Afro-

American was an amalgam. On the one hand he responded as an American with patriotism and loyalty in the hope that his participation would be recognized and rewarded; on the other, he resented his treatment both in and out of the forces and was inclined to feel he had nothing to fight for. Thus it was that only 66 per cent of blacks compared to 89 per cent of whites, in another survey, thought that the war was as much their affair as anybody else's. Twenty-one per cent felt that it was not as much their affair, and 13 per cent could not decide. Of the same group of soldiers, given a choice of questions they would ask the President if they could, 50 per cent of the blacks named discrimination, 23 per cent the progress and duration of the war, and 13 per cent conditions in the Army. The main concern of black soldiers appeared to be how the war would affect conditions at home vis-à-vis race relations. Yet expectations among the Afro-Americans were higher than among their white counterparts. When asked 'After the war do you think that you yourself will have more than you had before the war?,' 43 per cent of the blacks said more, 38 per cent expected to have just the same, and 6 per cent said less. The corresponding figures for whites were 19, 55 and 19 per cent.[34]

Such attitudes could change after experience of life in the Army. One soldier, in a letter to Truman Gibson, said that at the beginning of the war he had felt it was his 'patriotic duty' to serve in the forces but that having experienced military service he was now 'indifferent to the whole affair.'[35] With this type of disillusion often went an aggressive desire to bring about change. The NAACP was sent money as well as angry letters, and in 1943 received over $5000 from servicemen. By the end of the war donations from soldiers amounted to $25,000 and some 15,000 had joined the organization.[36] While many soldiers spoke of returning to demand their rights once the war was over, others suggested that if they were to fight and die for democracy they would be as well to start in the USA.[37] Rather than quietly suffer violence and humiliation, many fought back.

From the start of the war there were incidents of fighting between black and white soldiers, blacks and civilians, or blacks and policemen. In a typical incident described in the *New York Times* of April 3, 1942 three soldiers were killed and five others wounded after an argument between black and white soldiers over precedence at a telephone booth. Although the War Department attempted to play them down, such outbreaks were given conspicuous coverage in the black press. The stories of riots, of blacks destroying segregated facilities or battling with police, increased dramatically during 1943. In June the *Chicago Defender* reported four killed and sixteen wounded in five 'Dixie clashes' and the *Pittsburgh Courier* suggested that riots were 'sweeping the nation.'[38] War Department officials were alarmed by the 'general unrest' among Afro-Americans and one memorandum on black attitudes pointed out that 'most Negro soldiers have secreted ammunition.'[39]

Civilian aide Gibson, reporting on the disaffection and discontent at Forts Huachuca, Bliss and Clark, found that local Jim Crow laws were the main bone of contention and that black troops resented being denied the rights and privileges given to others in uniform. While he recommended that the segregation of officers' messes and base theaters be discontinued, he felt that commanders should withhold furlough passes from those men who refused to accept local laws and customs.[40] The McCloy committee did suggest that the policy of segregation, the main cause of black disquiet, should be reviewed and that a 'clear-cut policy be formulated and made known to all.'[41] The committee also fully recognized the lack of morale among black troops and successfully initiated some changes.

Together with the Research Branch of the War Department, the McCloy committee produced a manual *Leadership and the Negro Soldier* which offered careful guidance to the officers of Afro-American troops, as well as a brief history of black military participation in past wars. Also in 1944, following the example of the enterprising commanding officer of Camp Lee in Virginia, it became Army policy to arrange bus services between camps and neighboring towns solely for the use of military personnel and operated on a basis of first come, first served, with no segregation. In July the same year the McCloy committee ordered all on-base facilities to be used without restrictions because of race. Although the existence of separate facilities in many camps and the reluctance among some officers to implement the order prevented this from becoming universally carried out, the order marked a distinct change in Army policy.[42]

The need for 'morale-building information on the stake and role of the Negro in the war' was also realized, and in 1943 an educational program first suggested by Hastie was implemented to alleviate racial tensions.[43] Part of this program was the film *The Negro Soldier* which was previewed by an audience of 439 black and 510 white soldiers in 1944. The film, which stressed black military participation in previous wars as well as in World War II, was considered to be very good by the majority of both groups. Only three per cent of the black soldiers felt it was untrue, and only four per cent of the whites agreed—for reasons which were much the same in content but utterly different in emphasis. The blacks (rightly) thought that the film over-glamorized the treatment they received in the Army and their role in it, while the whites thought that 'it exaggerated the importance of the Negro soldier, showed too close contact between Negroes and whites, and suggested too ideal a picture of Negro treatment by the whites.'[44] About 80 per cent of the whole audience, black and white, thought that the film ought to be given a wide showing, and following distribution in 1944 it was seen in more than three hundred theaters in New York alone.[45] Following this success several more films were made about blacks and the war, including *The Negro Sailor* and the more emotive, if less exact, *Teamwork*, based on the black role in the European offensive.

The extremely popular black boxer Joe Louis was also used to boost black morale. After he had entered the Army in 1942 he spent most of his time touring Army bases and camps, giving talks and exhibition bouts. He also took part in the War Department film *This is the Army*, as well as being in a number of newsreels. For his services he was made a sergeant and awarded the Legion of Merit in 1945. His own attitude to the discrimination in the forces was summed up when, talking about the Navy, he expressed the hope 'that some day things would be better.'[46]

Another crisis arose in 1943 because of the concentration of Afro-American troops in service units and the delay in sending black soldiers overseas. While various war zones suffered manpower shortages, 425,000 of the 504,000 Afro-Americans in the Army were still stationed in the United States. This was due partly to objections raised by foreign governments who feared that Afro-American troops might cause unrest among either local black populations or, as in the case of Australia, among local whites.[47] In addition many overseas commanders refused to accept black troops on grounds of morale and efficiency. Abandoning altogether the attempt to achieve proportional representation of blacks in every branch of the service, the Army began to convert black combat units to service units (which were more acceptable to objectors) for posting abroad.

Early in 1944 the black 2nd Cavalry Division, which included the 9th and 10th Cavalry regiments created by Congress in 1866, was converted into a service unit after having two years of combat training. Hamilton Fish, Republican Representative from New York and a former officer of the black 369th Infantry, wrote to Secretary of War Stimson deploring the failure to use black combat soldiers and questioning the authority of this particular conversion. In reply, Stimson said that 'a relatively large percentage of the Negroes inducted in the Army have fallen within the lower educational classifications, and many of the Negro units have accordingly been unable to master the techniques of modern weapons.'[48] Fish made public this letter during a speech on the floor of the House on February 23. Not surprisingly, it created a considerable furor. Truman Gibson, who had earlier remarked on the waste of manpower entailed in keeping black troops at home, called the statement 'one of the most stupid' ever to come from the War Department; the *Pittsburgh Courier* described Stimson as 'a stubborn man . . . determined to continue color discrimination . . . war or no war,' and demanded his resignation.[49]

Most blacks assumed that Stimson was arguing that they were generally mentally inferior to whites, an assumption which he denied. In fact, the problem outlined by Stimson arose because of the policy of segregation which he and other military officials supported on grounds of efficiency. Whereas whites from poor educational backgrounds were scattered throughout the Army, blacks with the same deficiencies were of course concentrated in all-black units. There were in fact more whites than blacks

in educational groups IV and V, but their 'integration' into a wide number
and variety of units meant that they caused little difficulty. However, as a
result of the reaction of black people, newspapers and several politicians,
and on the advice of Truman Gibson, preparations were made to send
black troops into combat and the 92nd and 93rd Infantry were sent to Italy
and the Pacific respectively.[50]

The overseas service of black troops did create problems for both the
American military and foreign governments. It also had a considerable
effect on the servicemen. As one commander of a black supply unit pointed
out, black soldiers in Europe 'did things they could not do at home.' He
went on to say that the experience was 'something you can't expose a man
to and expect him to forget overnight.'[51] Written and film records tend to
bear him out: Afro-Americans were generally well received by the people
of foreign countries. In most of them the blacks were seen as just a part of
the armies of liberation and treated as such. Like other American soldiers,
they often had more money than local inhabitants and a ready supply of
such luxuries as cigarettes, gum, candy, chocolate, razorblades and nylon
stockings. On top of this, in many places a black face was a novelty and
racial prejudice was unusual; Afro-Americans often found that they were
treated better by the locals than by their fellow Americans. This would
certainly appear to have been the case in England.

It has recently been suggested that because of 'Jim Crow with a British
accent,' the black soldier in England faced an 'unenviable plight.'[52]
However, the most serious problem in Britain was in fact the importation
of discrimination and segregation by white GIs rather than the prejudice of
either the British government or the population. Although there had been
some blacks in Britain before the war, the number was small. Some West
Indians had remained in the country following their discharge from her
armed forces after World War I, a number of black seamen still in service
made their homes in British ports, and a few Africans studied at British
universities. While there was some conflict between blacks and whites in
particular areas such as Liverpool and Cardiff in 1919, it was short-lived
and highly localized. The influx of West Indian technicians, workers and
servicemen after 1940 was not sufficient to create any major problems.[53]
This is not to claim that the British were free from racial prejudice: their
imperial history demonstrated that this was not the case and later reactions
to the immigration of large numbers of *permanent* residents from the West
Indies, India and Pakistan confirmed it. However, during the war black
newcomers were regarded only as temporary visitors who were, after all, in
the country to help win the war. Their numbers were comparatively small
and because they were concentrated in a few areas most Britons were
unaware of their presence. Their arrival attracted some publicity but the
attitude of the British tended to be one of patronization: as one recent
writer put it, 'a Negro was regarded as an interesting curiosity.'[54]

The first black Americans arrived in 1942 and by the end of October that year there were over 12,000 in Britain. By May 31, 1944 the number had risen to 132,253 and while some were stationed in Northern Ireland, most were scattered throughout England. Both British and American authorities were concerned that the presence of black troops should not create friction which would in any way impair Anglo-American relations and to that end both sides embarked on public relations exercises to make known differences in racial attitudes. In 1942 General Eisenhower issued an order which declared that the 'spreading of derogatory statements concerning the character of any group of United States troops, either white or colored, must be considered as conduct prejudicial to good order and military discipline and offenders must be promptly punished.'[55] GIs were also familiarized with British customs and habits through the film *Welcome to Britain*, made in 1943 by the Ministry of Information and featuring Burgess Meredith in the leading part. As the white American soldier, Meredith discusses some of the differences between the two countries and indicates the do's and don'ts. In one scene racial attitudes are dealt with. A black soldier from Birmingham, Alabama is shown leaving a railway compartment which he has been sharing with a white lady from Birmingham in England. As the Afro-American prepares to depart, the woman remarks on the coincidence in the names of their home towns and she invites the black soldier to call on her. At this point Meredith turns to the camera and warns other Americans not to be alarmed by such occurrences: they might not happen at home, but in Britain there are fewer racial restrictions. This sequence is followed by a discussion in which General John Lee, head of Service and Supplies, urges black and white soldiers to work together and 'to live up to our American promises.'[56]

The British authorities had their own educational program and in an article in *Current Affairs*, the journal produced for British soldiers, American racial practices were explained and discussed. After giving a historical background, the article warned readers against embarrassing their American guests; there was no reason to adopt American racial attitudes, only to appreciate the reasons for them. British soldiers were urged not to interfere, no matter how angered or offended by cases of discrimination. The article also suggested that attempts to 'break down the various forms of social regulation accepted by the average American family' would be of little purpose and likely to lead to violence, 'especially where women are concerned.'[57] This type of reasoning lay behind the Home Office directive to chief constables which instructed local police forces not to implement or enforce any form of color bar. Segregation could only be enforced on the orders of, and by, American troops.[58]

Some members of the British government were prepared to accept and impose segregation. Professor Hachey quotes the views of the right wing Secretary of War Sir Percy James Grigg, and also those of John Spencer-

Churchill, a liaison officer with the United States troops and a cousin of Prime Minister Winston Churchill. However, to claim that the letter from Spencer-Churchill to his relative 'constitutes an indictment of British attitudes' is an exaggeration. The opinions of Spencer-Churchill and Grigg have to be balanced with those of the more influential government members such as Herbert Morrison the Home Secretary, Stafford Cripps the Lord Privy Seal, or Brendan Bracken the Minister of Information. While these men were prepared to permit the Americans to continue to segregate their own troops in order to avoid trouble, they consistently opposed the use of methods which would encourage Britons to accept the same social attitudes.[59] Given their reliance on American aid and troops, the British government was hardly in a position to demand that American military policies be changed.

Despite the rather uneasy compromise by the government, there were cases of American-style segregation and outbreaks of racial violence in Britain. By December 17, 1943 Truman Gibson could record that 'a rigid pattern of racial segregation' had appeared in Britain, 'community patterns in that country to the contrary nothwithstanding.'[60] By way of illustration he included a list of public houses and bars in Ipswich, eight of which were used exclusively by Afro-Americans. Publicans and dancehall owners sometimes did give way to American demands to exclude blacks, and women in branches of the British armed forces were warned not to associate in public with Afro-Americans.

However, fraternization between the races and sexes did occur and some two thousand 'brown babies' were born to British women as a result of their wartime friendships with black soldiers. Moreover, a poll in 1943 suggested that the British were overwhelmingly opposed to discrimination, and official records also revealed that Afro-Americans were often more easily assimilated than their white compatriots. One writer suggested that Afro-Americans were preferred because they were less brash and more careful and reserved than the white Americans.[61] Whatever the reason, the British public were sympathetic to the blacks and in some cases sided with them in conflicts with white GIs. After a clash between black soldiers and white MPs in Paignton in Devonshire some civilians protested against the subsequent court-martial of fourteen black soldiers; in a riot in Bristol involving white American paratroops and blacks of the Quartermaster Corps, it was found that British bystanders had encouraged the Afro-Americans during the fighting; in some cases the British actually joined in disturbances on their behalf.[62]

Instances like these reveal how mixed the racial pattern was in wartime Britain. It does seem clear that while the official attitude was one of strict neutrality, many civilians welcomed black soldiers and opposed any introduction of discrimination. Walter White, the executive secretary of the NAACP, toured the European Theater of Operations in 1944 as an accredited correspondent for the *New York Post* and after talking to black soldiers in England concluded that many there gained their 'first experience in being treated as normal human beings and friends by white people.'[63]

While service overseas could affect black soldiers, and on some occasions embarrass American military officials, it did not lead to any changes in military policy. Again the need to use all available manpower proved a more important factor. In 1942 selective service had been placed under the War Manpower Commission and all armed services were ordered to take their men from the draft. In 1943 Paul McNutt, the chairman of the Manpower Commission, wrote to Secretary of War Stimson and Secretary of the Navy Knox complaining that the separate calls for black and white registrants under the 'Negro quota' system had led to only six per cent of the armed forces being black. As a result of the segregation in the forces and the fact that blacks could only enter a limited number of black units, married whites were often inducted while many single Afro-Americans were passed over. McNutt therefore ordered that men should be drafted 'without regard to race or color.'[64] Although there was resistance to this order from all services, the Navy and Marine Corps did comply following pressure from Roosevelt. The Army was at first able to ignore the command because of the shortage of suitable black registrants due to high rejection rates for Afro-Americans on the grounds of educational deficiencies. However, in 1943 a shortage of both black and white manpower forced the Army to abandon its rigid literacy standards and to establish Special Training Units to give draftees a basic education. As a result, 'approximately 136,000 Negro soldiers received literacy training during World War II.'[65] However, while this change in policy had obvious benefits for the men concerned, it did not lead to any great increase in the number of black soldiers and the Army never did achieve proportional representation of Afro-Americans in its forces. Moreover, segregation remained intact.

The real test of segregation came in December 1944 when the Germans launched a last desperate offensive in the Ardennes. In the ensuing Battle of the Bulge, the American Army found itself critically short of infantry replacements and as a result white combat units were undermanned. In order to fill the gap General Eisenhower was persuaded to accept volunteers from black service regiments by the commander of the Communications Zone, General John Lee. In his original appeal to the black soldiers Lee proposed complete integration, but this was altered in order not to contradict War Department policy. Instead, black platoons of forty men were assigned to white companies of two hundred. The main elements of Lee's original call for volunteers were retained and some of them were quite remarkable. Non-commissioned officers were given the opportunity to accept a reduction in rank in order to enjoy 'the privilege of joining our veteran units at the front.' Lee also promised that volunteers would be able 'to share the glory of victory' and pointed out that this had been one of the black demands throughout the war.[66]

This document and the response it received from Afro-Americans clearly revealed the importance attached to military participation. Over 5000 blacks, many of them former NCOs, volunteered and finally the Army had to set a limit of 2500. After six weeks of intensive training thirty-seven platoons were attached to white units where they fought throughout 1945. Sadly, these platoons were either returned to their former duties or discharged from the Army once the war in Europe was won. While it would obviously be foolish to exaggerate the importance and relevance of the performance of highly motivated, volunteer platoons such as these, the experiment could not be ignored. Not only had these Afro-Americans proved to be capable soldiers, they had also been accepted by their white colleagues.[67]

The Army's contention that integration would be detrimental to morale had been supported by various surveys of white opinion in the forces. Although some white men—like Sergeant Alton Levy who protested against segregation and was reduced to the rank of private and given four months' hard labor as a consequence—might be in favor of integration, they were in the minority.[68] A 1942 survey of the attitudes of 2360 men to sharing facilities with black troops found that the majority favored segregation; another poll on the attitudes of whites toward the use of Afro-Americans in the Air Force revealed that while 65 per cent were agreeable to having blacks in the Air Force, all but a few wanted separate facilities to be provided. Nor was this prejudice purely sectional; 75 per cent of Northerners and 86 per cent of Southerners wanted segregation of the races.[69] Later opinion polls found little change. While about two out of five white enlisted men viewed plans for the greater use of black troops favorably, four out of five were opposed to the idea of having blacks and whites in the same unit even if they did not eat in the same mess or sleep in the same barracks.[70]

The survey of the units to which black platoons were eventually attached, although only of the attitudes of white officers and NCOs, indicated that experience of integration in wartime could bring radical changes in men's feelings.[71] Over 60 per cent of the 250 men questioned had viewed integration unfavorably prior to the event: after serving with black soldiers over 70 per cent had changed their minds and now favored the experiment. More than 80 per cent thought that blacks had performed very well in combat, 17 per cent said fairly well, and only 1 per cent said not so well. Equally important was the opinion held by 73 per cent of the officers and 60 per cent of the NCOs that the black and white soldiers had got along together very well. Seven per cent of the officers and 36 per cent of the sergeants said fairly well—the difference between the ranks presumably due to the NCOs' closer proximity to the enlisted men. The survey also found that those in closest contact with the black platoons, serving in the same company or regiment, viewed the experiment much more favorably than those with no contact at all.

Although it is impossible to say how permanent such changes of attitude were, or how the experience had affected soldiers' views on race relations in general, polls of the mixed companies seemed to show that white soldiers found integration less objectionable than they might previously have imagined. This was undoubtedly due to the fact that the Afro-Americans were sharing with them all the hazards of combat: misery likes company. After the Battle of the Bulge it was not as easy for the Army to argue that integration would lead to a drop in morale or efficiency, and later policy committees were to use the record of the integrated platoons to justify changes in military racial practices.

Surprisingly, in view of its policies at the beginning of the war, the Navy provided another case in support of integration. Although the Secretary of the Navy, Frank Knox, had accepted a wider use of black personnel in 1942, he did so reluctantly and remained a firm advocate of segregation. However, there were individuals within the Navy Department, such as the special assistant Adlai Stevenson, who were committed to the full and equal utilization of black manpower. A Special Programs Unit was established within the Bureau of Naval Personnel in order to suggest ways in which fuller use of black seamen could be brought about. The only way this could be achieved within a segregated naval force was to crew ships entirely with blacks—a suggestion accepted in 1944 when two ships, the USS *Mason* and the submarine chaser *PC 1264*, were manned by all-black complements.[72] This policy was carried further when Knox died in 1944 and was succeeded by the more liberal James Forrestal, who had earlier secured the integration of the WAVES, the women's branch of the Navy. Forrestal immediately accepted the program for integrating the crews of twenty-five vessels and later the integration of the whole auxiliary fleet. In 1945 he appointed Lester B. Granger, the head of the National Urban League, as adviser on racial policies. Granger found that his opinions were not only listened to but acted upon. At the same time the Special Programs Unit had also concluded that integration, rather than segregation, produced a more efficient fighting force. As a result, all restrictions on naval assignments for Afro-Americans were lifted in 1947 and the policy of total integration was confirmed in 1949.[73]

While the Navy had the most progressive policy at the end of the war, the Air Force began to move along similar lines as soon as it became an independent service in September 1947. Both the new Secretary of the Air Force, Stuart Symington, and the Air Staff were aware of the waste of manpower resulting from segregation and plans for integration began and were finalized in 1949.[74]

The least change occurred in the Army, but on October 4, 1945 a board of officers chaired by General Alvin C. Gillem was directed to prepare a broad policy statement on the use of black troops. In its report, presented in 1946, the Gillem board recognized 'that there is a limit to the amount of manpower available in the nation to form a modern military organization capable of prosecuting a major war' and recommended 'that every effort be expended to utilize efficiently every qualified available individual in a position in the military structure for which he is best suited.'[75] The report went on to point out that the Afro-American was a 'bona fide citizen enjoying the privileges conferred by citizenship under the Constitution': as such he was obliged to defend his country in time of peril.

After spelling out the links between citizenship and armed service and acknowledging the black man's equality, the Gillem board did not suggest the immediate end of segregation but proposed a plan which would have eventually led to integration. The 1940 policy statement was rescinded, the integration of recreational facilities was to continue, and the use of black platoons with larger white units was suggested as an alternative to full-scale integration. The Board still insisted on the 10 per cent quota of blacks in the Army and although this had already proved to be an obstacle in the way of full utilization of black manpower, it did guarantee blacks continued participation.

The Gillem Report received a mixed reception from Afro-Americans. Some felt that the Army was at least moving in the right direction, others felt that the new policies were little more than diluted Jim Crow.[76] However, the subject of black service continued to be an important issue in the post-war years and civil-rights organizations maintained their demands for full integration. Changed circumstances, a new President, America's position in world affairs, and the Cold War, made possible further changes and led to the beginning of full-scale integration. But the decisive first steps had occurred during World War II. The war had tested military institutions and found them lacking: segregation had not only hampered the full utilization of all available manpower, it had also threatened the morale of 10 per cent of the population and undermined America's democratic pretensions. As a result of wartime experiences all branches of the forces began to review their racial practices and at least to discuss the possibility of integration. Considering military policies in 1939, that alone was a remarkable change in a short space of time and it revealed the extent of the war's challenge.

3

Participation: The Impact of the War on the Employment and Economic Situation of the Afro-American

'The war years,' wrote Robert C. Weaver in 1946, 'have been unique in the Negro's economic history.'[1] During that period a number of forces combined to bring about greater industrial and occupational opportunities than Afro-Americans had previously experienced. Black protest and the necessities of war forced the federal government to order the full utilization of all available manpower and an end to discrimination in employment. While such action brought about some economic gains for blacks, the greatest force for change was the general expansion of industry and the shortage of labor as more men and women entered the armed forces. These manpower shortages gradually forced white employers and workers to forget their prejudices, if only temporarily, and accept black employees. By the end of the war the quantity and quality of jobs open to Afro-Americans had increased dramatically. However, the war emergency did not root out all discrimination and there was some indication that the blacks would lose the gains they had made once the war had ended.

When America began to prepare for war in 1940, the situation for Afro-Americans in industry, as in the armed services, was far from promising. Because of their second-class status in society, which meant that they were last hired and first fired, black Americans had been hit particularly hard by the Depression, especially in the industrial North where many were comparative newcomers. In 1937 the percentage of blacks in the North who were unemployed was 38.9 while for whites the figure was 18.1; in the South, where the majority of blacks still worked on farms, the percentages were 18 and 16 respectively.[2] Even there, however, the situation of the Afro-Americans could be apalling. In Norfolk, Virginia in 1935 80 per cent of the black work force were on relief, and in Atlanta, Georgia 65 per cent were in the same position.[3]

While the New Deal certainly did alleviate the plight of many people irrespective of color, it was not free from prejudice, nor did it provide programs for the Afro-Americans as a separate and especially needy case. The attitudes of certain heads of government agencies, such as Secretary of the Interior Harold Ickes or Harry Hopkins, the head of the Works Progress Administration, did ensure that blacks received some special consideration, as did the appointment of black advisers. It was one thing to formulate policies at the federal level but quite another to implement them locally where even those agencies headed by men sympathetic to Afro-Americans were administered in accordance with regional racial practices.

The National Recovery Administration had no sympathetic person at its head, nor any adviser on black affairs. Thus it laid down no minimum wage codes for domestic workers, an occupation dominated by blacks. Some officials of the agency even applied a dual industrial wage code with one minimum for whites and another lower one for blacks. In any event, many employers discovered that 'the codes could be evaded and ignored with impunity.'[4] The Agricultural Adjustment Administration also ran foul of local racial practices, and black farmers, particularly in the South, did not receive their fair share of the AAA benefits. In the 1930s approximately 192,000 black farmers were 'displaced' but the Farm Security Administration only resettled 1400. Even agencies such as the Tennessee Valley Authority, the Civilian Conservation Corps, and the National Youth Administration, which operated with a minimum of discrimination, normally conformed to local customs.[5]

If the New Deal had been free of prejudice, it is still unlikely that it could have helped all Afro-Americans, for it had not fully succeeded in easing the plight of whites. In January 1940 there were still seven million white, and one million black, Americans unemployed. The large pool of white labor meant that in the early war mobilization black job applicants could be, and were, overlooked. When manpower shortages did arise in areas of concentrated black population, some employers still refused to employ them and instead imported white workers. Because of this, from April to October 1940 the rate of unemployment among whites dropped from 17·7 to 13 per cent while among blacks it remained static at 22 per cent.[6] The proportion of blacks in the ranks of the unemployed rose as whites found new work: in Philadelphia in April 1940, 24·8 per cent of the total unemployed were black; by April the next year this had risen to 29·8 per cent.[7]

Far from discouraging such trends, the United States Employment Service actually encouraged them. Like many other government bodies, although it did have a Negro Placement Service Unit, the Employment Service had no clear-cut policy with regard to blacks. As a result regional offices largely followed local racial patterns. Not only did they accept requests from employers which specified 'whites only' but often they also classified black workers in 'traditional' occupations regardless of their individual skills or training. A young black man, qualified as a mechanic, told his wife that there was no point in registering for work because 'they don't hire colored people in factories for national defense.'[8] As well as discrimination in the Employment Service, discrimination in defense training also helped to reduce the opportunities for employment open to blacks. In the eighteen states with separate school systems where blacks made up 22·3 per cent of the population, only 6·6 per cent of the $6,591,741 allocated for defense training was used in equipping black schools and as late as 1942 only 4 per cent of those who benefited from the training program were black.[9] Those jobs which Afro-Americans were lucky enough to get were, therefore, largely the unskilled, hot and heavy. From October 1940 to March 1941 the greatest number of Afro-Americans placed in jobs by the Employment Service were in chemical industries, shipbuilding, and iron and steel works. The smallest number, a mere sixty-eight, were found work in the aircraft industry.[10]

The aircraft companies provide a good example of the obstacles faced by Afro-Americans at the beginning of the war and were in fact singled out by Robert C. Weaver, one of Roosevelt's 'Black Cabinet,' in a letter to Harry S. Truman, the Chairman of the Senate Committee to Investigate the National Defense Program.[11] The aircraft industry was a comparatively new one which had not used blacks in any great numbers prior to 1940. The work was of the type not generally given to them, being clean and light, and requiring skilled or semi-skilled labor. The policies of the corporations involved also limited the possibilities of employment for blacks. They were summed up by the head of industrial relations of the Vultee Aircraft Company when, in response to a query from the National Negro Congress, he said quite openly that it was not the policy of his company to employ people who were not of the Caucasian race: 'consequently, we are not in a position to offer your people employment at this time.'[12] Because of such attitudes, there were only 240 Afro-Americans in the entire aircraft industry in 1940, and the Fair Employment Practices Committee, at hearings in Los Angeles in 1941, was to find that of the 6000 people employed by Vultee Aircraft none were black. The Douglass Aircraft Company, like Vultee one of those named specifically by Weaver, had only ten Afro-Americans among its 33,000 employees.[13]

That such discrimination was common throughout all industry was illustrated by the response to a questionnaire sent out to 'hundreds of industrialists with large war contracts' by the US Employment Service in January 1942. When asked whether they would employ Afro-Americans, 51 per cent said they did not and would not, and only half of the remainder said, without reservation, that they would employ them.[14] Equally indicative of the levels of discrimination was the fact that from September 1940 to September 1941 blacks comprised only 1·6 per cent of the total number of men deferred from armed service because they were 'engaged in occupations necessary to the national health, safety and interest.'[15] The proportion among those deferred because they were involved in national defense work was even smaller—0·65 per cent.

Afro-Americans immediately began to fight for entry into war industries as well as the armed forces. 'The struggle of the Negro for equitable and decent treatment in the national defense program' was seen as 'another aspect of the race's continuing battle for full manhood.'[16] The NAACP and the National Urban League were joined by a number of organizations such as the Committee on Negro Americans in Defense Industries and the Allied Councils for Defense which concentrated on discrimination in employment. The Committee for the Participation of Negroes in National Defense acted as the co-ordinator of these different groups and was responsible for the mobilization of support for Senate Resolution SR 75, introduced by Senator Wagner, which would have authorized a Senate committee 'to make a full and complete investigation into the participation of Negro citizens in all industrial and other phases of the national defense program.'[17] Such a body would have been empowered to recommend legislation and other governmental action in order to end discrimination. However, a committee to deal just with discrimination was thought unnecessary by government officials because of the existence of the Senate Committee to Investigate the National Defense Program. The problem of racial discrimination was referred to that body although chairman Harry S. Truman frankly admitted that the committee was overloaded with work and would not be able to hear witnesses for some time.[18]

Nevertheless, the Truman committee did manage to hold a Preliminary Conference on Racial Discrimination on June 25, 1941 which was attended by several blacks including Mary McLeod Bethune, Colonel Campbell C. Johnson, John P. Davies of the National Negro Congress, and Rayford Logan. In an angry speech Logan attacked the government for its lack of action and accused it of giving Afro-Americans the 'run-around.'[19] On the very same day as the conference President Roosevelt issued Executive Order 8802 which authorized a Fair Employment Practices Committee to see that discrimination in defense industries was ended. His order, which virtually duplicated SR 75, was not so much the result of conferences but more of a threat of dramatic protest by A. Philip Randolph.

Randolph's career is one of the most interesting in contemporary black history.[20] As an opponent of participation in World War I and an angry critic of the Wilson administration, Randolph's writings earned *The Messenger* the title of 'the most able and the most dangerous of all Negro publications.'[21] During the inter-war years he devoted himself to trade union organization and gained prominence as the leader of the

Brotherhood of Sleeping Car Porters formed in 1925. Not only did he secure recognition of the union from the railroads, but in 1936 took it into the American Federation of Labor as an international union. From then on he and Milton Webster, the vice-president of the Brotherhood, consistently attended the AF of L's annual conventions where they attacked discrimination in both the unions and all other spheres of life. Because of his position in the labor movement he was elected president of the National Negro Congress, an organization which hoped to build a black mass movement by working with and through trade unions. After four years Randolph left the Congress in 1940 because it had become dominated by the communists, with whom he had been feuding since the 1920s.[22] The following year he achieved its aim of a black mass movement in the March on Washington Movement which resulted in Executive Order 8802.[23]

In January 1941, Randolph called on his fellow Afro-Americans to register their 'uncompromising demand for the right of Negro people to get their just share of work on all national defense work and also to be properly and equitably integrated into the armed forces of our country.'[24] Later that month, in an article headed 'Defense Rotten', he suggested that 10,000 Afro-Americans march on Washington to 'DEMAND THE RIGHT TO WORK AND FIGHT FOR OUR COUNTRY.'[25] At first there was little favorable reaction from other black leaders until it became clear that only such a protest would produce results from the government. In March 1941 a conference on Negro Participation in National Defense was held in Washington, and Walter White wrote to the President that 'it was the unanimous opinion of those present' that nothing short of presidential action would meet the situation.[26] In response to a request for a meeting to discuss the subject of discrimination, however, White was told by F.D.R.'s secretary that the President was too busy and that he should consult Sidney Hillman of the Office of Production Management.[27] Faced with this type of rebuff, White, like Logan, felt that blacks were getting the run-around, and in despair he, Logan, Lester B. Granger of the Urban League and others joined Randolph in a national March on Washington Movement Committee which called on 10,000 Afro-Americans to demonstrate in the capital on July 1.[28]

Sidney Hillman did act on receiving their complaints. On April 11, 1941, at the instruction of the Office of Production Management, he sent a letter to all holders of defense contracts asking for the removal of all bans on the employment of 'qualified and competent Negro workers' and pointed out that 'every available source of labor capable of producing defense material must be tapped in the present emergency.'[29] At the same time he created the Negro Employment and Training Branch and the Minority Groups Branch in the Labor Division of the Office of Production Management, with Robert C. Weaver and Will Alexander as their respective heads. This did not appease the black leaders, who insisted on a

meeting with Roosevelt and on much stronger action. The aim of those in
the MOWM was quite simply by exerting mass pressure to force the
President to issue an executive order abolishing discrimination in
government, industry and the armed forces. Similar demonstrations had
been staged before: in World War I a parade had been led by the NAACP
to protest against race riots and discrimination; in the 1930s the Jobs For
Negroes movement had campaigned for the employment of blacks in
ghetto shops and stores. What was unusual about the MOWM was its
proposed scale and the fact that whites were excluded. Randolph made a
point of asking sympathetic whites not to take part on the grounds that
there were some things the black man had to do alone: 'This is our fight
and we must see it through.'[30] He later pointed out that an all-black
movement would create 'faith by Negroes in Negroes,' but an additional
reason was that the exclusion of whites would prevent infiltration by
communists. While black communists were not barred as individuals, the
MOWM would have nothing to do with the Party because 'its policy was
rule or ruin.'[31]

While this racially exclusive tactic may have cost the wholehearted
support of the interracial NAACP and Urban League, it did not detract
from its mass appeal. By the end of May the number of marchers called for
had risen to 50,000 and Randolph, as national director, warned President
Roosevelt that between ten and fifty thousand were likely to take part.
Walter White wrote that the proposal to march on Washington 'had fired
the imagination of the disheartened Negroes throughout the nation,' and
Randolph was even more enthusiastic. In a letter to Eleanor Roosevelt
asking her to address the marchers on July 1, he said that nothing since
Emancipation had gripped the hearts of Afro-Americans like the question
of discrimination in defense plants.[32]

The initial reaction of the government was to attempt to have the march
called off. Roosevelt said that he could 'imagine nothing that will stir up
race hatred and slow up progress more than a march of that kind,' and at
the suggestion of one of his secretaries, Stephen Early, he had Eleanor and
the Mayor of New York, Fiorello La Guardia, meet Randolph and White
on June 13 and ask them not to go through with their demonstration.[33] The
two Afro-Americans not only refused to abandon their campaign, but also
managed to convince Mrs Roosevelt that they were in the right: she
promised to intervene on their behalf and to arrange a meeting with the
President. The following day a statement was released from the White
House containing the text of a letter dated June 12, to William Knudsen
and Sidney Hillman, the co-directors of the Office of Production
Management. The letter recognized the extent of discrimination in the
defense program and reaffirmed the policy of full utilization of manpower
as expressed by Hillman in April. It went on to say that no country engaged
in fighting totalitarianism could 'afford arbitrarily to exclude large

segments of its population from its defense industries' and that it was even more important 'to strengthen our unity and morale by refuting at home the very theories which we are fighting abroad.'[34] However, while seeming to agree with the arguments presented by Afro-Americans (and the military participation ratio theory), Roosevelt left it to employers, workers and the OPM to see that changes were made. The leaders of the MOWM still insisted on a meeting with the President and an executive order.

On June 18 Roosevelt finally acceded to their demands and held a meeting with White and Randolph at the White House; also present were Assistant Secretary of War Robert P. Patterson, Secretary of the Navy Frank Knox, Hillman and Knudsen. When informed by White that no less than 100,000 people would take part in the march, Roosevelt asked what he should do. He was told that the blacks wanted an 'unequivocal executive order to effectuate the speediest possible abolition of discrimination in war industries and the armed services.'[35] The President appeared to acquiesce to these demands and got Randolph and White to draft the kind of order they had in mind and leave it with him to consider. Knudsen had made his opposition to such an order clear at the meeting, and Patterson and Under Secretary of the Navy Forrestal also had strong reservations. They felt that an order abolishing racial discrimination in industry would arouse, rather than allay, racial prejudice and that it would be difficult to implement.[36] The black leaders, however, had made it obvious that they would not accept anything less. Finally Roosevelt issued Executive Order 8802 commanding an end to discrimination in defense industries on June 25, 1941 and the MOW was called off.

Obviously, the Afro-Americans had not achieved all their aims. No executive action was taken on discrimination in the armed forces, nor, at least not specifically, in defense training, government and trade unions. However, Executive Order 8802 stated national policy to be against 'discrimination in the employment of workers in defense industries or Government because of race, creed, color or national origin.' To that end, it did order the end of discrimination in defense training programs, the inclusion of a non-discrimination clause in all defense contracts, and the formation of a Committee on Fair Employment Practices to 'receive and investigate complaints of discrimination in violation of the provisions of this order' and to 'take appropriate steps to redress grievances which it finds valid.'[37] Thus, rather than several orders dealing with discrimination in employment, the blacks were given one which seemed all-encompassing. Dalfiume has argued that because several orders were not issued, the postponing of the March on Washington marked a victory for Roosevelt and that the President had decided from the start on the concessions he would make to black demands.[38] This seems unfair on White and Randolph who refused to accept a cut-down version of their draft order and who fought, with a certain amount of success, for an order with some power. The blacks were also well aware, from their meeting with Roosevelt and his advisers in 1940, that action against segregation in the forces was unlikely to be taken at that time. Their prime concern in 1941 was to ensure black participation in the war industries, and as far as Randolph was concerned their main objective had been secured.[39]

While the results of the MOWM may seem puny to present-day writers, in 1941 they were seen as a huge success. Pointing out that this was the first executive order relating to civil rights since Reconstruction, the *Chicago Defender* called it 'one of the most significant pronouncements that has been made in the interests of the Negro for more than a century,' and Mrs Mary McLeod Bethune said it came 'as a refreshing shower in a thirsty land.'[40] Coupled with this enthusiasm were reservations. The president of the *Pittsburgh Courier*, Ira Lewis, wrote that *if* 'this order is made workable and effective, the thirteen million Negroes in the United States can very well proclaim it to be an economic Emancipation Proclamation.'[41] *The Crisis* pointed out that the order was not popular with employers and unions, and that it was up to Afro-Americans to see that it worked.[42] When Roosevelt named the members of the Fair Employment Practices Committee, the *Pittsburgh Courier*, although pleased, felt that the recommendations of White and Randolph had been ignored and that therefore the committee was not truly representative. Its original membership included two blacks, Earl Dickerson, a Chicago alderman, and Milton Webster, vice president of the Brotherhood of Sleeping Car Porters. The other white members were the chairman, Mark Ethridge, editor of the Louisville *Courier-Journal;* William Green, President of the American Federation of Labor (AFL); Philip Murray, President of the Congress of Industrial Organizations (CIO); and David Sarnoff, President of RCA. Randolph seemed quite happy with these appointments and in a telegram to Roosevelt wrote 'You have gone right down the line with the Negroes.'[43]

Whatever their reservations, Afro-Americans were well aware that the threat of mass action had brought results. Randolph and the March on Washington Movement signalled a new departure in the methods of civil rights organizations. Indicative of the popular support for Randolph was the award of the Spingarn Medal at the 33rd NAACP convention 'in recognition of the dramatic culmination of his years of effort in the mobilization of Negro mass opinion in 1941.'[44]

Although the march was postponed, the Movement continued in being under Randolph's leadership. It immediately adopted a five point program to continue existing local committees, to collect facts and present them to the FEPC, to develop more local committees to gain pressure power, to gather information about job opportunities for unemployed blacks, and to encourage Afro-Americans to apply for jobs in industries with defense contracts.[45] As the war progressed, the militancy of the

MOWM declined. Although Randolph warned that a march could still take place after the transfer of FEPC to the War Manpower Commission under Paul McNutt, he had earlier spoken in terms of a 'non-march pressure campaign.'[46] It has even been suggested that the original threat of a march was nothing more than a bluff and that black leaders had little or no idea of how many people would take part.[47] If this was so, it is surprising that Roosevelt did not call the bluff, and that White and Randolph were so insistent on an executive order. Perhaps the warning from William Hastie that not only would a march take place, but also that if the 'responsible leadership' withdrew the march would be taken over by 'more radical elements', had some effect.[48] Moreover, three rallies were held in 1942, after America had entered the war, which demonstrated that the MOWM had some considerable following. On July 16 a crowd estimated at between 15,000 and 25,000 heard a number of speakers in Madison Square Garden; ten days later between 10,000 and 20,000 gathered in Chicago, and a third large meeting was held in St Louis in August.[49]

Only after job opportunities for blacks had increased and America was fully engaged in total war did this support fall away. When in 1943 Randolph adopted the plan for a non-violent protest campaign directed at segregation in areas other than the armed forces and defense industries, he was accused of using the 'most dangerous demagoguery on record.'[50] A *Pittsburgh Courier* poll in 1942 had found that 53·1 per cent of those asked were opposed to a march on Washington; in 1943 70·6 per cent were against the civil disobedience campaign.[51] Despite this lack of support at the time, there was something strangely prophetic when, describing the civil disobedience campaign, Randolph said, 'it appears that an important part of the future strategy and technique of the Negro must be in the field of demonstration, both non-violent mass activity and disciplined non-violent demonstrations of small Negro and white groups for civil and economic justice.'[52]

The idea for this type of demonstration seems to have originated from Bayard Rustin and James Farmer, two young members of the Chicago branch of the MOWM, who spoke in favor of non-violent direct action at the 1943 MOWM convention. Both were founder members of the Congress of Racial Equality (CORE), which sprang from the Christian-pacifist movement the Fellowship of Reconciliation in 1942. The members of CORE were very much influenced by the tactics and philosophy of Gandhi in India, and again it is interesting to note that Randolph made comparisons between America and India at the MOWM conference in Detroit in 1942. However, while CORE used pickets, boycotts and sit-ins to attack segregation in drugstores and department stores in a number of Northern cities during the war, the MOWM did not in fact use them.[53] In reality, although it lingered on until 1947 the MOWM lacked the support necessary for direct action, particularly after the outbreak of race riots in

1943. Besides, it was engaged in divergent activities, for as well as supporting Winfred Lynn in his legal battle against segregation in the forces, it was, from 1943 onward, active in the fight to save the FEPC, for which it had been largely responsible.

In his history of the FEPC, Louis Ruchames suggested that the President's committee demonstrated that customs and mores could be changed by law. However, he failed to demonstrate that 'guided' change of this nature in fact took place, and as he himself admitted there is no way of knowing how many Afro-Americans were employed as a result of the committee's actions.[54] While in operation, it not only suffered constant attack from political opponents but was also defeated by employers and unions in certain crucial areas. Afro-Americans did make considerable economic gains, but these generally occurred after 1942 and were the result of growing labor shortages rather than the work of FEPC.

The committee had limitations which sprang directly from the executive order. Most important, of course, was the unspoken fact that it was a temporary body, to exist only during the war emergency and to deal only with defense industries. The committee described the restrictions this placed on it, pointing out that it had no power to deal with 'privately owned and operated plants which do not hold government contracts or subcontracts and which are not engaged in activities essential to the war effort, even though they may be engaged in interstate or foreign commerce.'[55] In those areas where FEPC did have jurisdiction, it had little power to enforce its recommendations but could only hope that adverse publicity and persuasion would make a company change its hiring policies. When persuasion failed, FEPC lacked the final authority to back up its rulings.[56]

Another weakness was the committee's size, or rather the lack of it. The original order was amended on July 18, 1841 to increase the number of members to six, and again in 1942 to bring it up to seven. This small group had a staff not much bigger in size: in its first year FEPC had only seven field officers and five clerical workers and a budget of $80,000. Even when the personnel situation improved and the budget was increased to $431,609, FEPC remained well below the standards of other government departments.[57]

Because of its limited size and budget, the committee operated by holding public hearings in selected major cities. The first of these were held in Los Angeles in October 1941. The policies of ten firms, mainly aircraft manufacturers, and three unions were examined and the committee made several recommendations to end discrimination. Although no direct connection can be made, it is interesting to note that in 1944 Afro-Americans made up 6 per cent of the total number of aircraft workers compared to 0·2 per cent in 1940.[58] Later hearings were held in Chicago, New York, Birmingham, Washington, Philadelphia and Portland. The pattern of 1941 was invariably repeated, with the committee making recommendations and asking for periodic reports from those concerned.[59] During the hearings in Birmingham, Alabama Mark Ethridge, the former chairman, reassured anxious fellow Southerners about the committee's intentions and criticized black leaders who regarded Executive Order 8802 as a second Emancipation Proclamation. He went on to say that there was no power in the world '—not even in all the mechanized armies of the earth, Allied and Axis—which could now force the Southern white people to the abandonment of the principle of social segregation.'[60] His attitude was shared by the many whites in the South who did not object to the full utilization of black manpower or the principle of equal pay for blacks, but who did object to white and black working side by side on the factory line. Any attempt by the committee to bring this about led to violent reactions in the South and from Southerners in Congress. The opposition to FEPC appeared to have been successful when on July 30, 1942, without prior warning, the committee was transferred by President Roosevelt to the War Manpower Commission and placed under the supervision of Paul V. McNutt.

The black response at the time was to say that FEPC was being muzzled as a result of pressure from the South, and later writers have agreed. Ruchames wrote of the transfer that 'there can be little doubt but that its purpose was to restrict the committee's activities.'[61] According to Roosevelt's letter, however, the purpose of the transfer was to co-ordinate the activities of FEPC with those of the branches of the War Manpower Commission, and in response to critics he said that the intention was 'to strengthen—not to submerge—the committee, and to reinvigorate—not to repeal—Executive Order 8802.'[62] The official historian of the War Manpower Commission accepted this defense, but pointed out that neither greater co-ordination nor strengthening resulted. The War Manpower Commission consistently ignored the FEPC on matters of discrimination and failed to refer cases to it. There was disagreement and delay over changes in the US Employment Service's policies with regard to filling discriminatory applications for labor. It was not until September 3, 1943, when discrimination was defined to include the refusal to classify workers properly or hire workers of a particular color or race, that the Employment Service changed its practices.[63]

A greater condemnation was that no hearings were held while the FEPC was under McNutt's control. Public hearings on discrimination against Mexican-Americans were scheduled to be held in El Paso, Texas during August 1942: they were called off at the behest of the State Department for fear that Axis agents in South America would use them for propaganda purposes and damage relations between Mexico and the USA.[64] The important hearings on discrimination in the railroad industry were postponed on January 11, 1943. Although other railroad companies were involved, the parties most concerned were members of the South Eastern Carriers Conference—all Southern companies. It was suggested by blacks that the hearings were cancelled because of pressure from big business, the railroads and Southerners in Congress, and they voiced their fears that once again the FEPC was being muzzled.[65] McNutt accepted responsibility and took the blame, but it appears that he had been directed to postpone the railroad hearings by the President who was then out of the country. According to Schuck, it was reasonable for the President not to want such major hearings to take place in his absence—a rather facile explanation which did not satisfy the majority of Afro-Americans nor FEPC members McLean, Ethridge and Sarnoff, all of whom resigned.[66]

Following this debacle, Roosevelt held a conference on February 19, 1943 with all those concerned to discuss a revision of the scope and power of the FEPC. The principal recommendation, that the committee be reconstituted as an independent agency, was accepted. On May 27, 1943, by Executive Order 9346 the FEPC was re-established in the Office of Emergency Management of the Executive Office and given powers to conduct hearings, make findings and recommend measures to the War Manpower Commission.[67] As was soon to be demonstrated, despite this apparent strengthening many of its weaknesses remained.

On May 24, 1943 a four day riot began after the upgrading of twelve black welders at the Alabama Drydock & Shipping Company yards in Mobile, Alabama. The riot was inspired by the League for White Supremacy, a group organized to prevent the end of discrimination and segregation in the shipyards. The violence ended and workers returned to work only after federal troops were called in.[68] The FEPC and WMC then worked out an agreement which set aside four slipways where black workers could be employed as welders, riggers, caulkers and riveters. But even in those four areas they could not work as electricians, machine operators or pipefitters. While it condoned segregation and discrimination, this settlement was a victory compared to the committee's failure with the railroads later that year.

The postponed hearings were finally held in Washington, D.C. on September 15, 1943. After listening to 93 cases involving 22 companies and 14 unions, FEPC ordered an end to all discriminatory hiring practices and called for the upgrading of blacks on an equal basis. Of the 20 companies and 7 unions sent such cease and desist orders, 16 companies and 3 unions, all in the South, refused to comply. Four unions did not even reply to the request.[69] The companies argued that, rather than aiding the war effort, to enforce the committee's directive would disrupt their peaceful relations with employees, antagonize the public and 'result in stoppages of transportation, and would most gravely and irreparably impair the whole war effort of the country.'[70] When the committee referred these cases to President Roosevelt, he set up a three man mediation committee to examine them. In February 1944 Roosevelt reported that progress was being made, but then no more was heard and no action ever taken. As the FEPC later remarked, these cases 'proved that persuasion must be backed by final authority if conformity with the policy is to be realized.'[71]

Clearly, it was not just employers who were involved in acts of discrimination against Afro-Americans. Unions other than those on the railroads were cited in several FEPC hearings, either for excluding blacks from membership of a particular union and thus denying them employment in closed shop industries, or for segregating them in all-black auxiliary unions.[72] There were also a number of work stoppages when whites struck after the employment or upgrading of Afro-Americans even though the national union organizations had opposed discrimination in principle.

The many American trade unions or labor organizations were grouped in two separate bodies, the American Federation of Labor (AFL) and the Congress of Industrial Organizations (CIO), which united in 1955 to become the AFL-CIO.[73] The AFL, formed in 1881, began as a federation of craft unions and had a policy of non-discrimination. By the turn of the century unions which had excluded blacks altogether or relegated them to separate auxiliaries were admitted to the AFL, and such discriminatory practices became accepted if not explicit policies. The United Mine Workers Union was the only AFL affiliate with a completely egalitarian policy, and in 1902 its 20,000 Afro-American members accounted for half of the blacks in the AFL. In 1937 a number of industrial unions, led by the Mine Workers, broke away from the AFL to form the CIO, a federation of industrial rather than craft unions. Because it hoped to organize unskilled and semi-skilled workers in basic industries, many of whom were black, and because it attracted the liberal and left wing elements within the labor movement, the CIO adopted a policy of non-discrimination from the beginning.

The differences in the racial policies of the AFL and CIO became more apparent during the war. By agreement with the National Defense Advisory Commission the two organizations assumed responsibility for removing barriers against Afro-American workers in defense industries.[74] Yet at its conventions in 1940, 1941, and 1942, the AFL rejected resolutions condemning discrimination proposed by A. Philip Randolph: he was told that it was unnecessary for the ALF to adopt them because its opposition to discrimination had been stated in the past. Moreover, there was no need for such resolutions or the committee on discrimination proposed by Randolph until evidence of discrimination within the trade union movement was provided.[75] Randolph replied to these objections in 1943 when he presented details of prejudice among AFL-affiliated unions from a paper written by Herbert Northrup, a member of the regional War Labor Board in Detroit and consultant to the FEPC. Twenty unions within the AFL were listed as either excluding blacks altogether or affording them only segregated membership. In answer to these charges the president of the AFL, William Green, said that as such a small percentage of the AFL's 107 unions were involved, the situation was obviously improving; he hoped that it would continue to do so but did not recommend that the convention adopt the resolution abolishing segregated auxiliaries.[76] It was not until after the riots of 1943 that the AFL took any stand on discrimination and then in the form of a resolution condemning prejudice and bigotry in the country as a whole rather than another resolution which concentrated on racial practices within the Federation itself.[77] Lukewarm resolutions in support of the FEPC were adopted throughout the war period, but only after reference to discrimination in unions had been deleted. The AFL felt that to incorporate such a phrase would encourage government intervention in union affairs, and for similar reasons it was opposed to a permanent FEPC.[78]

While the black newspapers viewed AFL conventions as farces, they saw the CIO 'coming forward as the foremost organization in the country to fight for equality of job opportunity for Negroes.'[79] Their optimism had some justification, for the CIO maintained its pre-war policies and attempted to put them into practice. The 1941 convention not only condemned discrimination but also authorized the formation of a committee to abolish it within the Congress itself. Every year thereafter, the CIO reiterated its position and related the issue of racial prejudice to the war. A resolution at the 1942 convention delcared that not only was racial discrimination a 'characteristic of our fascist enemies,' but also that such discrimination was a direct aid to the enemy, 'creating division, dissension and confusion' at home. The resolution went on to say that the exclusion of minority groups 'hampers production by depriving the nation of the use of available skills and manpower.'[80] A resolution adopted in 1943 commended the FEPC for its work, demanded the prosecution of those 'whipping up hatred against minority groups' and called upon President Roosevelt to end the segregation of the armed forces; in 1944 the Committee to Abolish Racial Discrimination reported that a total of 85 local CIO anti-discrimination committees had been formed and that intervention by the CIO had led to policy reversals in certain government departments.[81] The CIO was also responsible for a case brought before the War Labor Board against wage differentials based on race used by the Southport Petroleum Company in Texas City, Texas: it ruled that rates of pay based on race or color were illegal.[82]

These were all points in the CIO's favor, but there were flaws. The main one was that it was easy to pass resolutions at conventions or for the Congress to intercede with the government: it was not as easy for it to impose its will on all branches of member unions, as indeed the Committee to Abolish Discrimination recognized.[83] While delegates at the 1942 convention adopted a resolution 'urging that employers be compelled to utilize in full the services of colored workers, aliens and women,' members of the CIO-affiliated Industrial Union of Marine and Shipbuilding Workers walked out of the Bethlehem-Fairfield shipyards in Baltimore in protest against the admission of two blacks to the welding school. When the union expelled five men for inciting discrimination, there was a further protest demonstration. It was the determination of the employers rather than union action which won the day.[84] CIO unions found themselves to be powerless in other disputes. In 1943, 700 workers at the Packard Motor factory in Detroit struck after the hiring of four black women, and in the conflict at the Alabama Drydock & Shipping Company yards in Mobile the CIO was reluctant to stress its anti-discriminatory position for fear of losing a forthcoming employee representation election to the AFL.[85]

FEPC faced a major crisis when the CIO Transport Workers Union proved unable to control its members in Philadelphia. Late in 1943 the FEPC ordered the Philadelphia Transportation Company and the AFL Rapid Transit Employees' Union to desist from discriminatory hiring and upgrading practices. The union notified the committee that it could not obey the directive and advised the Transportation Company not to comply.[86] At the same time the union brought the FEPC before the House Committee to Investigate Executive Agencies (Smith committee) which was opposed to the Presidential committee and encouraged the Transit Employees to continue their defiance.[87] However, in March 1944 the Transport Workers Union won the right to represent both maintenance and platform workers and a change in policy was expected. When the War Manpower Commission ruled in July 1944 that all hiring was to be done through the US Employment Service without discrimination, the TWU concurred. Following the upgrading of eight Afro-Americans the white workers, in defiance of their union and employers, the FEPC and the War Manpower Commission, went on strike on August 1, 1944 and effectively paralyzed the city. On August 3 at the command of President Roosevelt the Army moved into Philadelphia to curb violence and take over the running of the bus and trolley services. Major General Hayes warned the strikers that if they continued to stay away from work their draft deferment would immediately be cancelled and they would be declared 1A for draft purposes. That threat and the fear that they would lose their jobs permanently persuaded the strikers to return to work on August 5.[88] The FEPC also met with rebuffs from transport unions in Los Angeles and Washington, but although they took some time to settle those disputes did not require the Army to be called in.[89]

There were, of course, instances when the FEPC and unions did solve industrial disputes over racial issues. A dispute in 1942 over seniority rights

at the Chrysler plant near Detroit in which whites threatened to walk out
ended when the United Automobile Workers union advised the company
to fire all strikers. In 1943 other strikes by car workers were avoided after
concerted action by the UAW and FEPC.[90] In 1943 and 1944 alone the
FEPC satisfactorily solved twenty-five work stoppages involving more than
181,791 workers. Nine of those stoppages were caused by whites resisting
the employment or promotion of blacks, and eleven by blacks protesting
against demotions or other forms of discrimination. In one strike 500
white workers refused to return to work until the company agreed to end
discrimination against blacks.[91]

   While the union movement figures largely in the FEPC's successes and
failures, it also contributed to the opposition to it. In 1944 trade unions
subscribed $11,000 to the National Council for a Permanent FEPC, yet in
the same year the AFL voiced its opposition to a permanent agency at its
convention and before a Senate hearing.[92] As Brazeal said, 'their
opposition to a permanent FEPC is probably based as much on a desire not
to admit Negroes to an equitable membership as it is to labor's avowed and
traditional opposition to restrictive labor legislation.'[93] Even the more
sympathetic CIO showed signs of division: at the 1943 convention the
resolutions committee voted unanimously against support for a
permanent agency on fair employment practices; the following year the
CIO President, Philip Murray, urged all member unions to back a
permanent FEPC.[94] Support for those unions which chose to defy the Fair
Employment Practices Committee came from the Special Committee to
Investigate Executive Agencies, the Smith committee. Created in 1943, it
was a determined opponent of the FEPC and encouraged the transport
workers in Philadelphia to ignore its directives. It also challenged its
rulings in the Southern railroad cases, and although it finally dropped the
matter and even failed to issue a report on the FEPC hearings, the Smith
committee did provide a focus for the opponents of the FEPC among
unions, employers and politicians.[95]

   Support for the FEPC was mobilized by A. Philip Randolph in the
National Council for a Permanent FEPC which grew out of the 'Save
FEPC' campaign which had followed the transfer of the agency to the War
Manpower Commission. An interracial organization, the council attracted
a diverse following. However, the opposition proved to be too strong. In
1944 an independent Office Appropriation Bill was passed and it included
a direct attack on the FEPC. An amendment attached to the bill by Senator
Richard B. Russell of Georgia forbade the appropriation of funds for any
agency created by executive order and in operation for more than one year,
without the specific consent of Congress.[96] In 1946 a Southern filibuster in
the Senate prevented the passage of a bill of appropriation and the FEPC
died.

   Despite this gloomy history, it would be ridiculous to deny that it had
had some success. Conspicuous confrontations and defeats diverted

attention away from the thousands of individual complaints successfully dealt with. In the eighteen months from July 1943 to December 1944, 5803 cases were examined by the committee. Of these 64 per cent were dismissed for lack of merit while the remaining 36 per cent (approximately 1723) were processed and brought to satisfactory conclusions. Will Alexander of the War Manpower Commission pointed out that the committee also acted as a propaganda agency: 'it forced people to look, day after day, at this problem of the Negro's economic handicaps.'[97] During the war local and state governments followed the federal example. In July 1941 the state of Illinois declared it a misdemeanor for any war defense contractor to discriminate because of race or color. Similar bills were passed in New York state in September 1941 and in New Jersey in 1942.[98] A number of ordinances and bills against discrimination in employment were passed in various cities and states in the immediate post-war period. This was all to the good, but like the FEPC these bodies had only limited powers and, therefore, effect.

Most of the gains made by Afro-Americans in employment during the war came after 1942 when labor shortages began to affect hiring practices; more than half of them were made in areas of *acute* labor shortages. Faced with such facts one has to agree that 'such evidence of greater utilization as does exist cannot necessarily be attributed to government efforts but may be attributed to the general appearances of stringencies in the supply of labor.'[99]

Whatever the exact cause, employment opportunities for blacks did increase during the war. From April 1940 to April 1944 the total number of Afro-Americans in work rose by one million: from 4·4 million to 5·3. These figures are, by themselves, impressive, but again they obscure the fact that most gains were made in the latter half of the war. There was an increase in job opportunities for blacks during 1940 and 1941, notably in shipbuilding and iron and steel works, but 'until mid-1942 Negroes had not profited from the war boom to the same extent as had white workers.'[100] The main reason for this delay was the large number of unemployed whites who took precedence over blacks even if it meant importing them from outside areas. The lack of training and specific skills, at a time when unskilled workers were not in great demand, also made it difficult for Afro-Americans to enter new occupations. By 1942 the expansion of industry and the armed forces had seriously depleted the labor force and all available sources of manpower had to be tapped. At the beginning of that year three per cent of all persons engaged in war production were black; in September 4·6 per cent were black; in January 1943 this had risen to 6·4 per cent; by January 1944 it was 7·3 per cent; and in November 1944 it was 8·3 per cent. The number of blacks unemployed dropped from 937,562 in 1940 to about 640,000 in 1942; by 1944 this number had fallen to 151,000.[101]

The pessimism expressed by various writers early in the war vanished with this change in circumstances. Robert C. Weaver referred to 1942 as the 'crucial year', and the New York State War Council, which had described the employment situation of Afro-Americans in 1942 as 'extremely bitter', could in 1945 boast that there was not one war plant in operation in the Empire State which discriminated against blacks.[102] The Chicago Mayor's Commission on Human Relations reported that the employment of blacks in war production in Cook and DuPage Counties (Chicago) had risen from 80,347 in 1940 to 222,600 in 1945 and that this represented 11·7 per cent of the total work force. By September 1944 the *Chicago Defender* could record that the employment of Afro-Americans generally was at an all-time high.[103] While there were clearly rises throughout all sectors of war production, certain areas witnessed greater increases than others. The proportion of blacks among shipbuilding workers rose from 5·5 per cent in September 1942 to 10·2 per cent in March 1944; the aircraft industry reversed its pre-war employment patterns as 'companies like North American, Boeing, and Martin completely altered their policies in the face of all-out war, the need to utilize all available manpower, government pressure, and obvious morality and decency.'[104]

Among the additional million black workers were 600,000 women, who raised the total number of Afro-American women in employment to 2·1 million.[105] The pattern of discrimination was such that these women found work only after white women and black men, and as a result made up only 4 per cent of the seven million women in war production in 1944. Even so, the percentage of black women remained higher than that of white women in employment and like their male counterparts they made substantial gains in certain areas of industrial activity.[106] In 1940, in the Detroit–Willow Run region, the number of black women in factories was 14,451; in 1944 this had risen to 46,750. The Chrysler Car Company in 1940 included no blacks among its female staff; by 1945 it employed 18,148. An important area of increase was in government service—federal, state, county and municipal—where the number of black female staff rose from 60,000 in 1940 to 200,000 in 1944.[107]

The number and status of Afro-Americans of both sexes in government improved measurably during the war. President Roosevelt's letter of September 16, 1941 to all heads of departments required that all should examine their personnel policies in order that they could assure him 'that in the Federal Service the doors of employment are open to all loyal and qualified workers regardless of creed, race or national origin.'[108] When the FEPC received and reviewed the data on black employment in government it found increases in all departments: in 1943, of a sample of 1,957,858 federal employees, 12·5 per cent or 246,109 were Afro-Americans; in 1944 19·2 per cent of all persons in federal departmental service were black.[109] A great proportion of these were working in the traditional janitorial and custodial positions, but that proportion was much less than it had been before the war. One of the best departments, the Office of Price Administration, employed 1250 Afro-Americans in 1945, more than 70 per cent of whom held clerical and administrative positions. The OPA was also responsible for the inclusion of 396 Afro-Americans on local war price and rationing boards.[110]

With blacks in almost every government department and acting as advisers on race on selective service and in the Office of War Information, the Office of the Secretary of War, the Department of Labor, the Office of Education, and the Housing Agency, Afro-Americans had sufficient numbers and experience to assert their claims and maintain their role in the post-war period. As one historian has said, 'the changes in governmental service were remarkable, even against the background of changes in American society generally.'[111]

As in government, the gains made by Afro-Americans in the industrial sector of the economy were qualitative as well as quantitative. Between 1940 and 1944 the number of Afro-Americans employed as skilled craftsmen, foremen and semi-skilled operatives had doubled and by the end of the war black men and women were engaged in jobs which few had performed before.[112] Indeed, much of what happened in this period was contrary to accepted patterns of employment and was significant because of the departure from old, established practices. Even the numbers of blacks employed in domestic or personal service declined, but because of a greater drop in the number of whites in similar occupations, the proportion of Afro-Americans rose.[113] The increased opportunities and the higher wages in industry encouraged a further decline in the number of blacks working on farms and there was a considerable movement from the rural to urban areas. In 1940, 43·3 per cent of black men and 21 per cent of black women were engaged in agriculture; four years later the figures were 31·3 and 10·9 per cent.[114]

The primary motivation behind this movement was the possibility of achieving industrial employment with high wages during the war, and as a result of this trend Afro-Americans benefited from the general rise in real income. Because of regional variations in incomes it is hard to give overall statistics. However, it seems clear that the earnings of the average black urban worker more than doubled, rising from about $400 to over $1000.[115] Family incomes also increased as wives and husbands, sons and daughters, found work. In two housing projects in Atlanta, Georgia it was found that the average income of the 1281 families living there had increased by 65 per cent from 1940 to 1944, despite the fact that male wage earners had often been drafted.[116] Many of the increases were due to changes in occupation such as in the case of a black woman whose income increased from $312 to $2477 after she had left her job as a maid to become a drill operator. Even the earnings of those who remained in their pre-war employment increased. The average annual earnings of janitors rose from $709 to

$1245; of truck drivers, from $738 to $1340; and of pullman porters, from $1103 to $1795. These rises were not limited to the South, for in housing projects in the North and West the median annual income of black families rose from $867 in 1940 to $1967 in 1945.[117]

This economic progress was not always opposed by whites. The New York State War Council found that 'resistance of the white worker to the integration of Negro personnel has existed largely in the minds of some personnel directors.'[118] Just as in the Army some white soldiers found the thought of integration worse than the actual experience, so too on the shop floor. In an aircraft factory on the West coast, where 47·8 per cent of the white workers initially opposed the employment of Afro-Americans, after the event there was a progression from intolerance through tolerance to friendship, and by 1944 objections were weak and infrequent.[119] Also indicative of some accommodation between black and white workers was the increase in black union membership during the war as 'even iron-clad trade union tradition and practice were forced to bend, and at some points to give way.'[120] By 1945 the number of Afro-Americans in unions was 1,250,000, an increase of approximately 700,000 over the 1940 figure. Many employers found that hiring blacks did not lead to the disasters they had expected, or that Afro-Americans necessarily proved to be poor workers. The National Urban League survey of 300 war plants in 120 cities discovered that 288 of the firms had increased the number of their black employees. Of these, 215 were satisfied with their workers, 50 were fairly satisfied, and only nine said that blacks were not as good as whites. Of the 300, 253 indicated that they would continue to use Afro-American workers.[121]

While these facts point to considerable changes in the economic status of Afro-Americans during, and largely as a result of, the war, there are important reservations. I have already shown that there *were* several incidents involving the opposition of white workers to the hiring or upgrading of blacks. Employers *did* still refuse to hire Afro-Americans or resorted to only token compliance with Executive Order 8802 by employing a small number of blacks in menial positions. There was still a widespread tendency to give them only the hot, heavy, dirty occupations.[122] Bearing in mind the fact that blacks accounted for almost 10 per cent of the American population, the proportions of Afro-Americans in major occupational groups for 1940, 1944 and 1948 reveal the limits of wartime advances.[123] In 1944 black males accounted for 27·6 per cent of laborers, 21·1 per cent of farm workers and foremen, 21·9 per cent of service workers, 75·2 per cent of private household workers, and 10·1 per cent of the operatives and kindred workers. Although their representation had increased, they still comprised only 3·6 per cent of the craftsmen and foremen, 2·8 per cent of clerical and sales workers, and 3·3 per cent of professional and technical workers. The incomes of Afro-Americans rose during the war, but the discrepancy between their wages and incomes and those of whites still remained. In 1945 the average money income of all black families was only half that of white families. This was the highest it had ever been: it was also the highest it was to reach for some time.[124] As one writer pointed out, 'the gains of a decade, however striking, cannot seriously turn the tide of the seven preceding it.'[125]

Those gains which were made varied from area to area and from industry to industry. While the numbers of Afro-Americans employed in shipbuilding or the iron and steel industry were high, the numbers in textiles, electrical machinery, transportation and public utilities were extremely low.[126] The numbers of Negroes in the petroleum industry increased substantially in all regions, but in the rubber tire business very little.[127] William Schuck gathered a great deal of information which showed how conditions varied from region to region, for example that the employment of blacks in shipbuilding in Philadelphia, Baltimore, Seattle, San Francisco, Los Angeles and Galveston was good, and that in Mobile, New Orleans, Beaumont and Evansville it was poor. Similarly, the aircraft companies in Cincinnatti and Detroit employed more than those in New Orleans, Dallas, Atlanta, Evansville and Baltimore. There were regional variations in the ordnance industry, in non-electrical machinery, electrical machinery, iron and steel, rubber and textiles. His overall conclusion was that prejudice and old patterns retarded the progress made, especially in the South where he found little qualitative improvement in the employment of blacks.[128] Others, like Robert C. Weaver and Herbert Northrup, agreed with these conclusions. Northrup found that employment patterns in the automobile industry changed very little in the South and West, and that the greatest changes of all were made in Chicago and Detroit.[129]

The greatest reservation about the economic gains made by blacks was that any progress, no matter how slight, was made with the economy in full operation, with industrial expansion and a high demand for labor. On top of this was the 'disproportionate concentration' of Afro-Americans in war industries or government war agencies—the sectors of the economy most likely to experience cutbacks once the war had ended.[130] From past experience most Americans expected an economic recession in the post-war period and blacks were well aware that they would, once again, be last hired and first fired. Even without a recession, Afro-Americans feared that many of them would be displaced by returning white servicemen.[131] However, the economic gap between black and white had been closed and the Afro-American had tasted enough of prosperity to whet his appetite for more. It was clear that he would not be prepared to 'return to his prewar economic status without a constant and loud complaint.'[132]

4

Wartime Migrations and Urban Conflict: The Disruptive Effects of War

Commenting on the impact of World War II on race relations, the eminent black sociologist Charles S. Johnson spoke of the 'profound and sustained social shock' and the 'social upheaval of war.'[1] His description could not have been more apt, for during the 1940s, as a direct result of the American role in the world conflict, one of the most important of 'unguided' changes took place. Without any encouragement from government or other agencies, huge numbers of people of both races moved to the locations of defense industries. The influx of these newcomers, most of them from the South, into areas in the North and West had an effect which could only be described as disruptive. State and federal bodies, still attempting to cope with the problems of the Depression, were incapable of dealing with this added burden. Overcrowding in poor homes, racial conflict over housing, employment and recreational facilities, plus the anger of blacks at the continued insults their men suffered in the armed services, raised tempers to fever pitch. As a result, in 1943 there was an outbreak of rioting and conflict on a scale not to be witnessed again until the 1960s. But as well as creating friction between the races, urbanization had an influence on the health and education of Afro-Americans—generally for the worse. However, these ill effects were offset by wartime prosperity, the general rise in standards of living, and the realization that the mental and physical well-being of 10 per cent of the population was vital in times of emergency. Although the gap between black and white remained, it narrowed. It can be argued that this was another of the benefits of participation in the war effort.

The migration of blacks was no new development in American history. Following the Civil War some Afro-Americans had left the South and moved West, to Texas, Kansas and Oklahoma. In the late 1880s their numbers increased and their direction changed from westwards to northwards. This trend continued in the 1890s as the ravages of boll weevils and floods exacerbated the poor economic status of blacks in the South and as repressive Jim Crow laws and acts of violence further threatened already reduced civil rights.[2] The North became even more attractive with the outbreak of war in 1914, and the black population in a number of major Northern cities increased dramatically. The 'great migration' as it was called, continued in the post-war years and, despite widespread unemployment among Afro-Americans in the North, into the 1930s if at a slower rate. It led to an increase in their numbers in the cities, and a decline in the South. Even so, in 1940 only 48·6 per cent of all blacks were classed as urban dwellers, and 77·1 per cent still remained in the former Confederate states. Ten years later the corresponding figures were 62·4 per cent and 68·1 per cent.[3]

These last bald statistics reveal something of the changes which took place during World War II, but they do not tell the whole story. The movement of blacks during the 1940s was not merely a repetition of the earlier migration, nor just a continuation of the later trends. A major difference was that it was part of a general shift in population and came only after whites had flocked to the cities. There was little need for encouragement from friends or the press, nor was there any call for labor agents although some were reported in the South.[4] The departure between 1941 and 1945 of five and a half million people from farms and poor areas to seek work in towns and cities was encouragement enough. Even though blacks had to wait until their white compatriots found employment, the attraction was the same for both races: work in the Arsenal of Democracy. The location of the major war industries was responsible for the second difference between the two migrations. The movement during World War II was not simply from South to North: following the routes taken by whites, Afro-Americans went from country to town, to small cities as well as large, and to an entirely new region, the far West and Pacific coast. No matter where, the places which drew the largest numbers were inevitably centers of war production.

California, with almost half of America's shipbuilding and aircraft manufacture taking place within its boundaries, added over one million people to its population in three years. Between 1940 and 1944, more than 500,000 people moved to the San Francisco Bay area alone and 45,000 of them were black.[5] Although slower to start, the black migration soon surpassed that of whites, at least in percentage terms. Thus while the white population of San Francisco increased by 28·1 per cent between 1940 and 1946, the black population grew by an enormous 560 per cent, that is, from 4846 to 32,001. In Los Angeles the number of whites increased by 17·7 per cent; that of blacks by 109 per cent. In 1940 1·3 per cent of Afro-Americans lived in the West; ten years later this figure had more than doubled.[6]

But other areas had huge influxes too. In the Detroit–Willow Run area, another important center of aircraft production, the number of blacks increased by 47 per cent while that of whites rose by only 5·2 per cent. The Afro-American population in Michigan as a whole more than doubled but the white population increased by only 17 per cent. Between 1940 and 1950 the number of Afro-Americans in Washington, D.C., where government was the major war industry, increased by almost 50 per cent and that of whites by only 9·2 per cent.[7] In the country as a whole, 'by the end of 1947, 14 per cent (1·8 million) of all Negroes born in or before April 1940 were living in a different state from the one in which they had lived in 1940. During this period about 10 per cent of all whites moved to a different state.'[8]

The states which made the largest proportional gain in black population were California and Michigan, followed by Oregon, Washington, Utah, Colorado, Wisconsin, Illinois and New York. Oklahoma, Arkansas, Mississippi, Alabama and Georgia all suffered a decline in their black populations. Afro-Americans who remained in the South were moving into urban areas and between 1940 and 1950 Southern cities gained 750,000 blacks.[9] The largest increases were, however, made elsewhere.

Cities such as San Diego, Los Angeles, San Francisco, Salt Lake City, Denver, Milwaukee, Pontiac, Buffalo, Rochester and Syracuse had increases in black population of over 100 per cent in the ten years beginning in 1940.[10] In a sense these figures are misleading, for those cities generally had relatively small black populations prior to the war. Buffalo, for example, added only 8000 to the 17,694 Afro-Americans there in 1940. The number of blacks in Milwaukee in 1940 was only 9000: in 1945 it was still just 13,000.[11] In cities which already had sizeable black communities, the wartime growth did not appear as great in proportional terms. However, an additional 214,534 Afro-Americans entered Chicago during the war and 60,000 were added to Detroit's numbers—both greater increases than had occurred during World War I.[12] It is true, as Weaver said, that the impact of the migrants was probably greater for the cities which had had small black populations prior to the war than for the bigger cities which already had large numbers of Afro-American residents. But whatever their size, the problems were the same for all.

The most obvious and pressing was where to house the newcomers. The Depression had ended a boom in the building industry and construction was further curtailed during the 1940s as all resources were concentrated in the war effort. In the resultant general housing shortage blacks were harder hit than white. Even before the war, in both the North and South the worst housing was that occupied by Afro-Americans, and Southern blacks suffered more than others. Homes were often little more than overcrowded, unpainted, wooden shacks without toilets and often without running water.[13] Conditions in the North were little better; there Afro-Americans usually inhabited two-story wooden houses or older brick tenements long vacated by whites. In either case, they were generally dilapidated, overcrowded and rat infested.

Afro-Americans were concentrated in these poorer areas for a variety of reasons. New arrivals in a city normally sought the security and help of friends and relatives already established. Once settled, however, their low economic status and the prejudice of whites prevented any movement out of the ghetto. It was largely following the great migration, during the 1920s, that housing for blacks in the North became tightly segregated. As Robert Weaver, an authority on black housing, wrote,

> the idea of Negro ghettos in Northern cities became fixed. As years went on, colored Americans were identified with segregated areas, and it was often assumed that Negroes had never been other than relegated to a well-defined area of living. It was also assumed that the Negro ghetto in the North was indestructible.[14]

Attempts to break out of these physical confines were thwarted by real estate agents who refused to sell to blacks, by financiers who refused to loan money to them, and by restrictive covenants in property deeds which forbade the sale of a particular building to anyone other than Caucasians.[15] When such methods failed whites often resorted to violence, terrorizing Afro-Americans out of homes in predominantly white neighborhoods. As more and more blacks entered the cities the ghettos became increasingly congested and run down, affecting morals, health and race relations.[16]

The Depression, which led to widespread federal intervention in all walks of life, brought about some relief in housing. The near-total collapse in private construction, breakdown of finance, and widespread unemployment enabled the government to launch housing programs. Through the Home Owners' Loan Corporation, the Federal Home Loan Banks, and the Federal Housing Administration, the government endeavored to provide credit facilities for home-owners in difficulties and for prospective purchasers. This part of the federal program had little impact on Afro-Americans: increased credit mainly helped those people in the middle and lower-middle income brackets rather than the very poor. Secondly, the loans, although insured by the Federal Housing Administration, were still arranged through established real estate agents and financiers who for one reason or another were reluctant to lend to blacks. Finally, the federal authorities accepted and maintained segregation in housing and the use of restrictive covenants thus limiting black participation from the start.

The part of the government program which did help Afro-Americans was that which provided and funded low-rent public housing. Under the aegis of the Public Works Administration and later the US Housing Authority, black participation in this area was considerable. Of the more than 20,000 houses built between 1933 and 1937, about a third were for

Afro-American occupancy.[17] While this was an encouraging development, it hardly skimmed the surface, and with the onset of war their immediate housing situation deteriorated rather than improved.

The need to channel resources into the war effort prevented much new construction, and to 'the extent that new housing was constructed, it was reserved for essential inmigrant workers in urgent war production areas.'[18] Because of their late entry into war industry, Afro-American participation in the war housing program was delayed. As a statement from the Federal Public Housing Authority pointed out, additional housing for blacks would come only with the breakdown of barriers to employment.[19] This proved to be a correct assessment of the situation, for their inclusion to any great degree in priority war housing took place after mid-1942.[20]

Lack of co-ordination and contradictory racial policies among the various government housing agencies also served to limit the number of 'defense homes' available to blacks. A statement from the Defense Housing Co-ordinator of the Office of Emergency Management, which seemed to recognize the needs of war, declared,[21]

> Public interest and the war program demand that equitable provision of housing be made for Negro defense workers. This statement is to reaffirm and make effective this policy. A total war demands total participation by all of the people.

He went on to say that the lack of vacant sites for development in black areas should 'not constitute an impediment to the defense program through the failure to provide adequate housing for Negro war workers.' Government officials were called upon to take part in interracial and public relations work to prevent and overcome any problems that arose. Yet later the same year a memorandum from the Federal Works Agency stated that sites should be selected 'in accordance with our established racial policy, that is to avoid any disturbance of existing racial patterns for any communities affected.'[22] Such basic differences of policy were, theoretically, ironed out when the National Housing Agency was created, in August 1942, to oversee the war housing program. Although it had a policy of non-discrimination, the NHA lacked the machinery to put its principles into effect. Actions were also limited by the traditional racial viewpoints held by private financiers and by local laws, which in some areas forbade integration.[23]

This complex of forces restricted black participation in defense housing throughout the war. In 1941 only 4600 or 1·4 per cent of the total number of privately and publicly financed homes for war workers were for Afro-Americans although it was said that more than 20 million dollars were being spent on homes for blacks.[24] By the end of 1944, 8·6 per cent or 115,389 out of the total of 1,336,141 privately and publicly financed homes were for blacks. These figures obscure the fact that blacks received a greater number (and a greater proportion) of the publicly financed homes than they did of those privately financed: only 4 per cent, approximately 19,000, of the privately financed homes were for Afro-Americans in 1944, compared with 16·4 per cent or 96,461 of the public housing.[25] The better situation in public housing was, in part, due to the Federal Public Housing Authority (formerly the US Housing Authority) which was active in providing homes for black inmigrant workers. It was also due to the 'necessities of war, the enlightened policies of some housing authorities, and the constant prodding of the racial advisers in the Federal housing agencies' which 'yielded a growing number of racially mixed public housing projects.'[26] While this was all to the good, public housing could not keep up with the needs of Afro-Americans, or for that matter, of whites. Lack of money, authority and initiative all stood in the way of an adequate housing program. More important for blacks was the attitude of local white populations, which was accurately summed up by a government official who pointed out that 'even the demands of war' were insufficient to overcome the deeply imbedded objections to housing projects for blacks.[27]

   With such limitations on what little new home building there was, the housing conditions of Afro-Americans could not improve. Indeed, one survey found that during the war 'conditions of Negro housing in Chicago, Detroit, Cleveland, Buffalo, St Louis and other cities changed on the whole from bad to worse,' a view with which Weaver agreed.[28] There was, it is true, an increase in 'non-farm home ownership' among Afro-Americans in the war years, but in 1947 two-thirds of the black urban population still lived in rented property. Despite considerable increases in earnings, the purchasing power of black Americans was still limited by racial considerations. The prejudices of estate agents and their clients, reflected in the increasingly widespread use of restrictive covenants, prevented blacks from buying homes in new developments, most of which were in suburbs. Between 1940 and 1950 approximately two million whites moved out of the central cities while 1·3 million blacks moved in. There was, in short, an intensification of segregation in housing during this period, as a survey of 185 cities confirmed.[29]

   Whatever the shortcomings of his findings, and there are several, Cowgill's general conclusion that 'residential segregation in these American cities did in fact increase during the decade 1940-50' is borne out by other writers at the time.[30] The effect of this was to turn areas where some blacks had lived in 1940 solidly black, create new black areas, and add to the congestion of existing ghettos. Thus while the proportion of the white population living in overcrowded dwellings (i.e. with more than 1·5 people per room) declined from 4·8 per cent in 1940 to 3·6 per cent in 1950, for blacks, despite their generally improved economic status, the figures rose from 16·0 per cent to 16·7 per cent.[31]

This, of course, is a general view of the situation which omits variations from one place to another. A brief examination of a selection of cities in different areas will give some idea of the conditions faced by Afro-Americans. San Francisco and Los Angeles were both said to have no 'Negro problem' prior to 1941, largely because until then the number of blacks there was small. This situation changed almost overnight as thousands of Afro-Americans, most of them from Oklahoma, Arkansas, Texas and Louisiana, moved west.[32] The reason for this migration was, quite simply, economic: of 152 black immigrant families interviewed in San Francisco, the majority had come to seek better employment, to work in war industries, and to earn more money. A number had moved to join husbands in the forces who were stationed in or near the city. For most of them their hopes of economic advancement were fulfilled, and in the war boom prosperity the average gross monthly wage was $329.32.[33]

Despite their increased earnings, however, Afro-Americans were restricted in their choice of accommodation. Restrictive covenants in both Los Angeles and San Francisco forced blacks into the areas formerly occupied by Japanese. In San Francisco this meant that there were 10,000 people in a district previously inhabited by less than 5000 and where 55 per cent of the homes were rated substandard. War housing programs were completely inadequate: the black population of Los Angeles had increased by over 60,000; almost 30,000 blacks worked in war industry; but only 3825 units of war housing were provided for Afro-Americans. The number of defense homes occupied by blacks in San Francisco was 4784 although there had been over 20,000 black immigrants to the city.[34] While the public housing authorities in San Francisco insisted on segregation of the races, those in Los Angeles tried to ease the situation by dispersing Afro-American families throughout their projects. This was also true in Seattle and Portland, but in all cases white resistance limited the success of such ventures.[35]

The inflow of such huge numbers and the lack of vacant accommodation led to overcrowding. The average migrant family of five people in San Francisco occupied 3.3 rooms. For some, conditions were even worse: one family of three lived, ate and slept in one poorly furnished room; another in a 'substandard frame dwelling' without bathroom, toilet or hot water.[36] Living conditions in Los Angeles were described as 'appalling': in one case more than forty people used a single toilet; the sharing of beds by shifts was common—as one person got up to go to work, another took his place in the 'hot bed'. Similar conditions were recorded in Washington, D.C., the nation's capital. There, a journalist reported, were the worst slums of all where 'five or six persons to a room, occupying at times a single bed, is commonplace.'[37] Local housing authority plans to build homes for Afro-Americans outside the ghetto in Washington were abandoned in the face of white opposition. While 55,000 new war homes were built for whites, only 4000, half of them temporary, were built for blacks.[38]

Attempts to construct housing projects in Buffalo were also resisted by the local white population. With Bethlehem Steel and Bell Aircraft plants located there, Buffalo was an important center of war industry and therefore attracted a considerable number of black migrants, most of whom found work as labor shortages developed.[39] Finding accommodation was not as easy. When the Division of Defense Housing of the National Housing Agency announced, early in 1941, that it planned to build homes in north Buffalo for some of the black workers, protest was immediate. The NHA then suggested alternative sites in neighboring Cheektowaga and Tonawanda, but those too were unacceptable to whites.[40] Most of this opposition appears to have come from Polish and Irish Catholics, often led by their priests. In an address before the Catholic Inter-racial Council in New York, a representative of the Defense Housing Co-ordinator said 'the frequency with which Catholic priests have inspired, organized and led opposition to the Government's efforts to provide housing for Negroes has been very disturbing.' Buffalo, he went on to say, was 'the outstanding example.'[41] Pressure from Lester Granger of the National Urban League and from government officials persuaded representatives of the Catholic church to condemn the discriminatory actions of some of its priests and affiliated organizations.[42] Although the opposition to black housing projects then died down, it had already had effect. The federal and local authorities thereafter insisted on segregation in public housing and spent two years trying to find sites for projects while units in white areas stood empty for lack of 'suitable' applicants.[43] Despite the resultant hardship and wastage and the heated criticism of housing officials by the local Urban League, the policy of racial separation was adhered to until 1947 when the State Commission Against Discrimination ordered an end to it.[44]

The Chicago housing departments attacked the problem of war housing for Afro-Americans with considerable vigor, attempting to house blacks outside the 'black belt.' Their efforts were staunchly resisted by whites. The scene of the most intense covenant practices, 80 per cent of Chicago was estimated to be covered by racially restrictive housing agreements. When such 'legal' methods failed to keep blacks out of white areas, violence and intimidation were used. Between May 1, 1944 and July 20, 1946 there were 46 cases of fire-bombings.[45] In the face of this, public housing was the blacks' only hope, but with an increase of over 100,000 in the number of Afro-Americans in the city, the 7000 war homes were little help. For one project of 1658 units opened in January 1941 there were 19,000 applicants. By 1945, 300,000 Afro-Americans were crowded into the South Side, an area suitable for a maximum of 225,000. A survey of 69,000 homes in three black areas in 1944 found that 26·3 per cent (15,780) were overcrowded.[46] It was not surprising then that the Mayor's Commission found that 'most of the cases of racial friction . . . have occurred directly in relation to the housing situation.'[47]

Like the migration of Afro-Americans, interracial violence was not new to America, nor was its relation to times of war. During the Civil War there had been bloody clashes between blacks and whites in New York and Detroit. In 1917 at least forty Afro-Americans were killed in the riot at East St Louis; in 1918 there were more deaths in Philadelphia; in 1919 there were 26 race riots in various cities, the largest taking place in Chicago. The outbreaks during World War II, however, surpassed those of any previous period. There were clashes between servicemen of both races, between black soldiers and white policemen or civilians, and between black and white workers. These eruptions reached their peak in 1943 when there were 242 racial battles in 47 cities including Beaumont, Los Angeles, New York and Detroit.[48]

Attracted by the huge car factories converted to war production, over half a million people, more than 50,000 of them black, moved to Detroit and neighboring Willow Run during the war. The black newcomers found that Detroit had but two areas for Afro-Americans, one on the west side and a larger one called Paradise Valley, on the east. The Federal Public Housing Authority projects for war workers at Wayne and Willow Run were restricted to whites only, and of the total of 44,607 units built in Detroit only 3070 were for blacks. With an estimated shortage of 6000 to 20,000 dwellings for Afro-Americans, Paradise Valley was, in 1943, no paradise at all and an assistant to the US Attorney General was to describe the housing situation as 'deplorable.'[49] When in 1942 the Sojourner Truth Housing Project, a project named after a female black abolitionist but built in a white neighborhood, was opened for black tenants, white protests led to its reassignment to whites. Pressure from Afro-Americans led to the reversal of the order, but did not prevent a mob of whites from gathering to block their entry. Eventually, protected by state troopers, the Afro-Americans gained access to their homes.[50]

Whites also resisted the employment of blacks in Detroit, and as late as 1943 there were still plants which made little or no use of Afro-Americans despite the shortages of unskilled production workers. In the first six months of that year, three million man-hours were lost due to strikes after the upgrading or hiring of blacks in the US Rubber Company, the Vickers Company, Hudson Motors, Packard and several others.[51] Much of this race hatred was stirred up by white immigrants from the South, encouraged by men like the Reverend J. Frank Norris, Gerald L. K. Smith and Father Charles Coughlin, who were described, rather accurately, as 'religious political demagogues.'[52]

With this background of tension, it is not surprising that a major riot should have been forecast. After numerous violent incidents an editorial in *Opportunity* warned that 'unless the contructive forces of racial amity' took some positive action the violence would become a storm.[53] No action was taken, and on the evening of Sunday June 20 a riot began that was to last for three days, ending only after federal troops had been called in. The immediate cause was a confrontation between youths of both races on Belle Isle which in turn sparked off other clashes in the vicinity. By night time rumors of atrocities were circulating among both blacks and whites. The commonest story was that a black (white) baby had been thrown off a bridge, or that a white (black) woman had been assaulted.[54] The truth would have made little difference: the tensions of several years exploded. Blacks looted and destroyed white-owned stores, whites attacked blacks caught outside the ghetto. The police force could or would do nothing. In some instances blacks were beaten in the presence of police officers, in others the police themselves were actually involved in attacks, and of the 25 blacks killed, 17 died at the hands of the police.[55]

Despite the obvious inability of the forces of law and order to control the situation, both the mayor, Edward Jeffries, and the governor, Harry F. Kelly, hesitated to call in federal troops. It was Tuesday before such action was taken, and by the time soldiers arrived there was rioting in nineteen precincts and affecting three-quarters of the entire city.[56] After initially dispersing crowds, using bayonets and occasionally gas, the troops worked in patrols protecting especially the transportation system.[57] No further deaths were recorded after the soldiers' arrival, and gradually the city returned to order. By that time 34 people, 25 black and 9 white, were dead, more than a thousand injured, and a great deal of damage done. The general effect of the riot was 'to retard industrial production, to impair the morale of our armed forces, and to injure national unity.'[58]

The violence in Detroit caused some alarm among the administrators of other municipalities with large black populations. The mayor of New York, Fiorello LaGuardia, sent observers to Detroit during the riot and held a meeting afterwards in order to prevent a repetition of those events in his own realm. A few days later he wrote to President Roosevelt that, 'so far as conditions are concerned, I believe we have done more than any other city in the country.'[59] He must, therefore, have been sorely disappointed when a major disturbance broke out in Harlem on Sunday August 1, 1943.

During a minor fracas in a somewhat disreputable hotel, a twenty-six-year-old black soldier, Robert Bandy, was shot and wounded by a white policeman. Immediately a rumor that the soldier had been shot in the back and killed began to circulate among the black residents.[60] Whether or not the soldier was alive or dead was really irrelevant: what was important was the fact that such a confrontation had taken place. As Langston Hughes, the poet, summed it up,[61]

They didn't kill the soldier,
A race leader cried.
Somebody hollered,
Naw! But they tried! [italics his]

Unlike the Detroit riot, what resulted in Harlem was more of an implosion than explosion. Although there were a few attacks on white people who had mistakenly strayed into the area, most of the black rage was directed at white-owned property. After several hours of window smashing and general commotion, wholesale looting of shops and stores took place as Afro-Americans seized foodstuffs and clothing previously sold to them at exorbitant prices.[62] The only whites involved were police and city administrators attempting to restore law and order. As many people pointed out afterward, the eruption in Harlem was not a race riot in the sense that Detroit was.[63] It was not necessary for federal troops to be called into New York either: careful use of the police force and the assistance of prominent black leaders such as Walter White and Roy Wilkins of the NAACP was all that was needed to restore peace. Without the battles with whites that had occurred in Detroit, the black rage soon burned itself out. Five people, all black, were killed (compared with the 34 in Detroit), 500 were injured, and another 500 arrested. An estimated five million dollars worth of property was damaged. However, this was the last *major* riot of the war years, and in fact the last of its scale until the 1960s.[64]

The question of why these outbreaks should occur when they did was one which drew a variety of answers. The *New York Times* pointed out that both riots 'had similar powderkeg backgrounds in the rapid growth and overcrowding of Negro districts in recent years, charges of discrimination in the Army, Navy and war industry, demands for economic and social equality, and the rise of Negro radical agitators preying on these conditions.'[65] The Detroit Governor's Committee seized on the last of these points and in its report blamed Afro-Americans for starting the initial fight and black organizations and newspapers for stirring up the underlying tensions.[66] Afro-Americans, on the other hand, accused racist and subversive elements of causing trouble in order to prevent progress in civil rights and to weaken America's war effort. Walter White referred to the riots prior to that in Harlem as 'deliberately provoked attacks' designed to hamper war production and to limit black participation in the war effort.[67] Local and federal government officials rejected such arguments as unfounded, and Attorney General Biddle declared that there was no evidence of 'any Axis or Fascist or Ku Klux Klan incitement.'[68] They did, however, agree on some of the deeper causes of unrest, although their solutions to the problem generally differed from those offered by blacks.

One major contributory factor, as was pointed out by the *New York Times*, was the wartime migrations and resultant overcrowding. New York was no different from Detroit in that respect. Although the New York Housing Authority had a comparatively liberal policy, it could do little to counteract the prejudice that confined blacks to Harlem: even Afro-Americans in the higher income brackets could not escape despite their ability to pay. Newcomers from the South found themselves condemned to live in tenements which were 'a hundred delta cabins, plus tuberculosis.'[69] A senior official of the National Housing Agency singled out the shortage of housing as a major cause of racial friction, and the Vice-chairman of Labor Production in the War Production Board blamed the lack of 'adequate expansion in community facilities.'[70]

These and other similar reports led Attorney General Biddle to recommend that the President get a report 'on the advisability of putting into effect a program for building houses and recreational facilities in Detroit, particularly for Negroes, and in other areas where racial tensions are largely affected by the lack of housing and recreational facilities.' He also suggested that 'careful consideration be given to limiting, and in some instances putting an end to, Negro migrations into communities which cannot absorb them.' A hint of pessimism was included with his advice concerning the production of 'a simple manual to be used by local officials and corps commanders to expedite the sending in of troops when necessary.'[71] His gloom was probably justified given the impossibility of controlling migrations and the already proven failure of federal housing agencies to deal with the racial question. Moreover, President Roosevelt was reluctant to take action on civil rights in general, preferring to leave the problem until after the war. In the meantime, he was content to let his advisers and local civic committees handle racial affairs.[72]

Racial violence has been shown to be related to population changes and conflict over housing, and clearly poor housing and overcrowding played a large part in the disturbances in Detroit and Harlem.[73] But housing was just one of several causes of dissatisfaction and friction. While the lot of Afro-Americans could in general be said to have improved during and because of the war, all progress met with stubborn opposition. Employment opportunity did not come until necessity demanded it, and even then was limited by the attitudes of white workers and employers. Blacks in the armed services were segregated and discriminated against, and reports of violence directed at black soldiers appeared in the press with alarming frequency. There was still a rise in expectations and militancy among Afro-Americans, but when their aspirations were met by whites determined to maintain the racial status quo the result was anger and bitterness. Given the economic and social discrimination, the stories of racial violence elsewhere, and the physical restrictions of the ghetto, it is not surprising that a black area such as Harlem could be described as a 'cauldron of brooding misery and frustration.'[74]

Added to the racial tensions was the strain of war. The war fulfilled some of the conditions said to be necessary for riots to occur by preventing institutions from functioning properly and by delaying the resolution of grievances. In short, the war led to 'the disarrangement or distortion of the patterns of social interaction to the extent that the happening of major race conflicts was possible.'[75] People of all races were working long hours, subjected to rationing, irritated by shortages of material goods, and if not liable for the draft themselves, likely to have a relative or friend sent off to face the perils of armed conflict. Thus the war contributed directly and indirectly to the 'powderkeg' atmosphere. It only took fairly trivial incidents on hot, sticky days to provide the spark.[76]

The very violent nature of war may have encouraged rioting: it certainly would appear that armed service did, in more than one way. In Harlem, but more especially in Detroit, the majority of the rioters were young males. The governor's committee found that almost 61 per cent of the participants in the riot were under 31 years of age while less than 35 per cent were under 21.[77] This fact led Walter White and Thurgood Marshall to suggest two categories of young rioters.[78] The first was made up of those who had been rejected for armed service on physical, mental or moral grounds, or deferred by reason of occupation. Rioting for them was a means of demonstrating their masculinity and that they were as physically able as those who had gone into the Army. The second category consisted of those facing armed service, or likely to face it if the war continued for some time. A riot presented them with the chance of a 'final fling,' and armed service broke the pattern of their lives and destroyed the normal stabilizing influence of continuity. It is interesting to note that many of the rioters in Los Angeles and Detroit were men in uniform whose pattern of life had already been disrupted. The riots may have been an expression of their nervousness about their futures, a reaction against the restrictions of military life, or even a sign of resentment at young people who had avoided military service.[79]

One of the participants in the Harlem disturbance was later interviewed.[80] He was an eighteen-year-old Afro-American facing induction who had given up school in order to have some fun. When the disorder began he joined in, looting a number of shops. Of his future in the Army he said, 'I do not like it worth a damn. I'm not a spy or a saboteur, but I don't like goin' over there fightin' for the white man—so be it.' His role in the riot was obviously more than a final frolic prior to armed service: it was a conscious or unconscious protest against his social isolation, rejection and humiliation by white society. The same was probably true of most of those who took part with him.[81]

The war, then, served to damage race relations to the point of violence. By opening up employment opportunities in certain areas it encouraged large-scale migrations of people, both black and white. Unable to cope even with the increases in white population, most towns and cities were unwilling to tackle the problems facing Afro-Americans. Old ghettos were added to, new ones were formed. In either case housing was poor and overcrowded, and the general lack of decent accommodation and other facilities added to the many grievances felt at the time. Although generally having unpleasant consequences, the growth in the black urban population did lead to an increased sense of community and awareness. Attacks by whites were met by concerted action and news of racial incidents passed quickly through the entire Afro-American populace. As the war progressed and more immigrants entered the cities, tensions mounted and friction between the races increased. With the additional disruption of life by long hours in war industries, rationing and controls, and by armed service, open conflict became virtually inevitable. The war may well have 'pointed up the basic issues in the housing problem of Negroes in the North,' as Robert Weaver said.[82] It did not, however, produce much in the way of solutions for that particular problem or for the race relations problem in general.

As Gunnar Myrdal pointed out, 'housing is much more than just shelter': its relation to general health and welfare is of prime importance.[83] Inadequate accommodation, low economic status, and white prejudice ensured that the health of Afro-Americans prior to the war was far below that of the rest of the population. Measured by any indices, the difference between black and white was appalling. Two examples will suffice: in 1939 the number of deaths out of 100,000 due to tuberculosis was for whites 37.4, for blacks 134.3. The infant mortality rate per 1000 births for whites in 1940 was 43.2, for blacks it was 72.9.[84] Given the results of migration and urbanization during the war, one might expect a further deterioration in this situation. In fact, although the gap between the two races remained, it narrowed as the health of the black population continued to improve.

In many respects this was a continuation of the long-term trends in national health statistics. The greatest progress actually occurred before the war, during the 1930s, when federal intervention led to an improvement in medical care and facilities and in standards of living. That these trends continued, if at a slightly slower rate, during the 1940s was due to several factors. Housing in Northern ghettos was often superior to that in the rural South, and usually there was less discrimination in hospitals and by doctors in the North. Wartime employment and prosperity and the generally higher standard of living meant that Afro-Americans could spend more on hospitalization and medicine.[85] The mass treatment of those in the armed services and defense plants also had effect. Even in the South blacks could afford better foods with higher nutritional content, thus ensuring that they and their children received something approaching a balanced diet. By 1944 the figures for deaths per 100,000 due to tuberculosis had dropped to 32·7 for white Americans and 109·7 for Afro-Americans.[86] The statistics for infant mortalities also showed an improvement: in 1943 they had dropped to 37·5 for whites and 61·5 for blacks. This was even more remarkable given that the birthrate of both races rose during this period. In part this was due to the factors already mentioned, but also to the Emergency Maternity and Infant Care Program which provided free care for the wives and newborn babies of men in the lower ranks of the armed forces.[87]

However, many of the inadequacies in medical care for Afro-Americans still remained. Once again, the war served to highlight some of them. An editorial in the *Baltimore Afro-American* pointed out that 'it was not until war demands for manpower weighed our young folk in the balance of physical, mental and emotional fitness and found so many of them wanting, that many of us recognized the urgent need for better health and better homes,' a view with which a researcher for the NAACP heartily agreed.[88] The 921,000 black registrants for armed service declared IV–F, that is, physically, mentally or morally unfit, was a serious indictment of the American social system. The number of rejections was such that Southern politicians actually claimed that whites were being discriminated against.[89] Even so, little was done to change the underlying reasons for this state of affairs. While the general ratio of doctors to people in 1945 was 1 : 750, there were only 3810 black doctors—one to every 3377 Afro-Americans. In dentistry the ratio was even worse at 1 : 8800.[90] There were only two all-black medical schools, at Howard University and Meharry Medical College, and the number of graduates they produced was pitifully small. Once graduated, the students had difficulty finding places as interns. By 1948 the number of black patients per black doctor had actually increased to 3681.[91] The majority of Afro-Americans who qualified as general practitioners or specialists were located in the North where there was greater opportunity. In the South segregation of patients and practitioners led to wasteful duplication of facilities and a lack of hospital treatment for blacks. Separate was by no means equal. Despite the higher incidence of illness and disease among Afro-Americans, the proportion of beds per head of population was much lower for them than for whites. In Mississippi, for example, there were 0·5 beds per 1000 Afro-Americans compared to 2·3 per 1000 whites. In the entire state of Virginia there was no surgical treatment of tuberculosis available to blacks although it was one of the main causes of mortality among that section of the community.[92]

While the opportunities for black women to obtain training as nurses increased as a result of scholarships from the Public Health Service, and in 1943 through the US Cadet Nurse Corps, service in the Army Nurse Corps was segregated until 1945. Even the Red Cross refused to permit Afro-Americans to assist in its civilian first aid training program unless they formed segregated units on their own initiative.[93] Blacks did participate in the military medical services despite these limitations. As a result, they made some gains: co-operation between the National Nursing Council for War Service and the National Association of Colored Graduate Nurses helped to break down discrimination in nursing schools, and in 1948 the American Nurses Association voted individual membership to all black nurses excluded from state organizations on racial grounds. After the Arkansas State Nurses Association admitted blacks to full membership in 1949 only six other state nursing bodies barred Afro-Americans. By 1950 the National Association of Colored Graduate Nurses was disbanded because there was felt to be no further need for a separate association.[94] The previous year the American Medical Association named an Afro-American, Dr Peter Marshall, as a member of its policy-making body. He was the first black to hold such a position in 103 years.[95]

Hospital facilities for blacks also improved in the post-war years and a major advance was made with the passage of the Federal Hospital Survey and Construction Act in 1946. The Act, which provided federal funds for the construction or enlargement of hospitals, prohibited discrimination in the use of such monies. It required that separate facilities for Afro-Americans were to be equal and that the number of beds provided for blacks was to be in proportion to their numbers in the local population.[96]

Although encouraging, these were but small steps toward bringing the health of Afro-Americans up to the level of that of whites. *De jure* segregation in the South, *de facto* in the North, led to separation and thus inequality in all facilities—housing, recreational and hospital. The circle of prejudice and discrimination limited the very life of black Americans, and in a system based primarily on private rather than public health services the gap between the two races would remain as long as Afro-Americans were confined to the lowest economic and social strata of society.

The same was also true of education, another area in which Afro-Americans lagged behind whites as a result of discrimination and segregation. The educational gap between the races was apparent in the comparative number of years spent in school, the length of school terms, the amount of money spent per pupil, the ratio of pupils to teachers, and the difference in teachers' salaries. While there were differences in standards between black and white throughout the entire country, they were more pronounced in the eighteen Southern states which required segregated schools. In those states, the average length of school terms in 1934–5 was 167 days for whites and 146 for blacks. The salaries of black school teachers were generally half those of their white counterparts, ranging from $235 per annum in Mississippi to $667 in Texas.[97] While the situation was generally better in the North, *de facto* segregation and ghetto schools ensured that the educational attainments of blacks, while greater than those of both blacks and whites in the South, were lower than those of

whites in the same geographic area. There were considerable improvements in the education of both races during the 1930s under the auspices of
the New Deal: the Public Works Administration helped finance a
considerable number of schools, the Works Progress Administration
launched a huge adult education program, and the National Youth
Administration gave aid to students. An awareness of the racial problems
in education was revealed by government financed studies and by the
appointment of blacks to the Office of Education.[98] Also of importance was
the NAACP campaign begun in 1936 to equalize teachers' salaries: by 1941
it reported considerable success. As well as salaries, the length of school
terms and number of black pupils also rose in the years immediately prior
to the war.[99] Even so, the basic faults in the system which kept black
standards below those of whites remained.

Just as the war pointed up the inadequacies in housing and health
provision for blacks, it focused 'the attention of the nation on the
educational deficiencies of the Negro.'[100] Again, it was rejections for
military service which brought the lack of educational qualifications
among Afro-Americans to public notice. Between May and September
1941 five times as many black as white registrants for selective service were
rejected, and of these almost a third were due to educational
inadequacies.[101] The statistics also revealed regional variations which
reflected the differences in school systems. For example, while 0·3 per cent
of the white registrants and 1·8 per cent of the blacks from New York were
found ineligible for military service because of their inability to read and
write, 1·9 per cent of the whites and 15·4 per cent of the blacks from
Mississippi were deferred for the same reason. Even after the Army had
lowered its literacy standards, the gap between North and South, black and
white, was much the same.[102] Both the American Teachers' Association, an
organization of black school teachers, and Ambrose Caliver, the Senior
Specialist on Negro Education in the Office of Education, concluded that
these figures were indicative of the inequality in educational opportunity
and called for change.[103] Some Southerners argued that the high rejection
rate for blacks was a sign of discrimination against whites and expressed
concern that as the white male population was depleted through the draft,
white women were endangered by the large number of blacks left at
home.[104]

While such complaints may have had some effect, a more immediate and
serious cause for alarm was the rapidly developing manpower shortage in
the forces. By 1943 the situation was such that the Army could no longer
afford to refuse the illiterates and slower learners of either race. In June of
that year a special training program to give such inductees a basic
education in reading and writing was initiated. Approximately 136,000
Afro-Americans benefited from this course and their 85·1 per cent success
rate, compared to 81·7 per cent of whites, was regarded as a 'shattering

blow to racists.'[105] This program in particular and military service in general provided many blacks with some degree of education, if only in technical skills such as vehicle maintenance and electrical engineering.[106] A greater source of industrial education was the Defense Training scheme for war workers.

Although the role of blacks in defense training was discussed from its inception, there was nevertheless, in its early days, open discrimination. In the eighteen states with segregated school systems, where Afro-Americans comprised 22·3 per cent of the population, as of June 30, 1942 only 3910 or 7·0 per cent had taken part in pre-employment courses. Despite non-discrimintation clauses in the federal laws which appropriated funds for training, there was ample evidence that blacks received less than their fair share.[107] As the war progressed and shortages forced the breakdown in racial barriers, black participation increased. In the latter half of 1942 a total of 58,228 Afro-Americans took part in pre-employment courses, while another 13,066 took supplementary classes. In 1943 more than 112,000 completed war production, trade, professional and clerical studies. Over the four year period beginning in July 1940, 12·4 per cent or 323,496 of all trainees were black and 22,780 had taken engineering, scientific and managerial courses. These educational gains came about as a direct result of the war: as Robert Weaver remarked, 'were there no anticipated shortage of skilled workers, there would be no current federal program for their training.'[108]

The war had an impact on the very institutions of learning. First it stripped the universities and colleges of students and then flooded them with military and defense trainees who brought an influx of federal money to provide equipment and materials for their training. Second, there was, as the film *Negro Colleges in Wartime* illustrated, and emphasis on war-related skills: electronics, radio engineering, mathematics and the sciences. This raised questions about the place of non-related subjects on the college curricula and about the aspirations and the future place in society of those who completed such technical courses.[109] The wartime migrations, while alleviating the pressures on the inadequate school facilities in the rural South, added to the burdens of urban areas. Wartime prosperity enabled the Southern states to spend more money on *all* schools, and partly as a result of this, partly because of the urbanization of blacks, in the eighteen states with segregated schools there was during the war an increase in the average length of terms, an increase in the number of black teachers, and a 25 per cent increase in their salaries.[110] Similar developments were taking place elsewhere in America: more black children were spending longer in school at all levels, had slightly more money spent on them, and were taught by better paid teachers.[111] While the advances of the pre-war era were consolidated and continued, again the gap between black and white still existed. The average black teacher's salary in the South was still only 44 per cent of that of his white counterpart; the pupil-teacher ratio was still 20·7 per cent more than in white schools; the wide difference in expenditure per white and per black pupil still remained.[112]

For those already past school age, there was the opportunity to study under the GI Bill of Rights or the Project for Adult Education of Negroes. The latter, launched in 1946, was sponsored by the Office of Education with the financial support of the Carnegie Corporation of New York. Under the directorship of Ambrose Caliver, the Project aimed 'to raise the educational level of the large numbers of Negroes whom the Selective Service System and the 1940 census described as functionally illiterate.'[113] Most writers on the subject of education shared the sentiments inherent in that statement: they saw the failings in the existing school system which the war had revealed and emphasized, and called for improvement in order that America might be better prepared to meet any future test. Minorities would benefit from any such improvement. Charles H. Thompson, the editor of the *Journal of Negro Education*, summed up this feeling as early as 1942:

> We cannot afford to repeat the mistakes of the last war in believing that all of the problems of race relations are going to be solved merely because we are fighting a war for the preservation of democracy. And yet we do have reason to hope for a better post-war world.[114]

This applied as much to housing and health as to education. The war had exposed the inequalities; Afro-Americans had played their part in the war effort: they expected their just rewards.

5

Blacks in Film, Music and Literature during World War II

The impact of total war is felt in all areas of life, cultural as well as economic, social and political. This was perhaps more true of the countries where the actual fighting took place than those, such as America, which were some distance from it. Nonetheless, the war did have a similar effect in the United States: films were made, songs sung and books written about the war which revealed the response to the challenge it posed. By and large, patriotism and propaganda were the order of the day but the hopes and aspirations of the American people were also often treated in the different branches of the arts.[1]

Afro-American participation in these cultural activities reflected much of the impact of war, and while all three avenues are explored in this chapter it falls naturally into two parts, the first dealing with film and the second with music and literary works. The reason for this division is simple: the film world was essentially a white world and so any changes in the treatment of blacks shown in wartime films were due to changes in white attitudes. In music and literature, on the other hand, Afro-Americans had a more independent role and so could express themselves more freely. The songs, stories and poetry of the time dealt with *their* moods and reactions to the war.

With only one or two exceptions, movies made prior to 1941 treated Afro-Americans in a manner symptomatic of their general status in society. As one critic wrote in 1939, audiences regarded the black man 'as a clown, a buffoon, a gangling idiot or a superstitious fool,' an image which was 'fostered and fed by the unfair manner in which the negro is portrayed on the screen.'[2] From *Birth of a Nation* (1915) and *The Jazz Singer* (1927) to *Gone With the Wind* (1939), the characterization of the Afro-American was designed to demonstrate his inferiority. The failure of films made independently by blacks for blacks revealed the dominance of white-controlled Hollywood and its concern with the white censors and

Southerners. Following the outbreak of war, this situation began to improve and in the years 1942–5 'the Hollywood film industry demon-strated a conscious effort to bring a better understanding among most races and groups in this country and, in a broader field, among the nationalities and races allied with us in World War II.'[3]

In part, the change seen in films was directly due to the war. Of its own volition Hollywood produced films to encourage audiences in their support of the war. There were the patriotic propaganda type of films based on military and civilian life to bolster morale, and others, such as *Strange Incident* (1943), a western based on Walter van Tilburg Clark's novel *The Ox-Bow Incident*, which stressed the ideals of democracy. Of the 1313 feature films produced between 1942 and 1944, 374 were directly concerned with some aspect of the war.[4]

So important were movies that the government declared the film-making business an essential industry and created a Bureau of Motion Pictures under the Office of War Information to see that nothing damaging to the war effort was shown on the screen. In its information manual the Bureau advised the use of Negro extras in uniform in crowd scenes in order to demonstrate black loyalty and participation in the war effort. The Office of Censorship also forbade the export of several films showing racial discrimination for fear that they would tarnish America's image abroad.[5] Such government action was limited, however, due to opposition in Hollywood and Congress to such federal controls. The Bureau of Motion Pictures was forced to concern itself with regulating the amounts of money spent on film production and the use of manpower and other resources. More important, as far as Afro-Americans were concerned, were the pressures brought to bear by certain individuals and organizations, including actors themselves.

Wendell Willkie, the Republican presidential candidate in 1940, and Walter White, the executive secretary of the NAACP, were among the most active campaigners for better screen roles for blacks. The two men spoke out against discrimination and poor parts at the Annual Awards of the Motion Picture Academy of Arts and Sciences in 1940 and 1942, and at the Writers' Congress in Los Angeles in 1943. Dalton Trumbo, a screen writer and later a member of the 'Hollywood Ten' who refused to testify on their relations with the Communist Party before the 1947 House Committee on Un-American Affairs, also spoke at the Writers' Congress. He criticized the film industry for its failure to use blacks in crowd scenes and shots of war production lines, as well as its generally poor treatment of Afro-Americans.[6] Other pressures came from black actors and actresses such as Paul Robeson, Clarence Muse and Lena Horne, who refused to accept parts which denigrated the members of their race. Even Stepin Fetchit, the actor who played and gave his name to the archetypal black stereotype, was later to complain that he had trouble finding work after he had refused to play the old demeaning role any longer.[7] White actors, including Charles Boyer, Humphrey Bogart, Edward G. Robinson, Charles Laughton and Orson Welles, joined with Afro-Americans in organizations working for racial unity such as the Emergency Committee of the Entertainment Industry, the International Film and Radio Guild, and the Independent Citizen's Committee of the Arts, Sciences and Professions.[8]

Also of importance were the protests of the Afro-American population as a whole, but especially of servicemen, which demonstrated their growing social consciousness.[9] These forces together had some obvious and immediate effects. In 1942 Warner Brothers, Twentieth Century Fox and Metro-Goldwyn-Meyer gave assurances that black stars would be given roles more in keeping with their normal place in society, a promise reiterated by the movie moguls David O. Selznick and Daryl F. Zanuck.[10]

Several films made during and after the war reflected the changes that had taken place. A number of motion pictures featured Afro-Americans in small but significant parts; Dooley Wilson in *Casablanca* (1942), Canada Lee in *Lifeboat* (1944), Kenneth Spencer in *Bataan* (1943) and Rex Ingrams in *Sahara* (1943) all broke with established stereotypes in roles stressing unity and democracy. *Bataan* and *Sahara* showed black soldiers, one an American GI, the other a French officer, in an extremely favorable fashion—in fact Rex Ingrams's part in *Sahara* caused some controversy and at the preview the white actor Al Jolson recommended that one scene involving the black soldier and a white racist be removed. The advice was ignored and in another scene the main character, played by Bogart, emphasized the democratic ideals of the Allies compared with the racism of the Axis.[11]

A film which dealt more obviously with the question of racial discrimination was *In This Our Life* (1942) which featured Hattie McDaniel and Ernest Anderson in the story of a young Afro-American law student victimized by Southern prejudice. Not so far removed from the old stereotypes, on the other hand, were the all-black musicals *Cabin in the Sky* (1942) and *Stormy Weather* (1943). Whatever their limitations, these films were very popular and did provide opportunities for entertainers such as Lena Horne, Ethel Waters, Rex Ingrams and Cab Calloway. In fact, Ethel Waters's only comment on the effects of the war was that the tax man took a large slice of her salary as a result of the 1942 Revenue Act—a problem common to stars regardless of race and surely a sign of some success.[12] However, more important than the film musicals was the spate of 'Negro problem' movies produced in the immediate post-war years. In 1949 four motion pictures were released which showed clearly that Hollywood had moved into a new phase, treating Afro-Americans as a social problem; they were *Lost Boundaries*, *Pinky*, *Intruder in the Dust* and *Home of the Brave*.

In *Lost Boundaries*, produced by Louis de Rochemont and based on a real-life case, the family of a successful doctor practicing in a New England town suffer a traumatic period when it is discovered that they have black ancestry. Rejected by former friends and neighbors, the family faces the type of discrimination experienced by Afro-Americans in everyday life. They are eventually saved by the intervention of a white minister. While the film obviously had an important racial message, not one of the principal roles was played by a black person. Even so, it was banned in Memphis and Atlanta because of its potential to provoke violence and law-breaking.[13] *Pinky* had a similar plot, and indeed a similar limitation. Produced by Daryl F. Zanuck, this was a story about a young black girl also 'passing' as white, but as in *Lost Boundaries*, the title role was played by a white person, Jeanne Crain. Ethel Waters played the part of the young woman's elderly confidante who helps her face up to realities. The film focuses on the relationship between Pinky and her white boyfriend and with the community at large. When she is bequeathed the neighboring plantation, the girl suffers harassment from local whites and has to fight a court case in order to claim her inheritance. Mixed audiences in the South were reported to have wept and applauded during the final courtroom scenes in sympathy with the victorious heroine.[14]

While *Pinky* now seems outdated, *Intruder in the Dust* has stood up well to the passage of time. Like *Pinky*, it too received favorable reactions when first shown and, unlike most films with a racial content, was uncut by Southern censors.[15] Based on the William Faulkner novel of the same title, it tells the tale of a black farmer in the South, played by Juano Hernandez, falsely accused of murdering a white man. He is only saved from lynching by the intervention of a white boy whom he had earlier befriended. The boy, with the assistance of an elderly white lady, proves that the Negro was not the murderer.

The final film in this group, *Home of the Brave*, starred James Edwards as Moss, a black GI. In a piece of artistic license ignoring the segregation of the armed forces, Moss is sent with four white comrades to reconnoiter a Japanese-held island. When his closest friend in the group calls him 'nigger' in the heat of the moment, Moss wishes him dead; only to be racked with guilt after a Japanese soldier makes the wish come true. Still burdened with his sense of sin, Moss returns to base where he is cured after extensive treatment by a white psychiatrist. After nine profitable weeks in Manhattan the film opened in Dallas and Houston where it was greeted with good reviews from the critics. Far from provoking the expected race riots, *Home of the Brave* scored a box-office success.[16]

While it is undoubtedly true that these four films made 'explicit the nature of Hollywood's changed attitude toward Negroes,' they also revealed the new stereotype.[17] Afro-Americans were not treated as real, complete, people but as problems—almost as if they were permanently in the third person. Moreover, in each case salvation came as a result of whites' actions. The Afro-American was still portrayed as the passive victim of prejudice *and* the passive recipient of white largesse. Even if they were breaking new ground, there were serious doubts whether such films would continue to be made, as throughout the war movies were still produced which portrayed blacks in unfavorable roles. Alternatively, companies often wrote out black characters from scripts to avoid the risk of controversy.[18]

It was not until the 1950s that film producers and directors tackled the question of race with any honesty and Afro-Americans emerged on the screen as real people. While the war, with its stress on unity and democracy and America's new-found position among other nations, brought about some improvements, the forces for radical change were not sufficient to produce major results. Not as directly involved in the war as other countries, the American film industry did not react to fascism with the same speed or depth as its counterparts in Europe. Racism was not seen as a major war issue, and besides it was so ingrained in America that any great departure from old formulas would have been far ahead of its time. Seen in this light, such advances as were made were considerable.[19]

Government intervention clearly had little impact on the world of feature films; however, several agencies did play an important part in producing documentary films, designed to improve morale and further the war effort. The most important of these was *The Negro Soldier*, made by the War Department in 1944. Reactions to this film have been discussed in an earlier chapter, but it is well worth examining its content. A black minister's sermon to his congregation provides the vehicle for a film history of black military participation in wars past and present. On the issues involved in World War II, the minister contrasts *Mein Kampf* with the American Constitution, while for visual comparison the audience is shown the boxer Max Schmeling training in the German paratroops and Joe Louis, his old rival, in the US Army. After shots of a member of the congregation's son in the Army and various scenes of blacks in the forces, the minister emphasizes again what they are defending and calls for 'no let-up' in their effort. Aptly enough, the final credits are backed with the congregation singing 'Onward Christian Soldiers'. The film was clearly intended to be shown to both blacks and whites: on the one hand it urged continued black loyalty and participation, while on the other it demonstrated to whites that Afro-Americans had taken part in America's past struggles and were still doing so. Coming after the riots and violence of 1943, the film was a belated attempt to repair morale and bolster unity. To that end, it overlooked numerous historical contradictions and completely ignored the discrimination in the forces in the 1940s. As one reviewer who complimented the film on its 'distinct propaganda value' asked, 'When will truth and propaganda merge?'[20]

Following the Army's example, the Navy made a similar film in 1945, entitled *The Negro Sailor*. A twenty-seven minute documentary, *The Negro Sailor* told the story of a black, Bill Johnson, as a typical Navy recruit in the closing days of the war. Including scenes of black and white sailors together, the film was part of the Navy's campaign to show that it had adopted new racial policies. However, because the war had ended the Navy pigeonholed the movie until February 1946 when it was given a special showing in New York. Thereafter, the film was withdrawn from circulation, perhaps because some Southern boards of censors had refused to show it, or perhaps because it was considered out of date.[21]

While the Navy did little with film, the War Department followed up the success of *The Negro Soldier* with the more emotive *Teamwork* made in 1946.[22] The film opens with actors purporting to be German officers who, in the guttural accents and broken English peculiar to such parts, discuss how they will divide America by playing black against white. Thus, they theorize, they will rob the United States of a tenth of its strength without firing a shot. From then on, the film concentrates on the Allied attack on Europe and the importance of racial unity in that fight. Black service battalions are shown delivering vital supplies to the troops at the front on the famous 'Red Ball Express.' On scenes of blacks and whites rebuilding airfields, railway tracks, and roads, the commentator says, 'they were busy hating Germans, not each other.' A mixture of real and recreated clips shows black airmen supporting bombers flown by whites and downing enemy aircraft: here the comments are about the way in which these men are destroying Nazi myths. On the ground, black artillery and tank regiments are filmed supporting the men at the front. In a following sequence, again presumably acted rather than real, an Afro-American soldier under the anxious gaze of a white comrade reads a Nazi propaganda sheet which urges him not to fight. The black crushes the leaflet and joins the attack: the German strategy has failed. The film closes, after shots of the swastika being destroyed, with black and white soldiers marching to 'The Battle of Jericho.' As in *The Negro Soldier*, the segregation and discrimination in the forces is played down and the existence of racial strife completely ignored. Indeed, *Teamwork* exaggerates the degree of unity in the services and fails to point out that most blacks served in segregated regiments. The shots of blacks and whites together—sometimes achieved by careful intercutting—are in fact misleading: the only Afro-American combat troops to serve with whites were the few in the specially integrated platoons which fought during the Battle of the Bulge. The film makes no direct reference to this experiment. However, it did show something of black participation and unwittingly revealed the supportive, even subordinate, role of Afro-Americans in the Army. Also unwittingly, *Teamwork* provided an extremely strong case in favor of integration in the forces and an end to discrimination at home.

More exact, and perhaps more interesting from the historian's point of view, is the film *Negro Colleges in Wartime*, made by the Office of War Information in 1943.[23] Only nine minutes long, it still shows the extent to which black colleges and universities were affected by the war. Again the message is that blacks were playing their part. Pointing out that the need for trained men and women had led to the availability of courses geared to the war effort, the film moves from Tuskegee to Prairie View to Howard, and finally ends at Hampton Institute. The latter, we are told, was working on a twenty-four hour basis to train war workers, and certainly the range of activities shown taking place there and at the other institutions makes this credible. At Tuskegee men are trained for the Air Force while women learn automotive and other skills. The black nutritional and agricultural expert (and inventor of peanut butter) George Washington Carver is shown at work, adding his expertise to the war effort. Meanwhile, Dr Charles Drew, the man largely responsible for the use of blood plasma in storage banks, is filmed teaching classes at Howard University. Here too, laboratory experiments on various possible war materials are taking place. At Hampton, students are shown being trained as engineers, mechanics, chemists and nurses, and some women are taught to operate farm equipment. The institute is also used for Army and Navy courses, and students in mechanics and vehicle maintenance learn while servicing the trucks from nearby military bases.

Much more clearly than the written word could, this film reveals the extent and manner in which black colleges felt the effects of the war. Quite obviously there was an influx of federal money to finance many of these training courses, and even without such official stimulus the emphasis was put on teaching technical and practical skills, i.e. those relevant to wartime industrial and military needs. Many Afro-Americans must have learned trades and professions which might otherwise have remained closed to them, but the film leaves unanswered questions about economic discrimination, both during and after the war, which might prevent such qualified persons from putting their knowledge into practice. Like the other films of its type, it makes no explicit mention of racial prejudice or segregation although the fact that these colleges are wholly black is readily apparent. While Charles Drew is shown working in a field extremely vital to the war effort, no reference is made to the segregation of blood from different races in the Red Cross banks, a practice which drew considerable criticism from Afro-Americans. But despite these omissions *Negro Colleges in Wartime* would again give white Americans a good idea of the contributions blacks were making to the Allied cause.

Henry Browne, Farmer, made in Spanish and English by the Department of Agriculture primarily for export to Latin America, had a similar moral and compared the military and civilian contribution to the war of one black family in the South.[24] Henry Browne and his family labor in the fields producing valuable food products to feed the troops at the front and the workers at home. The film ends with the entire family going to town to visit their elder son stationed at the Army camp; the final shots are of the young

man flying off in his plane watched proudly by his parents. The message is
obvious, yet over and above this intended information we see fairly typical
conditions for Afro-Americans in the rural South. The farming is on a very
small scale; the plough and the wagon are drawn by horses or mules and
the farmhouse is a poor wooden structure. Of course this was not the point
of the film, and it is important to bear in mind that it and the others
described here were made during or after 1943, the year when race
relations in America were at their worst.

All four government-produced films were designed to improve the
racial situation by showing whites that Afro-Americans were loyal and
were participating in their country's struggle. Black audiences were shown
that they did have an important role to play and a stake in the war. While
no similar films were made by the government prior to 1943, there were
numerous newsreels with essentially the same type of message. Their visual
material is often less important to the historian than the commentary
which stresses the news value of the clips. Thus newsreels included such
things as black engineers at work building tank traps—ending with fairly
dramatic scenes of tanks crashing—or Joe Louis visiting camps in England,
or the first black pilots receiving their wings. Some news features were
produced specifically for blacks, such as the All American Newsreel
Company's piece on the black crew of submarine chaser *PC 1264*. Not
surprisingly, the Fox Movietone item on the Harlem riot of 1943 was never
issued—presumably for fear of the effect it would have on morale.[25]

One important documentary film made before 1943 and before
America had even entered the war was *One Tenth of Our Nation*, produced by
Henwar Rodakiewicz for the American Film Center and funded by the
Rockefeller Foundation.[26] A much more honest film, it restores some
balance to the impression made by the later government-produced
pictures. As well as showing, in great detail, the poverty of blacks in the
South, *One Tenth of Our Nation* also had a strong social message: its
emphasis is on the 'American-ness' of blacks and the conditions they have
to endure despite it. Palatial Southern mansions are contrasted with the
run-down, two-room wooden shack which houses a black family of ten.
The children's school and all its inadequacies are pointed out. Black
people are seen working in the fields and the commentator acknowledges
that they get few of the end products. Attention is drawn to the lack
of health facilities for Afro-Americans and to the difficulties which lie in the
way of their getting higher education. With final views of the school,
homes, fields and children, the audience is told that it is here that they
'must make a start' and that racial differences are 'not to be solved with
bombs: we must show the world democracy.' While not arising from
American participation in the war, this film did show the impact of the
European crisis and the rise of fascism.

The other films mentioned also showed something of the ideological impact of the war. If the better treatment of blacks in feature films indicated a change in Hollywood's attitudes, the official films showed an awareness in the federal agencies of the need for racial unity and harmony during wartime. In addition to improving morale, films illustrating black and white together fighting the enemies of democracy 'inevitably promoted ideals of integration.'[27] This supposed long-term educational value was either not appreciated or not desired by the government, and films like *The Negro Soldier* and *Teamwork* were withdrawn after the end of the war. Again, any changes promoted by the war seemed to be short-lived.

In black 'popular' music, the blues, and to a lesser extent jazz, the impact of the war went much deeper and was more permanent than for films. Enforced separation from the white cultural mainstream, first by slavery and then by social convention, had led blacks to produce music entirely their own, combining African and American elements in one form. The most obvious result was the spiritual or gospel song; less influenced by European forms and more purely a black phenomenon was the blues, usually with a distinctive twelve-bar construction, African-based rhythms, call and response, and blue notes—but also often using the European 4/4 time framework.[28] First sung in the fields and then by itinerant performers, the blues moved into the cities with the migration of Afro-Americans at the beginning of the twentieth century. The major white record companies, unlike the film industry, recognized a potentially valuable market and began to record black blues singers in the 1920s on records issued under separate 'race' labels. Such records were, almost entirely, bought and listened to by Afro-Americans. The relevance of such songs to the historian lies in the fact that they 'offered an indication of the hopes and fears of black people, sometimes their anger and sometimes their apathy. There was in the blues a gauge of the frustration within the colored community . . .'[29]

While the majority of blues continued to be about sex, unrequited love, loneliness and despair, a few related specifically to the war. Typical were Brownie McGhee's 'Million Lonesome Women' and Walter Davis's 'Hate to Say Goodbye,' both ironic comments on one effect of armed service but primarily variations on a common blues theme—the relationship between man and woman. Very similar sentiments were expressed in 'Training Camp Blues,' 'Uncle Sam Came and Got Him' and 'The Army Blues.'[30] Other songs such as 'Win the War Blues,' 'Letter to Tojo,' 'Pearl Harbor Blues' and 'Are You Ready' attacked the Japanese. Doc Clayton's 'Pearl Harbor Blues' compared the Japanese to stray dogs in the street: 'well, he bites the hand that feeds him, soon as he gets enough to eat'; 'Are You Ready' extolled heroism in battle, saying 'There'll be no turning back,' and asking 'Are you ready to go?'[31] A patriotic emphasis also existed in more 'serious' music by black Americans. William Grant Still wrote 'In Memoriam: the Colored Soldiers Who Died For Democracy' for the

League of Composers, and Paul Robeson's wartime 'A Ballad For Americans' was an enormously popular song on the subject of democracy.[32]

Although different in basic style and approach, these blues songs did not differ significantly from whites' songs such as 'You're a Sap, Mr Jap.' However, some blues were much more to the point, and Josh White's live performances of 'Defense Factory Blues' and 'Uncle Sam Says' raised basic issues and revealed the effect of wartime propaganda on black attitudes. In the first, White pointed out 'well it sho' don' make no sense, when a Negro can't work in the National Defense.' In the second, he drew attention to the fact that 'Uncle Sam says "We live the American Way",' so 'Let's get together and kill Jim Crow today.'[33] Other songs raised the question of the Afro-Americans' future after the war. Bill Broonzy sang 'I helped win sweet victory' and asked 'what you gonna do about the old Jim Crow' in 'Black, Brown and White,' and the sentiments he expressed were reinforced by Lonnie Johnson in 'Baby Remember Me':[34]

> And you can tell the world I'm fighting
> for what really belongs to me.

Such lyrics are by themselves interesting and informative, but more significant were the changes in musical style which came about as a result of the war and related social changes. White America reacted musically to the war with the bland sing-along ballads and songs of crooners like Bing Crosby and Perry Como. Hits such as 'White Christmas,' the biggest seller of the war, were meant to relieve wartime tension and anxiety and were completely lacking in excitement, stimulation or emotion. Black Americans, on the other hand, 'had seen fundamental changes take place in their lives as they moved from Southern rural areas to northern urban ghettos. They were eager for more radical changes to alter their status as second-class citizens.'[35] Urbanization, armed service, improved economic status, all served to whet black appetites for more change rather than stability. Discrimination, segregation and racial prejudice only made them more militant, more demanding. All of this was reflected in their music.

The increased mixing and urbanization which resulted from the migration of blacks to centers of war production led to an increased sophistication in their music and a fusing of what had been hitherto regional styles. Blues singers from Texas and the Southwest followed the movement of people to California and Northern cities, adding their styles and words. Performers such as Joe Turner, Louis Jordan and T-Bone Walker contributed a shouting kind of singing, boogie-woogie rhythms and all-round sophistication to the existing city blues. At the same time, among young Afro-Americans there was a rejection of the older 'down-home' blues and a desire for more aggressive music, while singers had to cope with crowded city dancehalls and bars. The two needs were filled by coupling the new, loud, harsh singing with electrical amplification. The end product, as sung by Muddy Waters, Howlin' Wolf and Sonny Boy Williamson, became known as rhythm and blues, later to form the basis of white rock-and-roll. The phrase 'rhythm and blues' was actually coined during the war as white record companies lost control of the production of 'race' records to small, independent, black companies which sprang up in the forties. To them, the term 'race' record was an embarrassment and so they resorted to 'ebony,' 'sepia' and 'rhythm and blues,' and the latter eventually stuck.[36] This, and the 'kind of frenzy' and 'extra-local vulgarity' of the music itself, was indicative of the 'profound changes in the cultural consciousness of Negroes' which had come with the war.[37]

In jazz, the parallel development at this time was bop or bebop. Rejecting the values of whites, middle class blacks and older musicians, men like Charlie Parker, Thelonius Monk and Dizzy Gillespie got together to play music with complex rhythms and jagged, varied melodies which was in complete contrast to the swinging jazz of the period. Even more than for the blues singers, this was a conscious act of rebellion and defiance, a declaration of their blackness which mirrored the aggressive, militant mood of many young Afro-Americans, particularly those who had served in the forces. They had no intention of accepting the pre-war social conditions nor the music that such an environment had produced.[38] The outward physical manifestation of this rebelliousness was the clothing worn by musicians and their audiences. While the jazz performers adopted berets and beards, young blacks wore zoot suits and were soon copied by white teenagers. The zoot suit was described later by Malcolm X, who was in his late teens and early twenties during the war, as comprising 'sky-blue pants thirty inches in the knee and angle-narrowed down to twelve inches at the bottom, and a long coat that pinched my waist and flared out below my knees.'[39] This was topped with a broad-brimmed hat. With the distinctive clothing went an equally distinctive and exclusive language, the hip or hep talk of chicks and cats, and groovy scenes in swinging pads.[40]

Nonconformity among young Afro-Americans seemed contrary to the efforts of the majority of black people to achieve integration and equality with whites. But it was clearly a sign of anger and a declaration of militance. For a black to wear a zoot suit meant that he wished to be recognized as a black, a nonconformist by virtue of his color, and to be given equality on those terms. It was also the reaction of youth to to the new pressures of urban society and wartime life. If the zoot suit became a popular fashion, it did so precisely because of its racial significance.[41] Thus while boppers created an in-group which white musicians could not penetrate, they demanded that their music be recognized as 'art' and that they be given equal treatment with white artists. Whatever the exact explanation, the musical changes in blues and jazz which accompanied the mode of dress were long lasting and remain in existence today, if in modified forms.

Some authorities have claimed that the war had an equally deep, if somewhat differently directed, effect on black literature. Rather than an emphasis on militant protest and a declaration of blackness, there was said to be 'a drastic reduction of the racial content, a rise in preoccupation with urban themes and subject matter both in the novel and the poem.'[42] The explanation given for this was that the discontent of the 1930s had been siphoned off by the war boom and that as Afro-Americans generally were moving towards integration, the black writers felt they should point the way by writing 'integrated novels.'[43] Another reason was given by the black writer James Baldwin: as far as he was concerned, *the* protest novel had already appeared before America entered the war, with the publication of Richard Wright's *Native Son* in 1940.[44] This may be no more than a question of semantics as most books by Afro-Americans seem, at least to me, to have some element of protest in them. There is plenty of evidence both for and against such claims, for whatever else was true, a considerable number of books with racial themes were written by blacks and whites during the war. One commentator said at the time that the 'loud acclaim' for books dealing with minority causes was unprecedented, and that in 'comparison, the famed Negro renaissance of the twenties is a mere whine.'[45] While this statement may be slightly exaggerated, the large number of literary works by and about blacks can be seen as the continuation of, or the second period of, the Harlem renaissance.

There was, of course, a long literary tradition among Afro-Americans, beginning in the eighteenth century with Phillis Wheatley and Jupiter Hammon. Later blacks wrote abolitionist tracts, slave narratives, biographies and novels. However, the general subordination of Afro-Americans, their poverty, lack of education and rural background, all served to limit such cultural endeavors to just a small number. Following World War I there was suddenly a great increase in the production of literary works by blacks. Urbanization, a degree of prosperity, wider educational opportunities and the post-war mood enabled a circle of black writers, centered at first in Harlem, to reach a wide audience. Afro-Americans like Claude McKay, Jean Toomer, Countee Cullen, Langston Hughes and many others were encouraged and joined by whites in writing 'Negro' literature. While the number of books and articles and the interest they attracted was more than sufficient to justify the term 'renaissance,' they were still the work of a small elite of Afro-American intellectuals: only Langston Hughes could be said to be writing of and for the common man.[46]

This literary renaissance ended with the economic depression; writers found it difficult to secure financial support, publishers found it difficult to sell books. Several of the black writers went abroad while others worked on the Federal Writers' Project. The few works which did appear in the 1930s differed from those of the previous decade. No longer dependent on white patrons (many of whom had gone bankrupt as a result of the Crash), black writers 'turned more and more to materials which genuinely interested them rather than to sensuous and bizarre themes which delighted American readers during the boom years.'[47] There was as much an emphasis on class as on race, and a use of characters drawn from real life rather than stereotypes. These new trends were best demonstrated in Wright's collection of short stories, *Uncle Tom's Children*, and his novel set in Chicago's South Side, *Native Son*.[48] Following America's entry into the war, there was a revival in literature about blacks as they and whites addressed themselves to the problems and issues of the conflict.

These various books, essays and poems give an extra dimension to the other more conventional historical sources. As well as adding to and confirming the information found in reports, pamphlets, articles and statistics, they provide a background and capture attitudes and moods. For example, a number of essays and short stories describe Harlem prior to and during the riot of 1943, an incident of some size and importance which is largely ignored elsewhere. In 1942 Ralph Ellison, who later included a riot in his famous novel *Invisible Man*, wrote an account of his conversation with a black woman which reveals the trials and tribulations of a typical Afro-American family. Her husband is dead, her eldest son in the Army, and her daughter desperately trying to enter a defense training scheme in order to get work. Both her daughter's and her nephew's experiences in search of employment lead the woman to dismiss the FEPC as 'doing something everywhere but here in New York.' She works herself to supplement the government checks from her son's Army pay—which always arrive late—and spends her time worrying whether the boy will survive his stay at Fort Bragg in North Carolina. Ellison comments on the 'war-made confusion' which affects this and every black family and points out that they 'do not ask for a lighter share of necessary war sacrifices than other Americans have to bear,' but that 'they do ask for equal reasons to believe that their sacrifices are worthwhile.'[49]

In an essay published in 1948, Ellison depicted Harlem as a 'ruin' of 'crumbling buildings,' 'ill-smelling halls and vermin-invaded rooms': 'the scene and symbol of the Negro's perpetual alienation in the land of his birth.'[50] Another black writer later to become equally famous, James Baldwin, agreed with this description. Deferred from armed service because of poor health, Baldwin was in Harlem in the summer of 1943 to attend his father's funeral. He felt and later wrote of the tensions of the time, saying that he 'had never before known it to be so violently still,' and commenting on the strains of war, he said, 'everybody felt a directionless, hopeless bitterness, as well as that panic which can scarcely be suppressed when one knows that a human being one loves is beyond one's reach, and in danger.'[51]

This kind of fear, common to many blacks, was the basis of Ann Petry's short story 'In Darkness and Confusion,' published in 1947.[52] A black man, anxiously waiting for news of his son in an Army camp in Georgia, finally hears the worst. After refusing to take a Jim Crow seat on a bus, the young man had been involved in a fight with white military policemen. In the struggle the black youth had taken the gun of one of his opponents and wounded him before being shot and wounded himself. Court-martialled, the boy had been sentenced to twenty years' hard labor. The father later witnesses an incident between a black soldier and a white policeman at a hotel in Harlem and, imagining his son in the place of the wounded soldier, his stifled anger and sorrow explode. Unconsciously, he encourages the gathering crowds to riot as does his wife when she joins him and is told the news. The rumor that a black soldier has been shot dead while defending a woman of his race spreads rapidly. The truth is ignored and is irrelevant: as Baldwin commented, the mass of Afro-Americans 'preferred the invention because this invention expressed and corroborated their hates and fears so perfectly.'[53] Although a fictional story, Petry's account of the actual riot is extremely realistic, no doubt drawing from her experiences as a journalist on the *Amsterdam News* and *The People's Voice*.

Two full-length novels by Afro-Americans dealt at least in part with the problems faced by blacks in the defense industries. Alexander Saxton's rather unsatisfactory book *Bright Web in the Darkness* (1959) involved both blacks and whites; the former in the quest for employment, the latter as representatives of labor unions. A black woman completes a welding course only to be told that there is no need for woman welders and is refused union clearance. Racial trouble in the shipyards increases and when the union fails to pass a no-discrimination resolution, the black workers walk out. In answer to a suggestion that they might damage the war effort, the Afro-American leader angrily exclaims, 'Don't you talk to me about this war! It's a white man's war. I've seen it.'[54] There were enough real cases of job discrimination and similar black reactions for the story to be based on fact.

The same was also true of the plot of *If He Hollers Let Him Go* (1945), which concentrates on one black man from the mid-West in the shipyards of Los Angeles. This, the first novel by Chester Himes, is a much better, if angrier and more militant, book than Saxton's and was reviewed favorably by the critics.[55] The chief character, Bob Jones, is from the start portrayed in conflict with his white-dominated environment, seeing even driving in heavy rush-hour traffic as a racial battle. At home Jones has problems with his girlfriend and her middle class family; at work he is troubled by a white foreman, apathetic union officials, and a white woman who is openly hostile and succeeds first in getting him demoted for using bad language and then falsely charged with raping her. Jones flees after being severely beaten by white workers, but he is caught by the police with a gun in his possession. Although the charge of rape is dropped at the request of the company, the judge persuades Jones to join the Army rather than be jailed for carrying a weapon.

Even amid all these adversities, the black man can still manage to feel a part of the mainstream, still subject to that feeling of 'twoness' described by DuBois in *The Souls of Black Folk* (1903). Driving past the shipyards and towering cranes, Jones feels 'the size of it, the immensity of the production.' Stirred by this sight, he 'felt included in it all,' something he had never felt before: 'it was a wonderful feeling.'[56] Later, as whites try to exclude him from this experience, he has doubts and wonders 'what would happen if all the Negroes in America would refuse to serve in the armed forces, refused to work in war production until Jim Crow was abolished.'[57] In the end, Jones is pushed into open revolt and defeated, losing everything.

In a short story published in *The Crisis* in 1943, Himes wrote of a black soldier on leave in Harlem after six months of active service in North Africa.[58] He meets and falls in love with a beautiful woman whom he eventually has to leave to return to the war. This is certainly not a 'protest' story in the sense of *If He Hollers*: the couple could have been white and their feelings must have been common to many, regardless of race. The same is not true of William Gardner Smith's novel about blacks in the American Army in Berlin at the end of the war. In *The Last of the Conquerors* (1949) Smith's theme is that Afro-American GIs received better treatment from the Germans than from their fellow Americans. Harassment on and off base, particularly in respect to relationships with German women, forces some of the black soldiers to flee to the Russian zone. The moral is obvious: the contradiction of discrimination in the armies of democracy in contrast to the acceptance of blacks by the former supporters of Hitler. Again the book met with considerable acclaim, although one reviewer thought it lacked 'the psychological penetration and daring which could have transformed it from an interesting historical document into a great and moving exposé of the inconsistencies and dilemmas of exported race prejudice.'[59]

Much less impressive was *Jigger Witchet's War*, written ten years later by Avery E. Kolb.[60] Also about black troops in Europe, it concentrated on humor rather than social comment, and suffers accordingly. Interestingly enough, a novel by the English author Nevil Shute also dealt with the question of exported racial prejudice. *The Chequer Board* (1947) included an account of racial strife between black and white American soldiers in an English town. The local publican refuses to exclude Negro soldiers and instead hangs up a notice which reads 'This House is for Englishmen and Coloured American troops only.' This appears to be based on fact, for Walter White, during his tour of camps in Britain, quoted signs saying just that in a number of pubs.[61]

The most impressive book on the subject of black military service was

And Then We Heard The Thunder. Its author, John Oliver Killens, had served
in the amphibious forces during the war, and although not published until
1962 the novel was clearly based on his own experiences. It has been
considered 'the most important novel about the Negro during World War
II.'[62] The story follows a black Army unit from induction and training at a
Southern base to service in the Pacific. The black soldiers hold widely
differing views, ranging from pro-Japanese to belief in the war for
democracy. The hero, Solomon Saunders, a moderate, initially considers
the racists from the South little different from Hitler or Tojo, but he has
ambitions to become an officer and do well once the war is over and so is
prepared to put up with a certain amount of the Army's brand of
discrimination. However, his attitude changes as time wears on. Referred
to as 'boys' by their commanding officer, abused by military and civil
police off base and given the dirtiest jobs to do, the unit eventually ends up
in Australia. There another clash with white American authority leads to an
all-out riot in which Saunders takes part, declaring 'there is no peace till
freedom.'[63] All of the incidents described by Killens are founded on fact,
including the final debacle which is based on the Brisbane riot. As well as
being accurate on the gloomier side of military race relations, the book is
not without humor and the sardonic wit of Afro-Americans despite all
adversity recurs continually, rather like the blues. One soldier comments,
'colored people join the service and white folks join the Army'; elsewhere,
the soldiers march to the tune of 'Hinky, dinky, parlez-vous,' and add the
lines 'They say this is a white man's war' and 'Well what the hell are we
fighting for?'[64]

   None of the works discussed so far could be referred to as
'integrated'—some were very angry protest novels—but a number of
books written during and published after the war justified that description.
Frank Yerby's historical romances of the South prior to, during and after
the Civil War use characters of all races, but the main ones are white.[65] Like
Yerby's books, the personae of Willard Motley's *Knock on Any Door* (1947)
are not black, nor was the book advertised by any reference to the author's
race.[66] Ann Petry's first full-length novel *The Street* (1946) was also classed as
'integrated' because, according to Butcher, 'the fact that her characters are
Negroes is only incidental to her theme.'[67] And yet it paints a gloomy
picture of race relations in America, describing the effect of segregation,
low incomes and slum environments on black people. However, in her
second novel *Country Place* (1947) the chief characters are white, but the
story of a veteran returning from the war to find he has been jilted by his
wife could have applied to any race or class of people.[68]

   As Afro-Americans wrote about whites, so whites wrote about blacks.
Prior to the war black subjects had been treated sympathetically by a
number of white authors, including William Faulkner and Erskine
Caldwell. During the 1940s a 'group of militant young liberals began

writing increasingly of the significance of the war for the Negro minority and the inevitablity of a revolutionary shift in Southern race relations following the war's conclusion.'[69] Howard Fast's tale of blacks in the South following the Civil War was dedicated to 'the men and women, black and white, yellow and brown, who have laid down their lives in the struggle against fascism.'[70] The moral of the story, about returning black soldiers denied their rights, needs no elaboration. More directly to the point was Hodding Carter's *The Winds of Fear* (1945), set in a Southern town during the 1940s where the white townspeople fear the return of 'the unruly Negro.' 'Maybe it's the war, maybe not. Things are happening too fast for them, things they don't like.'[71] When the sheriff is killed by an Afro-American, a replacement known for his violence and dislike of blacks is appointed. He eventually shoots a black soldier in uniform for no good reason, and the incident and its coverage by the national press divides the town into two camps, the blacks with white liberal support facing the racists. It is a confrontation guaranteed to lead to more violence.

Equally pessimistic is James Gould Cozzens's story of racial friction between black and white Air Force units in Florida, entitled *Guard of Honour* (1949). As one of the white airmen points out, it is dangerous to deny people their rights—'in the long run, you drive them to take their rights by force.'[72] Violence also features in *Trouble Follows Me* (1946), a popular thriller written by the author of the Lew Archer stories, Ross Macdonald, then writing under the name of Kenneth Millar. Part of the plot involves a black fascist organization called 'Black Israel' supposed to be involved in stirring up the riot in Detroit. While this type of story could hardly be thought to improve race relations, it does occasionally make social comments, such as a description of a black ghetto: 'Hemmed in by economic pressure and social injustice, the Negroes swarmed in the rotting hives which they had neither built nor chosen, three, five or seven to a room.'[73]

The violence inherent in America's race relations was the subject of a more serious work which was one of the best-sellers of the war years. *Strange Fruit* (1944), Lillian Smith's powerful novel, was remarkable both because its writer was a Southerner and a woman, and because of the reception it received. The story is of an interracial love affair in a Southern town. When the black girl, Nonnie, finds that she is pregnant, her white lover, Tracy Dean, arranges for her to marry his house servant. Nonnie's brother regards this as another example of white outrage against black womanhood and kills Dean. An incensed white mob then takes the falsely accused houseboy from jail and lynches him: this is the 'strange fruit' of America's race relations. As one of the more sympathetic whites comments, 'We lynch the Negro's soul every day of our lives.'[74]

As well as being a successful novel, *Strange Fruit* was one of several works about Afro-Americans which were produced on the stage. Others included

Deep are the Roots and *Jeb*, both about returning black servicemen and their readjustment to American society. In general, there was an increase in the number of theater productions with racial themes and in the use of black actors. One of the most significant performances was that of Paul Robeson as Othello in New York in 1943. The first time that a black actor and white actress had appeared together in this play, the production achieved the longest recorded run of any Shakespearian drama and lasted until 1945. The number of blacks in Broadway plays rose throughout the war, from three plays in 1940 to 20 in 1944 and 28 in 1946, and their roles 'indicated a trend toward unprecedented liberalism.'[75]

White liberalism was also revealed in the much-quoted poem by Witter Bynner, 'Defeat.' Commenting on the fact that German prisoners of war were treated as equals on a train in Texas while black soldiers were segregated, and referring back to the Civil War, Bynner wrote,

> Whom are we fighting this time, for God's sake?
> Mark well the token of the separate seat.
> It is again ourselves whom we defeat.[76]

Much less well known is the wartime poetry of Afro-Americans, a great deal of which was published in popular magazines and newspapers as well as in book form. Overall, such poems posed the same questions asked elsewhere. The worries of the black soldier overseas were encapsulated in the 'Draftee's Prayer':[77]

> So while I fight
> Wrong over there,
> see that my folks
> are treated fair.

Several of the poems of Owen Dodson were concerned with war issues. In one, he asks the American soldiers longing for peace if their home will be one of peace and equality and racial harmony, or[78]

> where a man will trample again
> his neighbor, shake no hands.

Similar questions were raised about the post-war world by other black poets. In 'Sonnet,' Alfred Duckett asked, 'Will we slip into old, accustomed ways,' while Allen Woodall in 'Questions' wanted to know whether America would be rid of 'These myths of nationality and race.'[79] One former black soldier supplied an apt comment on segregation in the forces when he wrote that troops in combat[80]

> were pulverized . . . Reduced . . . Wiped out—made uniform and *equal!*

White America was also warned that once the war had ended, instead of joining in singing the national anthem blacks might 'sing new words to another tune.'[81]

One of the greatest of black poets, and one of the few from the renaissance period still writing during the 1940s, was Langston Hughes. His many poems captured all the moods of war, and while he contributed to the war effort by providing jingles, verses and slogans for the Treasury Department and the War Writers Board, Hughes was well aware of the issues the war raised for his people. He pointed out that the fight for freedom

> means Freedom at home, too—
> Now—*right here!*

and commenting on the beating of Roland Hayes, the black jazz musician, in Georgia in 1942, he wrote,[82]

> Negroes
> Sweet and docile,
> Meek, humble, and kind.
> Beware the day
> They change their minds!

Like the blues singers, Hughes dealt with every aspect of black life—love and loneliness, prejudice and discrimination. But he could transcend simple racial themes and in reference to the war reveal his greatness and humanity. In 'World War II' and 'Casualty' Hughes brought out the basic suffering and loss involved in warfare; the loss of a friend, a husband or a son.[83] In a later collection published after his death in 1967, Hughes devoted an entire section to 'The Face of War,' and the poems included apply to any war, any race, at any time. His 'Peace' provides a final epitaph:[84]

> We passed their graves:
> The dead men there,
> Winners or losers,
> Did not care
>
> In the dark
> They could not see
> Who had gained
> The victory.

Clearly, it was true to say that 'Negro poets of the forties addressed themselves to the problem of war,' and the same could be said of the black authors and musicians.[85] In poem, story and song, Afro-Americans dealt with the question of equal military participation and the rewards they hoped it would bring. In the main this meant that their works were still primarily of protest, angrily denouncing discrimination and segregation in all areas of the defense effort. While this was easily visible in literal content, a change was also apparent in the very form and style of a music and literature which echoed the militant and aggressive mood of Afro-Americans: rhythm and blues and bop were the natural accompaniment to the March on Washington Movement, and to even more extreme groups. (It is interesting to note, for example, that a number of black jazz musicians took Muslim names at this time.)[86] Yet sufficient progress was made during the war to encourage some blacks to envisage a time in the not-too-distant future when integration and equality would be the norm. So much was this so that writers like Petry, Motley and Yerby could write what were later to be described as 'integrated' novels. These two radically different developments could take place simultaneously: the existence of one did not rule out the other. Indeed the two together reflected exactly the black mood—demanding *and* expectant. Promising economic and social advances were coupled with the broader portrayal of blacks on the stage and screen, and the sympathetic treatment of racial themes by white authors. That such efforts could be commercially successful also demonstrated the change in attitudes that had come about during, and because of, the war.

6

The Psychological Impact of War: Black Attitudes and the White Response

Songs and literature during World War II reveal a certain ambivalence in blacks' attitudes, between the sometimes militant rejection of white society and the equally militant desire to be included as equal participants. This was no new feature in Afro-American history, but the war had served to sharpen it by pointing up the discrimination which had long existed. That the majority of Afro-Americans wished to participate in the military and industrial war effort is clear enough. Why they should do so is perhaps not so readily apparent. To a certain extent, of course, participation was itself a reward, bringing increased economic opportunities and a sense of belonging and pride. However, underlying many of the black demands for greater and equal involvement was their desire for complete equality once the war had ended. If the Military Participation Ratio theory has any validity in this context, it was because it was unconsciously recognized by both blacks and whites. Thus, the black campaign to end discrimination and segregation in the armed forces and defense industries was coupled with claims for equality in society generally. Once they had taken part in the war, their position with regard to civil rights was strengthened considerably.

While white liberals might see the logic of the Afro-Americans' reasoning and agree with it, those with more prejudiced racial attitudes disagreed. Yet their very argument, that black involvement in the war effort would encourage 'uppity niggers' and moves toward social equality, itself recognized the importance of participation and the justice inherent in the black point of view. Just as blacks were determined to be included in their country's struggle, so, for really the same reasons, those whites were determined to resist them. The government, meanwhile, was intent on preserving national unity and winning the war. Aware of its position as a 'defender of democracy' and of the attitudes of the voters at home, it temporized and compromised and so postponed any confrontation until a later date.

When the United States entered the war in December 1941 Afro-Americans faced a considerable dilemma. Given the discrimination in the war effort, they had to decide whether or not to fight overseas under existing conditions, or to concentrate first on the struggle for equality at home. For most, that dilemma was resolved in the slogans in the popular black newspapers which worked to encourage a positive attitude toward the war. While the *Chicago Defender* urged 'Remember Pearl Harbor and Sikeston, too,' a reference to Sikeston, Missouri where a young Afro-American had been lynched in January 1941, the *Pittsburgh Courier* adopted the 'Double V'—for victory at home *and* abroad—which had been suggested by one of its readers.[1] The 'Double V' symbol was immensely popular and was displayed throughout the newspaper, in texts, photographs and in advertisements for the NAACP. The *Courier* also received requests from the public for 'Double V' buttons, stickers and pins, and according to Roi Ottley, the black journalist and writer, the campaign had the support of 'nearly every newspaper and pulpit.'[2]

The attitude of the NAACP was not dissimilar to that of the black press, combining the concern for civil rights with the wish to participate loyally in the war. Walter White declared that Afro-Americans 'will fight for our country, but at the same time, demand the right to fight as equals in every branch of our country's military, naval and aviation service,' and *The Crisis* editorialized, 'With our country at war for little more than a month, the CRISIS would emphasize with all its strength that now is the time *not* to be silent about the breaches of democracy here in our own land.'[3] This was far removed from the statements mad in World War I and W. E. B. DuBois's 'Close Ranks' editorial in particular.

This new belligerent attitude was not peculiar to black leadership. In fact, as Lee Finkle has shown, black newspapermen often lagged behind the temper of the masses.[4] Various surveys conducted during the war found a new militancy among the black public on questions of civil rights. One commentator said, 'The war has brought about a new stage in the Negro psychology where *aggressiveness on behalf of rights and privileges is given full-hearted support by the masses while compromise is scorned*'; a poll reported in the *Courier* which found that 88·7 per cent of those asked felt that the Negro should 'not soft-pedal his demands for complete freedom and citizenship and await the development of the educational processes' bore him out.[5] Government surveys of black attitudes also found considerable militancy. Of 1008 blacks interviewed in New York, 42 per cent felt that it was *more* important to make democracy work at home than to defeat Germany and Japan when questioned by a black interviewer. This figure dropped to 34 per cent when the interviewer was white.[6] The degree of aggressiveness also varied from one locality to another, and a survey requested by William Hastie before his resignation as civilian aide to the Secretary of War found that the 'militance which was widespread in Harlem was conspicuously absent in Memphis.' The reason for this was that the 'Memphis Negroes were fearful of expressing their views, and were more ignorant about war issues and more apathetic about them than New York respondents.'[7]

Perhaps in response to attitudes such as these, black spokesmen argued that involvement in all avenues of the war effort was imperative to the black struggle for civil rights. It was both means and end. Not only did Afro-Americans 'see in war an opportunity to prove their patriotism and thus lay the nation under obligation to them': the war also provided the chance to demonstrate that they were in fact first-class citizens.[8] The situation was aptly summed up by Lester Granger of the National Urban League when he said that 'the quest of the Negro for full partnership in the war is an expression of his desire to assume full citizenship responsibilities.'[9] From the very beginning, the duties and the privileges attached to citizenship were thus linked together and demands for participation in the war effort were coupled with specific demands relating to civil rights.

A. Philip Randolph, the leader of the March on Washington Movement, put forward a program in 1942 which 'in the interest of national unity' demanded 'the abrogation of every law which makes a distinction in treatment between citizens based on religion, creed, color or national origin.'[10] The MOWM went on to call for the complete end of Jim Crow, enforcement of existing statutes and additional legislation in order to end lynchings and the disenfranchisement of Afro-Americans, the abolition of segregation in the armed forces and government, an end to economic discrimination, and black representation in all government agencies. The *Chicago Defender*'s National Negro Defense Program included similar points and, explaining why it was necessary to launch such a scheme at that particular time, the paper argued that 'Negroes CAN and MUST profit from the discipline that war will impose on all American citizens and BEGIN NOW under a planned program to secure all of the things which have previously been denied.' Earlier, in a reference to the March on Washington Movement, the paper had also pointed out that 'effective protest during emergency is infinitely more productive of results than ten times the effort during periods of comparative normalcy.'[11] Expanding on its 'Double V' slogan, the *Pittsburgh Courier* suggested that blacks 'would be less than men if, while we are giving up our property and sacrificing our lives, we do not agitate, contend, and demand those rights guaranteed to all free men . . . this would be neither patriotism nor common sense.'[12]

Along with this desire to fight for equal rights was the feeling that participation in the war effort would be rewarded; in fact the two ideas were inextricably interwoven. George Rouzeau, one of the *Courier*'s war correspondents, urged black soldiers to 'insist on combat duty' and asked, 'is it not true that only those who spill their blood are in a position to demand rights?'[13] A black soldier, in a letter to the *Baltimore Afro-American*, said that black soldiers 'fight because of the opportunities it will make possible for them after the war.'[14] The mutual obligations of the citizen and the state were also spelled out. For a man to enter the forces, risk life and limb, was 'just and reasonable' if the nation was 'fighting for the purpose of providing a better life for the people who compose the citizenry.'[15] Forty-six per cent of the blacks polled in the New York survey felt that they would be treated better once the war was won; of that number, 14 per cent expected better treatment because of their war effort, while another 10 per cent thought it would be due to black initiatives in demanding rights.[16]

Another important reason for rising expectations was the feeling that the war was a revolutionary force capable of transforming society. 'War—and a global war in particular—is a social revolution.'[17] Robert C. Weaver's opinion, that unsolved social issues would come to the fore and demand attention, was shared by other people. Gunnar Myrdal, in *An American Dilemma*, spoke of the wartime 'revitalization of the American Creed of Democracy,' and some Afro-Americans even went as far as to say that the longer the war, the more blacks would benefit. George Schuyler was one of these, and argued that previous wars had not provided a sufficient test of American institutions to bring dramatic changes; Joseph Bibbs in the *Pittsburgh Courier* said, 'war may be hell for some, but it bids fair to open up the portals of heaven for us.'[18] There were arguments against this point of view: Benjamin Mays, the president of Morehouse College, argued that 'a world crisis does not destroy customs, mores and prejudices that have their roots anchored in centuries.' The black historian Benjamin Quarles put a similar case based on precedents. While he saw the possibility of economic gains, he saw no reason to expect that participation and valor would be rewarded. Moreover, he warned Afro-Americans that the war might 'create a national psychosis which would indefinitely delay a solution to the American race problem.'[19]

While the editors of *Crisis* felt that Quarles had undervalued the war's potential to bring change, the historian's pessimism was shared by some Afro-Americans. Thirty-eight per cent of the respondents in the New York survey expected to be treated just the same after the war as before, and 5 per cent actually thought they would be worse off. Only a third of those asked in Memphis felt that a United Nations victory would bring any improvement in their lot.[20] The continued maltreatment of black soldiers and civilians throughout the country encouraged this mood of despair. Sociologist Horace R. Cayton, Roi Ottley, and the New York politician Adam Clayton Powell, Jr all asked their fellow Afro-Americans if they were 'Fighting for white folks?,' and the now well known epitaph for black soldiers 'Here lies a black man killed fighting a yellow man for the protection of a white man' originated during this period.[21]

Although important as representatives of the extreme view among Afro-Americans, the number of blacks who openly and actively opposed participation in the war effort was very small. In 1941 there were only 33 black conscientious objectors or 2·6 per cent of the total number of COs. In the period 1941–6 there were 2208 black violators of the Selective Service and Training Act. Of these, 166 were classed as conscientious objectors; the remainder had failed to appear before their draft boards either deliberately or because of misinformation, lack of knowledge or carelessness.[22]

One group which initially encouraged opposition to the war and American entry into it was the Communist Party of the United States and its black socialist sympathizers. One prominent socialist, A. Philip Randolph, was, as we have seen, intent on ensuring a black role in the war effort. His view, that America had more to offer to the black man than Hitler did, was shared by his friend and former fellow editor of the *Messenger*, Chandler Owen, who wrote the text of the morale-boosting Office of War Information Pamphlet *Negroes and the War*.[23] Such activities were opposed by the CPUSA which, after the Nazi-Soviet Pact of August 1939, opposed American support for the Allies. The Communist line on race relations at this time was that 'you can't defend Negro rights without fighting against this war.'[24]

When Hitler attacked the Soviet Union in June 1941, American Communists and socialist sympathizers performed a *volte-face* and called for complete support for the war effort and a halt to protests, such as the March on Washington, which might hinder it. Thus the author Richard Wright, a former opponent of the war, could in December 1941 offer his literary services to the government for 'the national democratic cause.' No doubt because his political affiliations were known, his offer was not accepted. He did, however, write the text to *Twelve Million Black Voices* as his contribution to the war effort.[25]

It does not appear that these political adversaries of the war supported or encouraged draft evasion in the short period of their opposition. The groups which did so were almost entirely nationalist-separatist sects which originated in the period of disillusion following World War I and during the Depression. To them, America was a white man's country in which they had no stake and therefore no obligations: the war was a white man's war from which nothing could be gained for blacks. To the majority of their fellow black Americans and the integrationist press, these people were no more than 'foolish fanatics,' 'crackpots and starry-eyed cultists,' or members of 'obscure religious sects.'[26] If not foolish, they were, like the black conscientious objectors, certainly brave, for the FBI attempted to prove that most of those concerned were, if not the tools of enemy agents, at least pro-Axis, and as such they would be liable to a maximum of forty years in prison. Luckily for them, these charges were hard to substantiate, and the majority of people accused of sedition were instead convicted of draft evasion.

The largest group charged with sedition were the followers of the Temple of Islam (Black Muslims), 63 of whom, including their leader Elijah Muhammad, were arrested in the Chicago roundup of September 1942.[27] Altough the Muslims were sympathetic to the Japanese (because they were also colored), no acts of sedition were proven. Indeed, 'observers felt that the charges of draft evasion cleared the defendants . . . of any connection with Japanese espionage. The government's case of sedition against them evidently collapsed.'[28] On conviction for draft evasion the Muslims were jailed for three years and their leader for five. Muhammad was released from Milan, Michigan in 1946 and returned to a movement which had grown during and perhaps because of his imprisonment. Gulam Bogans, known as Elijah Mohamed, the leader of another sect of Muslims with temples and universities in Washington, D.C., Detroit and Milwaukee, and 'several hundreds' of his followers also refused to register for the draft: 50 of them were given three year prison sentences.[29] A sole Muslim, James Barnes, was jailed in Mississippi—but for breaking the Jim Crow laws of the state rather than for evading the draft. He was, however, sentenced to ten years or *for the duration of the war*.[30]

The remainder of those arrested in Chicago in 1942 were members of the Peace Movement of Ethiopia (formed in 1932, an offshoot of Garvey's UNIA supporting massive resettlement in Africa) and the Brotherhood of Liberty for Black People in America. The members of the Peace Movement of Ethiopia were treated comparatively leniently, perhaps because they were led by a woman, Mrs M. L. Gordon. While she was sentenced to two years in prison, her followers were released on probation.[31]

A tiny number of Afro-Americans *were* found guilty of sedition. Five supporters of the Ethiopian Pacific Movement in New York, led by a former Garveyite, Robert O. Jordan, were indicted for sedition in 1942. Known in both the black and the white newspapers as the 'Black Hitler,' Jordan's pro-Axis sympathies were common knowledge. He and his followers were accused of 'urging soldiers and others to resist service in the armed forces of the United States and to support Japan, holding that Japan was going to liberate the darker races.' The *Chicago Defender* referred to them as 'agents of fascism' and urged the court to 'convict them all.'[32] Although convicted, they were not given the maximum forty year sentence—the court held that their activities had been ineffective—but were jailed for periods of four to ten years, with an additional $10,000 fine for Jordan.[33]

Still another offshoot of Garveyism, the Pacific Movement of the Eastern World, was supposed to be 'sponsored by Japanese agents . . . to spread confusion and dissension and disrupt America's war effort.' Only two of its members, in St Louis, were found guilty of both sedition and draft evasion:

one was given four year sentences on both charges, the terms to run concurrently, and the other two two year sentences.[34] Seven followers of the House of Israel from Newark, New Jersey were sentenced to three years in jail for evading the draft, although they had 'been inciting other Negroes ... not to fight the Japanese because they are another colored race.' The local FBI director said that their violations of the Selective Service Act were not based on their religion but on 'an almost fanatical conviction that they had nothing to fight for in this war.'[35]

A variety of other groups throughout the country faced similar charges to these after refusing to participate in the war for a mixture of racial and religious reasons. Twenty-one members of the International Reassembly of the Church of Freedom League who refused to serve overseas were imprisoned in New Orleans for draft evasion; other movements included the Ethiopian Women's Work Association and the African Nationalist Pioneering Movement; individuals as far away from the East coast as San Diego, California were convicted on charges 'of a subversive nature.'[36] The FBI attempted to relate such beliefs to Japanese agents and propaganda, and in some instances this alleged relationship was given credence by fellow blacks such as Randolph and Ottley. Ottley devoted an entire chapter of his book *New World A'Coming* to such charges, but he failed to point out that indictments for draft evasion were generally substituted for those of sedition.[37]

Rather than the subjects of Japanese espionage agents, it seems more likely that, given their ideological backgrounds, the defendants were, in the words of the American Civil Liberties Union, 'the victims of over-zealous race conciousness, while others were religious zealots.' Alternatively, their actions could be, and were, described as 'passive resistance to the American war effort as a protest at racial discrimination in the United States.'[38]

Although these people obviously represented a minority of Afro-Americans, the fact remains that a number of blacks shared their sympathy for the Japanese. The government surveys found that in New York 18 per cent of those interviewed thought they would be better treated by the Japanese than they were by the Americans, and in Memphis the proportion was higher. Few of those asked thought they would be any better off under German rule. The interviewers attributed these attitudes to apathy or lack of knowledge about the comparative war aims of the Axis and the Allies.[39] Richard Wright suggested that the attack by the colored Japanese on the white Americans might have awakened the racial consciousness of some Afro-Americans; that 'when looking at the dark faces of the Japanese generals' they could 'dream of what it would be like to live in a country where they could forget their color and play a responsible role in the vital processes of the nation's life.'[40] A more likely reason was that these were extreme reactions to the continued discrimination in America during the war. By and large, however, the militance of most

Afro-Americans was directed to ensure equal participation in, not withdrawal from, the war effort. In return, they hoped that their demands for civil rights would be recognized.

If white Americans were not aware of the black attitudes or had ignored them, the belligerence of Afro-Americans and the riots of 1943 forced them to take notice. In 1944 a book was published 'at the request of the Press' entitled *What The Negro Wants*. Edited by the former chairman of the Campaign for Participation of Negroes in National Defense, Rayford Logan, the book consisted of essays by fourteen well known blacks of various political persuasions, including W. E. B. DuBois, Mary McLeod Bethune, Roy Wilkins, George Schuyler and Willard Townsend. The degree of unanimity among these diverse contributors was remarkable. All noted that the war had heightened racial issues and spoke of the 'abnormal' and 'unprecedented' changes which were taking place. All demanded 'first-class citizenship' for the Afro-American and full 'economic, political and social equality.'[41] In another collection of essays, pointedly called *Primer for White Folks*, both black and white writers commented on the importance of the war to race relations and emphasized the paradox of fighting for democracy abroad while denying it to minority groups at home.[42] That blacks had participated in the war effort despite the often considerable limitations imposed on their service, was stressed in these and other publications. One book of eighty-five short stories from the *Baltimore Afro-American*'s war correspondents declared *This Is Our War*, while the black role and achievement was listed in *Democracy's Negroes* and various yearbooks.[43] On VE Day, Afro-Americans could justifiably proclaim 'On Land, On Sea, in the Air, We Did Our Part,' and as one black soldier wrote from 'somewhere on Okinawa,'[44]

> Our people are not coming back with the idea of just taking up where they left off. We are going to have the things that are rightfully due us or else, which is a very large order, but we have proven beyond all things that we are people and not just the servants of the whiteman.

A number of white Americans agreed that the Afro-American had played his part and supported his demands for equality. One white writer suggested that the 'common hardship' shared during the war 'may bring the races closer to a better understanding' and that whites should extend to the black man 'consideration for his wellbeing as partner in our struggle.'[45] Several popular magazines devoted entire issues to the question of race relations in the United States and the significance it had achieved because of the world conflict. While the June 1942 issue of *Fortune* was entitled 'The Negro's War,' *Survey Graphic* for November the same year was concerned with 'Color: Unfinished Business of Democracy.' Various books by white authors served a similar function on a larger scale; prominent among them were Gunnar Myrdal's *An American Dilemma* and Lillian Smith's novel

Strange Fruit. Later works also stressed the manner in which the war had brought questions of prejudice and tolerance to the fore and pleaded for unity and understanding.[46] Afro-American participation was lauded in all of these, as well as in the House of Representatives where it was noted in 1946 that 'Negro heroes in this war achieved their proud records under handicaps that did not have to be overcome by most of their white fellow citizens.'[47]

One of the most important and influential supporters of the Afro-Americans' case during the war was undoubtedly Wendell Willkie, Republican presidential candidate in 1940. He sided with the black press in urging 'fight for democracy at home as well as abroad,' and argued that 'the correction of certain injustices can be made under the pressures of war which years of peaceful effort have failed to bring about, such as the discrimination against the colored citizen in industry, in labor, and in the armed service of the nation.'[48] Willkie pointed out in his best-selling book *One World* that America could not in all honesty fight 'the forces of imperialism abroad and maintain any form of imperialism at home': he wanted the United States to adopt policies and practices in keeping with Allied propaganda and so demonstrate its good faith to India, Africa and China.[49] In taking this stance he was, according to writer and journalist Carey McWilliams, reflecting 'a growing interest and concern with racial minorities on the part of a large section of the majority.' This ferment could not be written off as 'crisis patriotism.' Following his untimely death in 1944, Willkie was mourned in the black press as the 'nation's number one patriot,' and the Afro-American's 'foremost champion.'[50]

Willkie's views on race were shared by, among others, the well known novelist Pearl S. Buck. In a widely publicized letter to the *New York Times* she too attacked American hypocrisy and suggested that the government could at least guarantee equal economic opportunity to all Americans and see to it 'that colored people in this democracy shall not suffer insult because of their color.'[51] It is interesting to note that these comments were made in November 1941, before America had entered the war, and were presumably intended to reinforce Executive Order 8802 issued the previous June. Later Buck urged blacks to stand by their white countrymen 'in this imperfect democracy' because America was the place where 'the hope of democracy is still clearest.'[52] The *New York Times*, the paper to which she had originally written, took a stand on race relations itself, and on April 3, 1942 in an editorial headed 'A Minority of Our Own' urged Americans to demonstrate their sincerity to their allies: the racial problem had to be solved if America was to avoid 'the sinister hypocrisy of fighting abroad for what it is not willing to accept at home.' This concern among whites increased following the riots of 1943 which made evident the deterioration in race relations that had occurred despite their pleas.

A survey of opinions conducted by the Office of War Information after the Detroit riot found that people were 'shocked,' 'outraged,' 'alarmed,' and occasionally 'shamed' by the racial violence. While the correspondents showed an awareness of black discontent, they put the cause of the riots down to the 'belligerence' of Afro-Americans and the resentment this caused among whites.[53] Yet there was evidence to suggest that white Americans had been *unaware* of the black mood prior to 1943. In a National Opinion Research Center poll taken in 1942, 62 per cent of the whites interviewed felt that blacks were 'pretty well satisfied with things in this country,' while 24 per cent thought that blacks were dissatisfied. By 1944, only 25 per cent thought that blacks were satisfied, and 54 per cent said the opposite, a considerable reversal in attitudes.[54] Indicative of the panic and fear felt by whites after the riots was the appearance of numerous race relations committees and organizations. By the summer of 1944 over two hundred local state and national commissions had been established to deal with racial problems; in Chicago alone there were twenty such agencies, including one set up by the mayor.[55]

Although such bodies could only be to the benefit of the communities concerned, their effectiveness was limited. In the first place, the vast number of organizations was misleading: in many instances the same people were members of more than one committee, thus duplicating membership and reducing the real number of activists.[56] Second, the committees were born out of fear of riots. In order to prevent further outbreaks they centered their attentions on building goodwill and understanding rather than attacking root causes such as poverty, poor housing and discrimination in employment. Typical was the American Council of Race Relations founded in 1944 with a six point program designed to do little more than disseminate information to other bodies, schools and the mass media; another body, the Chicago Mayor's Committee, was criticized for failing to attack discrimination and it was suggested that the commission was just 'a convenient cubbyhole' where complaints were filed and forgotten.[57] Of course the spreading of knowledge was an important and valuable function, and the very existence of the committees demonstrated that civic leaders and authorities recognized their responsibility for the maintenance of good human relations. However, public opinion polls taken throughout the war did not reveal any comparable enlightenment of the mass of people.

Although a survey of 12,622 students in 63 colleges throughout the country revealed that 73.6 per cent of them felt that in order for America to implement the 'four freedoms' in the world as a whole, she should take steps to end discrimination against blacks, other opinion polls were less encouraging. Surveys of factory workers and high school pupils taken in 1942 showed that the majority were opposed to working or living with Afro-Americans.[58] Later polls showed that there was considerable confusion in white attitudes. In 1944 the majority of interviewees thought blacks were dissatisfied with their lot but 60 per cent thought that Afro-Americans were treated fairly. Again 85 per cent felt that there was equal opportunity in education while 71 per cent suggested that blacks did not have the same chance as whites of finding employment. Expectations about the future were decidedly gloomy: most surveys showed that whites feared that more jobs for blacks would lead to fewer for whites and that this would cause conflict.[59] Perhaps because of such fears, opinion was divided on the question of fair employment laws. In a survey in 1945, 43 per cent of those interviewed favored a law which would require an employer to hire people regardless of race or color, while 44 per cent were opposed to it. The statistics for particular regions were more revealing. In the North and mid-Atlantic states 58 per cent favored such a law compared to only 30 per cent in the South where the majority opposed it.[60] There was little in this to suggest that the war had altered the climate of opinion in the South, and in fact, if anything, racial intolerance in that region seemed to increase during the 1940s.

Despite the migration of Afro-Americans during both World Wars, the South still had the largest black population and its long ingrained racial prejudice and intolerance remained. The numerous outbreaks of violence directed against blacks and the utterances of racial demagogues indicated that many Southerners were immune to propaganda about democracy and the rights of man. The campaigns for equal service in the armed forces and for an effective policy on fair employment were consistently opposed by Southerners. Any form of integration was to be opposed regardless of the war and America's role in it. In 1944 the South Carolina House of Representatives reaffirmed their 'belief' in and 'allegiance' to the system of white supremacy and pledged their lives and 'sacred honor' to maintain it; the Senator from Mississippi, James Eastland, was quoted as saying that he had no prejudice in his heart, 'but the white race is a superior race and the Negro race is an inferior race, and the races must be kept separate by law'; even more incongruous was the sign in a bus in Charleston, South Carolina which urged bus passengers to observe the Jim Crow laws on the grounds that 'co-operation in carrying them out will make the war shorter and victory sooner.'[61] This was one of the paradoxes of the war: it brought changes which threatened existing racial patterns, and outspoken reaction against such changes.

The war clearly did affect the South; its 'cataclysmic' forces had shaken and loosened many traditions.[62] The economic, social and political advances made by blacks during the war, and their militant demands for further progress, caused widespread alarm in the South. A variety of rumors were common throughout the region; domestic servants were supposedly leaving *en masse* for better paid jobs in defense factories, while those that remained in service were said to be joining 'Eleanor clubs' and demanding higher wages as well as behaving in an offensive manner. Such clubs were named after the President's wife, Eleanor Roosevelt, whom many Southerners regarded as being responsible for black militancy. Neither the researches of the white writer Howard Odum nor the investigations of the FBI resulted in the discovery of any such club; they were purely myths which represented the fears of white people. Other tales were of black men threatening white women when their husbands joined the forces. Equally widespread was the feeling that black servicemen would return to America with ideas above their station.[63]

The whole issue of black military participation highlighted the often contradictory position of many Southerners. On the one hand they feared that Afro-Americans would lay claim to white women if only white men were called to serve (revealing some of the basic sexual phobias involved in race prejudice), or that the whites would bear the brunt of war casualties. On the other hand, they were opposed to the equal and integrated armed service of blacks because it would recognize the Afro-Americans' claims to equal citizenship and destroy the principle of white supremacy. Besides, even if they believed that they were incapable of becoming good soldiers, the prospect of blacks with guns and military training remained a traditonal fear.[64] In the event, a solution was forced upon them by the manpower shortages which required the fuller utilization of all sections of the community.

It would be as foolish to write off all Southerners as bigots blind to their own logic as it would be to consider all Northerners free of prejudice. A number of liberals in the South were aware that the racial beliefs and practices were in complete contradiction with America's war aims. Several joined with blacks from the South in forming the Southern Regional Council in 1944; it sprang from a number of conferences that took place in 1942 and 1943 and its objectives were spelled out in the first meeting of blacks at Durham, North Carolina.[65] Recognizing that the war had 'sharpened the issue of Negro-white relations,' the Durham conference called for the abolition of the poll tax, the white primary and other forms of disenfranchisement. It also demanded equal, but not necessarily integrated, educational and economic opportunities for Afro-Americans; segregation was condemned, but for the time being the conference wished only to improve race relations within the existing framework.[66] Other interracial committees were formed elsewhere in the South to perform similar functions.

Also influential were the liberal newspaper editors Hodding Carter, Virginius Dabney, John Temple Graves and Thomas Sancton. Following the breakdown of segregation in public transport in and around Richmond, Virginia due to the pressure of numbers, Dabney, the editor of the Richmond *Times-Dispatch*, urged the repeal of the segregation laws 'on the ground that under the stress of war conditions these laws no longer work'. He reported that he had received hundreds of letters of support in this demand, and only a few which were unfavorable.[67] However, even sympathetic whites were alarmed by the tenor of black demands and they urged the Afro-Americans not to push events. John Temple Graves accused Northern black leaders of going crazy, 'making plain beyond question an intent to use the war for settling overnight the whole, long, complicated, infinitely delicate racial problem.' They were, he said, alienating the little support they had in the South. Dabney agreed. While he attacked white demagogues for fanning the flames of prejudice, he was also critical of the intemperance of black organizations and newspapers. He warned that 'a group of Negro agitators' and a 'small group of white rabble-rousers' were pushing the country 'closer and closer to an interracial explosion which may make the race riots of the First World War and its aftermath seem mild by comparison.'[68] In the face of violent and sudden criticism from the North, the threats of bodies such as the March on Washington Movement, and the outbreak of riots in 1943, the liberals tended to side with their more extreme brethren rather than the blacks. The same was also true in Congress where the issue of race generally united Southerners in opposition to the rest of the country.

As the political scientist V. O. Key pointed out in his mammoth study of Southern politics, the region was not as wholly united nor as reactionary as was commonly imagined. Although it was almost entirely Democratic, there were within the party's ranks differences ranging from left in Louisiana to right in Virginia. The Southern congressmen did not always vote *en bloc*, but when they did so in opposition to those from the rest of the nation, it was invariably on matters involving race or federal intervention in the states.[69] Civil rights measures were opposed on both counts.

This opposition could not be ignored nor overruled because the South was vital to the Democratic party and to the President, both in getting reform and then war measures passed in Congress and in securing victory in presidential elections. Not only did a number of Southerners serve as chairmen of important committees due to their seniority, but also, after the defeat of many Democrats in the North and mid-West in the elections of 1942, the Dixiecrats formed the backbone of the party in Congress. So strong were they in the party that at the 1944 Democratic convention Harry S. Truman, the Senator from Missouri, was nominated as Roosevelt's running mate instead of the more radical former Vice President, Henry Wallace.[70]

But if Roosevelt had to be careful not to offend the South, he also had to pay attention to the Afro-Americans. The number of black voters in urban areas, particularly in the North, was increasing and becoming of strategic importance; their support had already played an important part in the election of 1940. Caught between these conflicting camps, Roosevelt also had to direct America's war effort, and in the end he concentrated on that.

The President and his advisers were well aware that the war had affected race relations in the United States: their files contained hundreds of letters from both blacks and whites about the situation. That federal agencies felt it necessary to carry out surveys of opinion and to study the Afro-American press was an acknowledgement of how important the issue was.[71] It was even suggested in 1942 that the editors of the more flamboyant black newspapers be indicted for sedition, but that idea was rejected by Roosevelt. Instead, meetings were held between black editors and the heads of various government departments, and in 1944 the President himself met members of the Negro Newspaper Publishers Association. When asked to temper their demands, the black representatives declared that while deploring 'any and all forms of disunity that threaten the winning of victory for democracy,' it was their 'duty and obligation to fight for every right guaranteed by the Constitution' and 'to refrain from doing so would impair our democracy . . . by weakening the principles on which it is founded.'[72]

As well as the minorities at home, the federal government also had to consider the attitudes of both allies and enemies abroad. The credibility of America's war aims was vital in securing support in the Far East, Africa and Latin America. As so many commentators pointed out, America had to practice at home what she preached abroad. The Axis powers could, and did, make great play of the poor race relations in the USA. Japanese radio programs beamed to North and South America dealt with the Ku Klux Klan, the riots in Detroit and the discrimination in the armed forces.[73]

One way of counteracting such radio messages and easing racial tensions was to produce propaganda of one's own. At home, pamphlets such as *Report to the Nation* stressed the need for unity in the face of total war, but did not mention race relations specifically. More to the point was *Negroes and the War*, the seventy page illustrated record of black life written by Chandler Owen for the Office of War Information. The emphasis was on the gains made and being made rather than on the disadvantages faced by Afro-Americans. Hitler's writings on race were compared to the pronouncements made by Roosevelt, and the reader was told that no matter how bad things were they would be worse if America lost the war.[74] The government-produced films *The Negro Soldier, Negro Colleges* and *Henry Browne, Farmer* had similar messages, and like many others, some of them were intended for export. What Afro-Americans wanted, however, was not so much propaganda as action.

President Roosevelt was neither willing nor able to act on civil rights unless forced to do so. Executive Order 8802 was, as I have shown, only issued after a militant campaign by blacks which, if it had been allowed to come to fruition in the March on Washington, would have been extremely embarrassing. Once America had entered the war, the President was even less prepared to respond to black demands. By 1942 he could not find time to meet Afro-American leaders to discuss the status of blacks in the war emergency and, in reply to a request to establish a 'commission on race and color in the present world struggle,' he said 'I think we must start winning the war with all the brains, wisdom and experience we've got before we do much general or specific planning for the future.'[75] Even so, Roosevelt did appear to realize the importance of black participation and America's race relations to the war effort. In a message to the 1942 NAACP convention he suggested that they reverse their theme from 'victory is vital to minorities' to 'minorities are vital to victory.' The following year, in a statement to the annual National Urban League conference, he pointed out that the 'integrity of our nation and our war aims is at stake in our attitude toward minority groups at home.' Racial strife, he said, 'destroys national unity at home and renders us suspect abroad.'[76]

If the underlying theme of these messages was unity and a call to put aside grievances in order that the war might be won, Roosevelt was prepared to suggest that participation would bring rewards. In a radio message to the nation from the White House in October 1944, the President called for the right to vote for all citizens 'without tax or artificial restriction of any kind' and went on to say that 'We must be able to present to our returning heroes an America which is stronger and more prosperous, and more deeply devoted to the ways of democracy than ever before.'[77] He reinforced that message when writing to the Sixth Congress of the Southern Negro Youth Congress in December 1944 that the thousands of young blacks had fought 'not only to defend America but to advance America.' Their goal, he said, was 'to establish a universal freedom under which a new basis of security and prosperity can be established for all—regardless of station, race or creed.'[78]

Despite these various declarations, Roosevelt remained unresponsive to demands for civil rights legislation. Even after the outbreak of riots, which he deplored for their damaging effect on the war effort, plans for a government investigation and a committee on race relations were dropped. In place of them a Presidential aide, Jonathan Daniels, was appointed to correlate information on racial problems, and the flow of morale-boosting material was increased. Once more, attention was not to be distracted from the immediate problem of winning the war, and the prevention of future riots was left to the local community organizations which sprang up after the summer of 1943. The counsel of patience and moderation at a time when blacks were most impatient was even put forward by Eleanor Roosevelt, normally an outspoken defender of the Afro-Americans' cause. Like her husband, she felt that militant civil rights campaigns could only detract from the war effort.[79]

As well as his overriding concern with winning the war and his political pragmatism, in the Roosevelt philosophy there was an inherent feeling that special legislation for blacks was unnecessary. In all the New Deal programs not one act was aimed at helping the black community alone.

Rather, all policies were expected to apply equally to all underprivileged groups, and it was left to the administrators of particular agencies to see that there was no discrimination within their areas of jurisdiction. Where local laws and customs prevented this policy from becoming practice, little was done to correct the imbalance. To do so would have alienated the South, as would have any public support from the President for civil rights legislation against lynching or poll taxes. After the war had begun, the support of Southerners was even more vital to ensure the passage of war measures, many of which increased federal power and could be seen to threaten states' rights. Roosevelt still maintained that such domestic measures as were passed would apply equally to all Americans, without the need for special consideration. For example, when Walter White asked that a qualified Afro-American be appointed as assistant administrator in the Veterans Bureau, Roosevelt replied that such an appointment would not be necessary. Blacks, along with all veterans, were provided for in the Serviceman's Readjustment Act, the GI Bill of Rights.[80]

There was some justification for Roosevelt's approach. Afro-Americans had gained with the rest of the population from participation in the war effort and from wartime policies. Employment had risen, better wages were paid, rents and prices were controlled and even cut back, and defense training and armed service had given blacks some skills which could be used later in civilian life. However, as their spokesmen were well aware, those gains had been made under exceptional circumstances and had still been limited by discrimination. In all areas, housing, health, employment or education, the advances had not been sufficient to bring blacks up to white levels and there was still an immense gap between the races. Moreover, Afro-Americans, even more than whites, suffered from 'depression psychosis'—the fear that the war would be followed by mass unemployment and that the gains they had made would be lost and the gap between black and white would widen.[81]

Such fears were not groundless. Even without discrimination, the disproportionate concentration of Afro-Americans in industries directly related to the war meant that they would be the first to feel the effects of peace. As early as 1944 layoffs were reported in a number of plants in Missouri, Connecticut, Minnesota and Indiana in which black employees' seniority was being ignored.[82] In seven 'war centers' studied by the Fair Employment Practices Committee during the period of reconversion, all but one showed a heavier loss of jobs by blacks than by white workers, and by 1948 Afro-Americans in San Francisco had dropped back halfway to their pre-war employment status.[83] Once laid off, black workers were less likely to be re-employed or at least not at the levels they had experienced during the war.

These early developments caused considerable alarm among Afro-Americans, particularly about the fate of the returning black veterans. It was the servicemen who were most conscious of the part they had played in the war and so most likely to have high expectations for change. Even if the majority of black soldiers had performed only noncombatant duties, their experiences were still likely to encourage optimistic ideas about their future. Indeed, the soldiers in service of supply regiments had perhaps greater reason to be hopeful. Many of those in the engineering, technical and mechanical units had been taught skilled and semi-skilled trades which might otherwise have been denied them, and would expect to put such expertise to good use in civilian life. A man who had gained such qualifications would 'not be satisfied, in the light of the training which he has received and in the light of the occupational changes which have occurred among non-whites, to return to his former occupational status.' What the black soldier would want, said the National Urban League, were 'jobs, opportunities to complete their education, a chance to go into business, and the privilege of sharing completely in the future development and prosperity of the nation.'[84] This, of course, was the wish of every American, black or white, and to a large extent their wishes were met in the GI Bill, the Serviceman's Readjustment Act.

The GI Bill is possibly the major example of reward or compensation for military participation in modern society. It enabled the former soldier to claim a $20 weekly readjustment allowance, loans for home purchase or improvement, loans to buy farms or businesses, and educational grants of up to $500 for tuition plus $65 monthly subsistence allowance for the single man.[85] By the 1950s several million veterans had availed themselves of these benefits; unfortunately there is no record in the Veterans Administration of the number of Afro-Americans who profited in this way. However, it is clear from information on the plans of black soldiers that many intended to make use of the GI Bill to improve their lot in life.

Among black enlisted men 43·5 per cent hoped to return to school, college or university for part or full time study. Another indication of their expectations was the fact that only a fifth intended to return to their old jobs and employers, and only a third planned even to return to the same type of work.[86] The Afro-American veterans not only hoped to find new and better jobs, but were also prepared to move in order to do so. Only 65·7 per cent, compared to 82 per cent of white soldiers, said that they would return to their former homes. Most of those planning to move were going to leave the South and following the patterns of wartime migration head for the North and the far West. Indeed, by 1947 some 75,000 black veterans were reported to have left the South.[87] Many were going to join families and relatives already in the new regions, but a great proportion of the departures were undoubtedly due to the repressive and limiting atmosphere of the South which prevented the use of newly acquired skills and training. Sadly, the black veteran was to find that similar problems faced him no matter where he went.

The various provisions of the GI Bill were dependent on factors largely

outside federal control. To receive an educational grant a soldier had to
be accepted by one of the colleges approved by individual states. For blacks
this raised immediate obstacles: the 112 black colleges were already
overcrowded and segregation in the South, prejudice elsewhere, limited
the alternatives available. By 1947 some 20,000 black veterans had
managed to enter college but another 15,000 had been unable to secure
places. Of those accepted, 70 per cent went to black institutions.[88] In order
to obtain loans whether for homes, farms or businesses, the ex-soldier had
to satisfy the lending agency, governmental or private, of his suitability and
the likelihood of the project being a safe investment. In the area of
housing, restrictive practices and the prejudice of builders and agents
meant that there were too few new homes and too little of the existing
supply available to Afro-Americans. Houses in the old, deteriorating
neighborhoods were unlikely to qualify for grants.[89] Low incomes
presented yet another problem in securing loans and purchasing houses.

No matter what the provisions of the GI Bill or the expectations of the
soldiers, blacks were faced with the same patterns of prejudice as had
prevailed before the war. The number of Afro-Americans employed by
either the Veterans Administration or the US Employment Service was very
small, particularly in the offices in the South. Information was therefore
often denied to black veterans, or the jobs offered were menial and
unskilled. In one survey of 50 cities, the movement of blacks into peacetime
employment was found to be lagging far behind that of white veterans: in
Arkansas 95 per cent of the placements made by the USES for Afro-
Americans were in service or unskilled jobs.[90] There was even
discrimination in the redistribution centers provided for returning
servicemen. In reply to complaints about the inadequate and segregated
facilities for black soldiers, Secretary of War Stimson said that they were
'essentially' equivalent to the centers for whites. Afro-Americans, he said,
were more able to rest, relax and readjust in the 'congenial' atmosphere of
black areas and all-black centers.[91] Given such widespread discrimination
it is not at all remarkable that blacks accounted for 25 per cent of re-
enlistments in the first year after the war. For some at least, Army life was
better than civilian life.[92]

Re-entry into armed service offered not only greater economic security
but also more personal safety, for with the end of the war there was an
increase in the violence directed at Afro-Americans and at black veterans in
particular. In 1946 it appeared that the 'red summer' of 1919 was to be
repeated. In February rioting whites in Columbia, Tennessee killed two
blacks and wounded ten others. The following August more than fifty
Afro-Americans were injured in a riot in Athens, Alabama, and there were
smaller disturbances in Philadelphia and Chicago.[93] Even more horrifying
were the bloody murders of two black men, one of them a veteran, and
their wives in Walton County, Georgia in July 1946. Shortly afterwards in

Taylor County, Georgia another veteran, Maceo Snipes, was shot to death for voting in the local elections.[94] Snipes was just one of a number of blacks who tried to exercise their political rights. In Atlanta, several hundred veterans met to work for their share of democracy and in Birmingham, Alabama, 100 black veterans marched on the courthouse to register their votes: the majority were rejected on the grounds that they could not understand or interpret the constitution.[95]

Whether trying to exercise their rights or not, throughout the South returning black servicemen were involved in incidents on buses and trains, and many of them suffered injuries at the hands of police and transport officials. One of the worst, and also the most publicized, examples of this sort of brutality occurred when Isaac Woodard was beaten in a town in South Carolina. Woodard, on his way home after three years in the Army, was arrested for being drunk and disorderly at the request of a white bus driver. The black soldier, who did not drink, protested and as a consequence was hit about the face. His eyes were damaged to the extent that he was permanently blinded. This and other incidents caused widespread revulsion, and in response a National Emergency Committee Against Mob Violence was formed in August 1946. One of its first acts was to arrange a meeting with the President in order to put its case.[96]

By 1946 the man in the White House was Harry S. Truman, the Vice President who had succeeded to office following Roosevelt's death on April 12, 1945. Despite the fact that most of the traditionally Republican black papers had opposed his re-election in 1944, Roosevelt's death was mourned in the Afro-American newspapers. They were very doubtful whether Truman would continue with the general humanitarian approach of his predecessor: he was from a Southern state (though not one in the deep South) and had been chosen as Vice President in order to appease the Dixiecrats. Truman's record on civil rights as a senator was not outstanding one way or another. Rather, his position had been that of a liberal Southerner, a defender of equality of opportunity *and* of segregation.[97] Yet as President he was to take actions on the Afro-Americans' behalf which far surpassed those of Roosevelt, and which, moreover, threatened to jeopardize Southern support of the Democratic Party.

In his first year as President, Truman gave strong verbal support for a permanent Fair Employment Practices Committee, appointed a black lawyer to the US Customs Court, and nominated William H. Hastie for the governorship of the Virgin Islands. In July 1946 he instructed the Justice Department to investigate the murders in Georgia, and in September he met the members of the Committee Against Mob Violence. According to Walter White, the chief spokesman at that meeting, Truman was shocked by the details of the violence. As a result, he promised to institute a committee by executive order to investigate violations of civil rights and make recommendations.[98] Such a body was formed in December 1946.

The reasons for the delay between the meeting in September and the announcement in December are not clear. It may be that the President withheld his statement until after the November elections for fear of losing the votes of Democrats. If so, the decision had little effect: the Republicans scored widespread victories. The President's advisers reacted to the electoral defeats by urging on him a liberal program, including civil rights, and Truman agreed. On December 5, 1946 by Executive Order 9808 he set up a committee to study, report and recommend 'effective means and procedures for the protection of the civil rights of the people of the United States.'[99] In speeches to Congress in January and February 1947 Truman again referred to the need for civil rights action and called for FEPC legislation. Later that year he addressed the NAACP meeting before the Lincoln Memorial—the first President ever to speak publicly to an NAACP conference. In his message, which was broadcast nationally on the major radio networks, Truman said that the country's 'immediate task is to remove the last remnants of the barriers which stand between millions of our citizens and their birthrights.' However, he felt that 'we cannot any longer await the growth of action in the slowest state or the most backward community. Our national government must show the way.'[100] America's vulnerability on the racial issue became more apparent when delegates from the USSR tabled a petition, presented to the United Nations by the NAACP, at the UN Commission on Human Rights. Although the motion was denied, the attempt brought publicity the United States could ill afford.[101] Further pressure was exerted on the President with the publication in October 1947 of the report of the Committee on Civil Rights.

In a comprehensive document covering every aspect of black life, the committee spelled out four essential rights due to all Americans: the right to safety and security of the person; the right to citizenship and its privileges, including armed service and voting; the right to freedom of conscience and expression; and the right to equality of opportunity. The black claims concerning the importance of military participation were accepted and reiterated. 'Any attempt to curb the right to fight in its defense', said the committee, 'can only lead the citizen to question the worth of the society in which he lives.' Further, the report said that underlying 'the theory of compulsory wartime military service in a democratic state is the principle that every citizen, regardless of his station in life, must assist in the defense of the nation when its security is threatened.'[102] In order that this be achieved, the committee recommended an end to all discrimination and segregation in the armed forces. The general separation of the races was also attacked. Segregation was described as 'the cornerstone of the elaborate structure of discrimination' and separate facilities were said to be 'far from equal.' The committee called for the elimination of discrimination and segregation from American life by means of fair employment and fair education laws, the ending of segregation in public and private health facilities, the outlawing of restrictive covenants, anti-lynching laws, and guarantees of Afro-American voting rights. As well as legislation, the committee wanted the civil rights section of the Justice Department reorganized and strengthened, the formation of a civil rights unit in the FBI and permanent federal and state commissions on civil rights.[103] On February 2, 1948 President Truman included many of these recommendations in his Civil Rights Message to Congress. He emphasized that 'the world position of the United States in the world today makes it especially urgent that we adopt these measures to secure for all our people their essential rights.'[104]

It has been suggested that Truman's stand on civil rights and this speech in particular were merely a political maneuver to win black votes away from the Progressives and Republicans prior to the 1948 presidential elections. It is clear that political considerations were involved in the decision to push civil rights, but as McCoy and Ruetten point out, in picking that issue the President 'was walking a tightrope.'[105] If this were the only reason, then Truman had taken a brave gamble, for the Southern Democrats, predictably, reacted violently, some even threatening to bolt the party. At the Democratic convention in July 1948 the administration supported a general civil rights plank on the lines of that of 1944 in order to mollify the South. In a floor vote this was overthrown in favor of a more liberal and specific plank. Several Southern delegations then walked out of the convention and shortly after the States Rights Party with Strom Thurmond of South Carolina as its presidential candidate was formed.[106] Yet in face of this open opposition Truman issued two more executive orders later in July 1948; one to set up a Fair Employment Board within the Civil Service Commission, the other to bring equality of treatment and opportunity in the armed forces.

Executive Order 9981 which ordered the beginning of integration and established a Committee on Equality of Treatment and Opportunity in the Armed Services (the Fahy committee) to see this policy implemented, came as a result of several pressures. Segregation in the military had been singled out by the Civil Rights Committee when it said that 'prejudice in any area is an ugly, undemocratic phenomenon; in the armed services, where all men run the risk of death, it is particularly repugnant.'[107] At the same time, as we have seen, the military were themselves moving toward integration in the post-war years and were attempting to formulate methods to best achieve this. Another reason for change was the threat of a militant civil disobedience campaign from A. Philip Randolph and a black former Army chaplain, Grant Reynolds. Their appeals to blacks to refuse to serve in segregated forces had some support: an NAACP poll among black students found that 71 per cent supported the campaign, and in an angry meeting with Truman, Randolph told the President that he had met blacks throughout the country 'not wanting to shoulder a gun to fight for democracy abroad unless democracy was obtained at home.'[108] Other black leaders, including Lester Granger, warned that they would no longer advise the government on troop policies so long as segregation continued.[109]

The Executive Order, the third dealing with race relations in eight years, marked a major departure in federal policy and had a considerable effect on black attitudes. Although Truman attempted to play down the civil rights issue during his whistlestop campaign, he did visit black areas, and he became the first President to speak in Harlem. As a result of his speeches and actions, Afro-Americans contributed to his remarkable upset victory over the Republican candidate, Thomas Dewey. An estimated 69 per cent of all black voters in 27 major cities across the country backed Truman, while in the South the Dixiecrats carried only four states and 22 per cent of the entire Southern vote.[110] However, Southern Democrats in coalition with conservative Republicans did block the legislation on lynching, poll taxes, the FEPC and civil rights which Truman submitted to Congress early in 1949. After 1950 the position of the South was further strengthened as its congressmen held a majority of the Democratic seats in the House and only lacked one seat to have a majority in the Senate. Coupled with this was the increasing fear of communism, the McCarran Internal Security Bill, and the rise of Joseph McCarthy, of all which created 'an atmosphere when anyone who believed in equal rights for Negroes must ipso facto be a "Communist".'[111] It was not until after 1957 that any of the Truman proposals became legislation, and then only in a general and rather unsatisfactory Civil Rights Bill.

This is not to detract from Truman's achievements. He was the first President to discuss publicly the issue of race relations and demand civil rights legislation. His Executive Orders, the report of the Committee on Civil Rights and desegregation of the forces marked a shift from federal support of segregation to a policy of integration: instead of following public opinion, the government attempted to lead it. If the administration had little success in the legislative area, it was more fortunate with the judiciary and particularly in the Supreme Court. During the New Deal and World War II there was a marked change in the membership and opinion within the Supreme Court and as a result several important decisions were made. In cases during and after the war, the Court ruled against segregation in interstate transport and against segregated higher educational institutions. Segregated schools were also attacked by the President's Commission on Higher Education in its report of 1948.[112]

Encouraged by Truman, Attorney General Tom Clark prepared *amicus curiae* briefs against restrictive housing covenants, and in 1948 the Supreme Court ruled that such covenants were not enforceable in law. The Federal Housing Authority thereafter refused to insure mortgages on property with restrictive covenants in the deeds.[113] Also of some benefit to Afro-

Americans in the field of housing was the 1949 Housing Act, which aimed to provide 'a decent home and a suitable living environment for every American family.' By furnishing federal funds to local authorities, the act launched a direct attack on poor housing. However, it was still up to individual cities and towns to embark on programs of slum clearance; the government provided financial aid, but not the initiative. Of the 205,706 dwelling units built under the act's provisions, 55,826 or 27·1 per cent were for black families.[114]

Afro-Americans were also affected by the amendments to the Fair Labor Standards Act which raised the minimum wages in 1949 and again in 1950. Although they were still concentrated in the lowest paid jobs and suffered a higher rate of unemployment than whites, blacks were still better off economically than they had been before the war because of the generally higher levels of employment. The early post-war layoffs did not continue and nowhere did Afro-Americans drop back to the level of the 1930s.[115] With continued prosperity, there were also signs that the Afro-American was gaining recognition as an equal citizen under law. In a series of Supreme Court cases the white primary, which had excluded blacks or their primary votes from the local Democratic Party conventions in the South, was declared unconstitutional. Partly as a result of this, and partly because of their increased political and social consciousness, the numbers of registered black voters in the South increased throughout the 1940s. Afro-Americans still were subjected to harassment at the polling stations by the Ku Klux Klan, but less so after that organization had joined the Communist Party on the Attorney General's list of subversive movements.[116]

It is clear from this that not all the black expectations had been met during or after the war: indeed, it would have been remarkable if they had been. It would take considerably more than America's involvement in the war, and a longer period, to change the attitudes and mores of the majority of whites. However, there were real signs of progress. In the executive and judicial branches of the federal government there was a change from grudging acquiescence to black demands to open support for them. Liberal white opinion was also outspoken in the black man's defense. Change was due to the new role in international affairs which the war had forced on the United States and to the constant campaign of blacks themselves. Neither world opinion nor black voters could be ignored: action had to be taken on civil rights. While progress continued, black expectations remained high. When those hopes were crushed with the widening of the economic gap between the races and the outbreak of open opposition to social and political reform in the 1950s and 1960s, the second 'revolution' in American race relations began. As Lerone Bennett, Jr pointed out, the seeds of that revolt had been sown during World War II.[117]

7

The Postwar Years: World War II in Perspective

The importance of the war to Afro-Americans can only be judged in the context of both earlier *and* later developments. While the war years stand out in sharp contrast to the Depression, the changes which took place over the period would be less significant if there had been a reversion to the pre-war state in 1945, or if the war had brought few long term consequences in race relations. This is, however, where World War II differs in impact from World War I. Black participation in the military and industrial effort of the 1940s was much greater, and consequently brought more economic, social and political gains which they were determined to hold on to and increase. At the same time they were helped to do so by the post-war situation: as Malcolm X once said, 'Stalin kept up the pressure' which had been applied during the war.[1] America's new-found dominance in world affairs, role in the Cold War and later involvement in Korea, coupled with developments in the domestic economy, all made it possible for blacks to maintain the advances made during World War II. But when those pressures were removed, progress, particularly in the economic sphere, halted and the promise of the Truman years was unfulfilled. Black expectations were frustrated and the militancy of the 1940s returned. If there was a 'Negro revolt' in the late 1950s and early 1960s, it was precisely because America failed to continue during peacetime the racial progress made in war.

While the actual achievements of the Truman administration were slim, they were still sufficient to encourage, and to a certain extent satisfy, black Americans. The President's uncompromising stand on civil rights, the beginning of real desegregation in the armed forces, the Supreme Court decisions, and above all a fairly high rate of employment, convinced Afro-Americans that the progress would continue. American involvement in the Korean war from 1950 to 1953 further bolstered black hopes: 'once again

. . . armed conflict and national danger brought the Negro advancement toward his goal of full citizenship.'[2]

However, because of the limited nature of the conflict, the racial issue did not reach the prominence it had in the earlier war. Truman refused to establish another Fair Employment Practices Committee but instead ordered the inclusion of nondiscrimination clauses in defense contracts. Although the order was neither very strong nor by itself very effective, unemployment among blacks, which had been rising before 1950, dropped by half. Income levels rose too, and by 1952 the median non-white family income had risen to $2338 compared to $1614 five years earlier. Black membership in labor unions also grew, increasing from 1·5 million in 1949 to 2·4 million in 1953. As in the 1940s, war and 'unguided' change succeeded where government action failed.[3]

Progress also continued to be made in areas other than employment: the number of black voters registered in the South rose from 750,000 in 1948 to 1·3 million in 1952; more blacks bought their homes and went to colleges; in Washington, D.C. the attack on racial segregation began to show some results with the beginning of a breakdown in residential separation and segregation of recreational areas.[4] On the national level the Supreme Court continued to undermine the legal basis of segregation, and equally important, public opinion surveys showed that white opposition to integration in housing, transportation and education continued to decrease through the 1940s and into the 1950s. In 1942 fewer than a third of respondents in one survey favored school integration; by 1956 almost half favored it. Even in the South, the number of people who felt segregation would remain the normal practice was declining. There were indications that some Southerners were reacting to, and resisting, such progress—that the 'white backlash' hinted at in the 1940s was becoming more visible. One sign of this was the increased display of Confederate flags and the outbreak of racial violence in the early 1950s.[5] However, despite this reaction, the progress or promise of progress in civil rights was such that black leaders urged Truman to run for re-election in 1952. Though Truman refused to stand for a second term (he was the last President to be able to do so), because he thought no-one should be President for more than eight years and because he feared his candidacy would split the Democratic Party on civil rights questions, he did nonetheless play an active part in the campaign and prevented any compromise on civil rights. Black allegiance to the Democrats remained strong and Afro-Americans, unlike the majority of their white countrymen, voted overwhelmingly for Adlai Stevenson and his running mate John Sparkman from Alabama rather than Dwight D. Eisenhower.[6]

Eisenhower's election in 1952 marked the end of one era in civil rights and the beginning of another. The strong executive leadership on race issues was gone. In line with his general outlook, Eisenhower preferred not to lead or intervene in racial matters; where he was forced to act, he responded with a hesitancy and ambivalence which often served to encourage the forces he wished to counteract. It was unfortunate for America, and for Afro-Americans, that this should coincide with a period of reaction and crisis.

In 1954 the Supreme Court followed up its earlier decisions and concluded a series of cases presented by the NAACP when it ruled, in *Brown v. Topeka Board of Education*, that segregation in public schools was unconstitutional. The next year the Court ordered that their integration be carried out 'with all deliberate speed'. These decisions marked a landmark in the history of US race relations and together destroyed the legal foundation of segregation. The response of the white South was immediate and overwhelming. The Ku Klux Klan re-emerged and White Citizens Councils were formed; the Supreme Court was denounced by 100 Southern senators and representatives who urged massive resistance; and mobs in towns in Texas, Tennessee, Kentucky and Alabama gathered to prevent the entry of black children into formerly all-white schools. In 1957 the governor of Arkansas, Orval Faubus, used the local National Guard to keep nine black students out of Little Rock Central High School. Faced with this challenge to the federal laws and courts, Eisenhower, as Commander-in-Chief, took control of the National Guard and sent federal troops to escort the black children into the school. His action ended such open defiance of the Supreme Court, but his own caution on the entire issue served to stiffen Southern resistance. Eisenhower made no public commitment to the idea of desegregation, and throughout his term in office refused to comment on the morality of the issue. Fourteen years after the initial court order, not a single school in South Carolina, Georgia, Alabama, Mississippi or Louisiana had been integrated.[7]

While some white Americans prepared to resist any attack on the racial status quo, blacks prepared to launch a direct assault. In Montgomery, Alabama in 1955 Afro-Americans began a boycott of the segregated bus services which lasted almost a year and brought national prominence to the Reverend Martin Luther King. In the following years there were similar campaigns by blacks in other cities in the South, and sit-in demonstrations against segregation in restaurants and lunch counters throughout the entire country. Sympathetic whites joined in these campaigns (and shared the very real risks) and the early 1960s witnessed a number of drives against segregation led by interracial organizations like CORE, the newly-formed Student Nonviolent Coordinating Committee (SNCC), and King's Southern Christian Leadership Conference (SCLC). The 'freedom rides' through the South and protests against *de facto* segregation in the North culminated in 1963 with a massive March on Washington for Jobs and Freedom attended by over 250,000 people of both races. Appropriately enough, one of the spokesmen at that gathering was A. Philip Randolph, the leader of the March on Washington Movement of the 1940s. By 1960 the militant but non-violent Gandhian methods advocated by Randolph and the members of CORE twenty years earlier had become widely accepted by both black and white activists. There had indeed been a revolution in civil rights.[8]

The reasons for this dramatic change are complex, but their roots lay in 'the deepening mood of despair and disillusion that gripped the American Negro after World War II.'[9] Blacks were divided between the older generation of optimists who emphasized the progress made since the war, and the younger group of pessimists who replied that the progress was too slow. The latter, with some justification, pointed out that the advances of the earlier years were more apparent than real and were anyway being gradually eroded. Whites too were now more aware of the moral issues involved in racism as a result of both World War II and the Cold War, and the violence which met civil rights demands increased white liberal support for the black cause. However, the Civil Rights Acts of 1957 and 1960 were too little, too late. They dealt almost entirely with the voting rights of blacks in the South and did little to mollify the young Afro-Americans, who pointed to the continued widespread segregation in both North and South of housing, schools and recreational facilities.

The slow rate of progress in America was made even more galling by the rapid developments in Africa where 36 colonies gained their independence between 1957 and 1965. James Baldwin was quoted as saying 'At the rate things are going, all of Africa will be free before we can get a lousy cup of coffee.'[10] Such fears were borne out by the violent reaction of whites in the South to integration and to the peaceful demonstrations. To counter such violence, some black veterans of World War II and Korea formed a para-military organization, the Deacons for Defense, and Robert F. Williams, another veteran of the war, was dismissed from the NAACP in North Carolina in 1959 for advocating armed self-defense. In both cases, the blacks acknowledged that their military experiences had had an important effect on their attitudes.[11]

As well as being alarmed by and responding to the setbacks faced in the South, the more militant Afro-Americans drew attention to conditions in the North. The migrations which had accelerated during the 1940s had continued at a high rate in the post-war years. In 1950 the proportion of the black population still in the South was 68 per cent; by 1964 it had dropped to 54·4 per cent, and 73·2 per cent of the total black population lived in urban areas.[12] This movement and urbanization led to increased separation of the races as the newcomers joined and expanded the existing ghettos in cities in the North and far West. In 212 metropolitan areas in 1960, 78 per cent of blacks lived in the blighted city centers while 52 per cent of the whites lived in the suburbs. Where there was urban renewal and slum clearance, it actually led to a reduction in the number of homes available to Afro-Americans and to greater overcrowding. Rebuilding programs were never able to keep up with the clearances and blacks had limited access to housing in areas outside the ghettos.[13] While poor housing affected schooling and employment opportunities, the concentration of blacks in low paid jobs or among the unemployed made it impossible for most of them to consider house purchase and limited their choice to low rent homes of inferior quality.

The deteriorating economic situation of Afro-Americans was, in fact, one of the chief causes of anger and pessimism among young blacks. Afro-Americans were hit particularly hard in the recessions of 1953–5 and 1957–60: their unemployment rate rose from 4·5 per cent in 1953 to 9·9 per cent in 1954; in 1958 it reached 12·6 per cent and thereafter was consistently over 10 per cent and always more than double the rate of unemployment among whites.[14] The gap between the races in income and occupational status began to widen once more and the earlier gains began to disappear. In 1947, 17·7 per cent of all the families with incomes below $3000 were black, but by 1960 this category had risen to 20·8 per cent. As one commentator said, although 'the majority of the poverty-stricken are not Negro, the majority of Negroes are poverty-stricken.'[15]

Given this situation, many Afro-Americans gave up integrationist aspirations in despair and joined separatist-nationalist movements such as the Nation of Islam—the Black Muslims. This organization, in existence since the 1930s, attracted public attention in the years after the Korean War because of its dramatic growth and its public castigation of white society. Other young Afro-Americans, however, responded in an entirely different fashion and sought to enter the one occupation in which there seemed to be equality—the armed forces. The process of desegregation ordered by Truman in 1948 had advanced slowly, notably in the Army. The Korean War speeded up the changes and led to the abandonment of the 10 per cent racial quota and to integration of fighting units. In 1951 integration of all branches of the Army in the Far East was ordered and by 1952 this had been extended to Army units in America and Europe. In the other services integration also continued—so much so that the armed services were often ahead of the rest of society in racial matters. As a result Afro-Americans were faced with the ironic situation that armed service, even with the risk of death, offered 'a chance to learn a trade, to make it in a small way, to get away from a dead-end existence, and to join the only institution in this society that seems really to be racially integrated.'[16]

Even more ironic was the change in black attitudes towards armed service. Whereas the majority had insisted on participating in World War II in the hope that this would improve opportunities in civilian society, twenty years later, black opposition to armed service in Vietnam was considerable. In part, this was due to the widespread questioning by all Americans of their role in Southeast Asia, but it also reflected the increased disillusion among blacks about white society. The Black Muslims were joined in their opposition to black military service by the militant Black Panther Party, an organization which achieved prominence through its open display of weapons and vaguely revolutionary philosophy. Point four of the Panther's ten point program was that all black men should be exempt from military service. Even more moderate spokesmen questioned the black man's role in the forces in Vietnam, and many blacks agreed with Floyd McKissick of CORE, Stokely Carmichael of SNCC, and Martin Luther King when they publicly pointed out that it was contradictory to fight for freedom in Asia while it was denied at home.[17]

An additional cause for concern was the high casualty rate among black servicemen in Vietnam. While blacks comprised 9·8 per cent of military personnel, they made up 20 per cent of the combat forces and accounted for 14·1 per cent of those killed in action.[18] Despite this, the number of blacks in the forces continued to be high, no doubt because of the lack of opportunity and security in civilian life. However, as the Black Power movement spread at home, and as black spokesmen became increasingly critical of the Vietnam War, discontent among black servicemen grew. An additional reason was the continuation of discrimination in the forces. In the Army, where blacks comprised 13·4 per cent of enlisted men, only 3·5 per cent of the officers were black. In the late 1960s there were several outbreaks of racial violence in both the Army and Navy, and one survey found that not only did the majority of Afro-American GIs feel they had no business in Southeast Asia, but also that most of them were prepared to use violence to secure their rights at home.[19] The fears held by some whites throughout American history had been realized: to train, arm, and commit Afro-Americans to combat without recognizing such service with equal citizenship had increased the possibility of armed insurrection at home.

In conclusion, we have to ask how World War II relates to the later period and what effect, if any, the war had on the Afro-American's status. The sociologist Robin Williams pointed out that poverty and unemployment are not enough by themselves to provoke social protest and militant action, and went on to say that 'organized and sustained protest is most likely not when the economic position of a population is continuously low and oppressive but rather when conditions have been improving, especially if advancement is abruptly blocked or reversed.'[20] This was true of the revolutions in France and Russia; it was also true of the 'Negro revolt'. World War II and its aftermath had provided that crucial period of progress before reaction.

Participation in the war effort, while it did not close the gap between the races, did bring Afro-Americans increased employment and economic security which lasted into the 1950s, and fostered a growth in political and social consciousness. The campaigns for greater involvement in the military and industrial effort, the migrations and resultant urbanization of the black population, and the issues of the war all pushed the American racial question to the fore 'in a disturbing and challenging manner unequalled since the days of Reconstruction.'[21] The expressions in black literature and song, the increased circulation of black newspapers, the growth in civil rights organizations, and the formation of the March on Washington Movement indicated that Afro-Americans were aware of this new situation and were prepared to take advantage of it. By threatening mass demonstrations during the war and the use of their often decisive voting power after it, they were able to secure executive actions on their behalf which marked a definite change in federal policy. There were also signs that the war, and America's position in post-war international affairs, had forced many whites to re-examine their attitudes to race. It was surely no coincidence that the first President since Lincoln to take a stand openly sympathetic to Afro-Americans, and at the risk of dividing his own party, should do so in the immediate aftermath of the war. This was both a reward for military participation and a response to new political circumstance.

However, not all the effects of the war were to the Afro-American's benefit. Urbanization intensified inadequacies of housing, health and education. Nor were changes sufficient to break down all racial barriers or to overcome white prejudice: there were signs even then that some whites were prepared to fight to delay change. Such opposition grew during the Truman era and prevented any legislation being passed until the 1950s. Coupled with the post-war economic recessions which practically destroyed the gains of a quarter of a century, this intransigence on the part of whites was sufficient to frustrate and anger Afro-Americans and their white sympathizers. They, however, had learned from the experiences of World War II. The tactics espoused by the March on Washington Movement and put into practice by the Congress of Racial Equality during the 1940s, became commonplace during the 1960s. When even those methods failed to produce the desired results, or produce them quickly enough, there was an explosion of the greatest black militancy yet experienced. Seen in this context, the importance of World War II is hard to deny.

Epilogue: The African American and the Second World War Fifty Years Later

Many recent historians see World War II as the point at which modern America emerged in a form still recognizable today. While some writers have seen the war as transforming all of American society, others see the war as having particularly special importance in black history.[1] According to A. Russell Buchanan, 'Black Americans especially felt the impact of World War II.' Others have claimed that the war 'brought massive changes,' and 'altered the political, economic, and social status of Negro Americans', or that it marked 'the watershed of Afro-American history', and was 'a turning point in the Negro's relation to America,' serving 'as the catalyst in the struggle for equal rights.' No longer could it be said, as Richard Dalfiume had done in a subsequently much-quoted phrase, that the war years were 'The "Forgotten Years" of the Negro Revolution.'[2]

If anything, those who 'discovered' the forgotten years may have over-stated their significance, and some views may now need modification and qualification. War often creates an appearance and expectation of change which only masks underlying continuities. World War II was certainly no exception. Everyone at the time was aware of the general effects of the conflict and what the black sociologist Charles S. Johnson described as the 'social upheaval of war,' but he and many others suggested that the war would particularly affect the place of African Americans. The Swedish sociologist Gunnar Myrdal, whose now classic study *An American Dilemma* was published in 1944, predicted that 'there is bound to be a redefinition of the Negro's status in America as a result of this war.' Even earlier novelist Pauli Murray could write to President Roosevelt 'It is my conviction that the problem of race, intensified by economic conflict and war nerves, will eventually occupy a dominant position as a national domestic problem.'³ Such statements were a reflection more of hopes than of reality. The fact that it took almost another twenty years for race relations to assume the 'dominant position as a national domestic problem' only points to the need to place the war years in perspective. Not even the Second World War was an independent cause of social change—its influence was shaped both by existing forces and by the circumstances which followed it.

Rarely, if ever, does war produce change not already begun in some way—the preconditions for change are usually already evident. Thus, black participants in World War II brought memories of earlier experiences with them and used them to shape their responses to the new conflict. The First World War was a constant source of reference and comparison as African Americans recalled their high hopes and expectations—and the sense of disillusionment which had followed. Just a few days after Pearl Harbor the *Chicago Defender* could state, 'In pledging our allegiance to the flag . . . we are not unmindful of the broken promises of the past.' As late as 1944 singer Josh White could still recall that 'My father died, died fighting across the sea, Mama said his dying never helped her or me,' reflecting both on past experience and a growing disillusionment about the effects of World War II.⁴ Nonetheless, the mood of the black leadership was far different from the apparent moderation of DuBois's famous 'Close Ranks' editorial in 1917. From the beginning of the conflict in 1939 there was an attempt to secure the inclusion of African Americans in the defense effort, and A. Philip Randolph's threatened march on Washington seemingly produced a significant breakthrough in 1941.

The MOWM has often been seen as representative of new militance and as the forerunner of the nonviolent protests of the 1950s and 1960s. However, August Meier and Elliott Rudwick have argued that the movement was as much the culmination of past developments as the start of new ones.⁵ Blacks had protested against race violence by marching in New York following the riot in East St. Louis in 1917, and the 1930s had witnessed a considerable rise in black protest in the form of picketing and the widespread 'Don't Buy where You Can't Work' campaigns, antilynching protests, and court actions against segregation. Randolph himself built upon a base established as a leading black trade unionist and the organizer during the 1920s of the Brotherhood of Sleeping Car Porters. In addition, of course, black organizations such as the NAACP had grown in the 1930s and more important had gained access to the White House through the 'black cabinet,' sympathetic New Dealers, and the good offices of Eleanor Roosevelt. A number of studies have drawn attention to the significance of the New Deal for African Americans, and it may well be that the 1930s and 1940s ought properly be seen together.⁶

It is tempting to see the MOWM and Executive Order 8802 as a high point in civil rights because both the threat of direct protest and the promise of presidential action diminished thereafter. Although the MOWM continued in existence, groups like the NAACP and National Urban League withdrew their support, and Randolph's call for a civil disobedience campaign in 1943 was generally dismissed by other black spokesmen. Lee Finkle has written critically of this apparent conservatism among black leadership and suggested that the black media lagged behind the masses.[7] Low attendance at MOWM rallies after 1941 suggests, however, that popular support had waned; membership in the NAACP, on the other hand, increased during the war years from 54,000 in 1939 to more than half a million in 1945. Given the duration of the war and the military difficulties experienced overseas in 1942 and 1943, it is perhaps not surprising that the tone of the black press moderated. The increasingly unresponsive attitude of the government, which urged concentration on the war effort as a priority over domestic social concerns, was also significant.

Roosevelt has been much criticized for his apparent unwillingness to listen to black demands after 1941, but in fact he may have acted as a moderating influence. Patrick Washburn has argued that both Roosevelt and Attorney General Francis Biddle were called upon to indict black pressmen for sedition in 1942 but resisted. Moreover when the black press stood its ground Biddle, mindful of the excessive use of sedition legislation in World War I, refused to bring the indictments some whites wanted. Indeed, the attorney general reflected the mood of liberals when he expressed concern about the 'poor treatment of black servicemen, and the contradiction between our profession of faith in democracy and our acts.' Biddle was still much more in favor of positive government action than Roosevelt even after the outbreak of racial violence in 1943.[8]

1943 has been identified as the point at which a shift in black protest occurred. That it did so was hardly surprising. Midway through the war, victory was far from assured, and the strains of the conflict took their toll, even in America. Most significant in terms of race relations was the outbreak of racial violence that year. Throughout the early years of the war race tensions had mounted as blacks demanded more change and some whites demanded less. Tensions exacerbated by overcrowding in defense areas, competition for jobs, conflict over housing, and the stresses of wartime exploded in the riots in Detroit, Harlem, and other places (described in chapter 4).

Following those events it was hardly surprising that the black press moderated its language and called for unity. To suggest, however, as Harvard Sitkoff has, that the 'old-line Negro leadership retreated . . . to entrust white liberals with the job of winning the Negro his rights' may be too severe.[9] Although the black civilian aide to the secretary of war, Truman Gibson, could say in December 1943 that 'relations with the Negro press have never been better than they are at present,' and report that black servicemen were told 'to be good soldiers in spite of the many things they hear about and see,' racial incidents in the military, and letters of complaint from black soldiers were still published in the African-American news-papers. In 1944 there was a widespread call in the black press for the resignation of Secretary of War Stimson—described by the *Pittsburgh Courier* as 'a stubborn man who is determined to continue discrimination and segregation in the army war or no war.'[10]

Another moderating influence on the tone of black protest was the fact that by the end of 1943, despite the continuation of discrimination and the outbreak of race violence, African Americans could feel that some progress was being made as a consequence of both government policy and the exigencies of war. As a black man later recalled, 'For me the war period was a very compelling, very exhilarating era. There was a feeling that you had hold of something that was big and urgent and was not going to last forever. There were opportunities for change which could not exist after the war was over.'[11]

The most obvious area of progress was in employment where, according to one writer, the war brought 'the greatest improvements . . . than at any time before with the exception of the abolition of chattel slavery.'[12] While one might not wish to go quite that far—the First World War, after all, had seen a significant shift in black employment—there can be little doubt that the war did bring considerable economic progress. As a black woman remembered, 'the war and defense work gave black people oportunities to work on jobs they never had before. It gave them opportunity to do things they had never experienced before . . . ,' and she remarked significantly, 'Their expectations changed. Money will do that.'[13] Not much has been written about these economic advances (which are dealt with in chapter 3), but they were generally maintained into the 1950s and were of consider-able significance in shaping the wartime and postwar mood of African Americans.

The same positive comments could not be made about the employment of black women, a group about whom I had little to say in 1973. This was a major omission, for 'Rosie the Riveter' was just as likely to be black as white. Of the one million additional black workers who joined the labor force during the war, 600,000 were female, and much has now been written about this group of workers. Qualitative changes were, however, marginal. The increase in the number of black women workers in manufacturing was half that of black males, and most of the gains came late in the war and in particular occupational areas. Most of the new jobs were in heavily male areas of work, notably the foundries and shipyards; advances for African Americans in traditional categories of *female* employment were negligi-ble.[14]

The greatest area of employment for black women was still the service sector, but there was a shift from private domestic service to public service. The loss of black house servants was much bemoaned: one white Alabaman recalled her black servant giving up her employment for $15 per week to earn $100 per month in the torpedo factory. In such instances it might be said that if 'Lincoln freed the Negroes from cotton picking . . . "Hitler was the one that got us out of the white folks' kitchens." '[15] Overall, however, as Karen Anderson rightly suggests, rather than a 'Second Emancipation' what is significant about the war experience for black women 'is the extent to which barriers remained intact.'[16]

One of the most important and liberating consequences of the war for black women and men alike was the movement of population. While one black woman recalled that during the war 'we got a chance to go places we had never been able to go before,' another spoke for many Americans regardless of race when she said, 'The impact of the war changed my life, gave me an opportunity to leave my small town and discover there was another way of life.'[17] Of course, African Americans had experienced a 'Great Migration' during World War I, and the exodus from the South had quickened in the 1920s. During the Depression the number of African Americans leaving the former Confederate states fell from 749,000 between 1920 and 1930 to 400,000 in the thirties. In that sense, the movement of half a million blacks, (17 per cent of black Southerners as opposed to only 3 per cent of whites) during World War II was merely a resumption of the pre-Depression trends.

In 1973 I gave most prominence to the northern movement of African Americans, but as Pete Daniel has pointed out, demographic change was part of the wartime reshaping of the South.[18] Although many blacks remained in the South, a considerable number still moved from the country to the city as a consequence of the further disintegration of sharecropping and the increase of job opportunities elsewhere. The rising urbanization of southern blacks contributed to a breakdown in traditional race relations and, with the wider effects of the war, created a mood of change. Jo Ann Robinson, for example, recalled that the Women's Political Council began in Montgomery, Alabama, in 1946 after the arrest of people challenging segregation on the buses. 'By 1955, we had members in every elementary, junior high, and senior high school, and in federal, state, and local jobs.'[19] Thus the foundations of the Montgomery bus boycott could be said to have been laid in the postwar era.

Other evidence of the new black mood in the South could be seen in the 10 per cent rise in the number registered to vote. Spurred on by the Supreme Court's decision against the all-white primary in *Smith* v. *Allwright* in 1944 (the culmination of the NAACP campaign which began in 1923), African Americans in Mississippi, Louisiana, Georgia, Virginia, and South Carolina organized voter registration drives and other political campaigns. Such campaigns were often led by or involved returning servicemen, a group that has been seen as having a significant role in shaping the new postwar mood of black Americans.[20]

Nothing so encapsulated the ambivalence of wartime experience for blacks as military service, and the history of African Americans in the armed forces continues to be a subject of great interest. As I pointed out in chapter 2, the combination of political pressures and the practical demands of winning the war helped bring about a considerable shift in military policy. The maintenance of segregation was declared to be official policy in 1940, and at a conference for the black press in 1941 in Washington, D.C., War Department officials insisted that the military would not act as a 'sociological laboratory.' However, in practice segregation proved to be inefficient, unworkable in some areas, and clearly harmful to black morale. In one example George Flynn pointed out, 'The armed forces could not build their Jim Crow facilities fast enough to cope with the inexorable operations of the draft's selection by numbers,' and so slowed the recruitment of black servicemen.[21] The inability to provide segregated recreational facilities for all those in camps led to the beginning of an open access policy in 1944. Conflict over transportation between Southern military bases and neighboring towns led to the introduction of a first-come, first-served service with no segregation the same year. The most radical departures were, of course, those that came in the Navy and in the Army during the Battle of the Bulge.

By the end of the war more than one million African Americans had served in different branches of the military. Despite the changes there can be little doubt that for many armed service was a bitter and disillusioning experience. As one soldier wrote to civilian aide Truman Gibson, 'When inducted I honestly believed that as a Negroe [*sic*] I comprised an important part of this nation and it was my patriotic duty to avail myself when my country was in peril. My attitude now is really changed. I'm indifferent to the whole affair.'[22] Despite such comments, however, a recent study of the attitudes of black servicemen suggests that a much higher proportion of blacks than whites (41 per cent to 25 per cent) expected to be better off as a result of their service, and that for many black soldiers service was 'an eye-opening experience.'[23] In fact, as one soldier wrote, black soldiers 'fight because of the opportunities it will make possible for them after the war.'[24]

How are we to explain this apparent contradiction between the attitudes of black servicemen and their experiences? It appears that whatever the limitations—and clearly there were many—military service gave many African Americans a modicum of self-respect and often provided training and skills. Service outside the South or even overseas (in Britain, for example) provided a first taste of equality which could have a lasting effect (see chapter 2). John Modell and his associates have shown that black veterans were twice as likely to have moved to a different region after the war as whites, and by 1947 it was estimated that 75,000 black veterans had left the South. There is also evidence of attitudinal change: Modell suggests that 'the impact of military service influenced the structure of [black] aspirations in a way that contributed to their unwillingness to accept the prewar structure of racial dominance.'²⁵ A former member of a black tank crew expressed this more clearly when he said, 'After the close of hostilities, we just kept on fighting. It's just that simple.'²⁶

There was much left to fight for. Although many white Americans supported racial change, the occupational and demographic changes affecting African Americans almost always met with some resistance from whites, particularly in the South. While I dealt with the wartime riots in Detroit and Harlem when I wrote in 1973, I nonetheless tended to stress positive aspects of the war's impact upon white Northern attitudes, and said very little about Southern resistance. Of course attempts 'to keep Negroes in their place' in the South were not new—they were often evident amid the uncertainty and economic competition of the Depression years—but they reached new levels and were possibly even more widespread during the war years. The Rankins, Bilbos, and Talmadges were vociferous in their defense of white supremacy, and challenges to the color line were often met with violence. Pete Daniel lists 'six civilian riots, over twenty military riots and mutinies, and between forty and seventy-five lynchings' occurring during the war.²⁷ As Mark Ethridge, first chairman of the Fair Employment Practices Committee and a Southerner, declared, 'All the armies of the world could not force southerners to end segregation.'²⁸

Of course, the very fact of heightened white resistance was a sign that things were changing. In countless ways white Americans were encountering blacks in new roles at work, in cities north and south, in politics, and in the armed services. Many did not like it. A theme which had its origins in the 1930s and which would reach greater intensity in the postwar era was already evident, namely the charge that those demanding improvements in America's civil rights were 'the crackpots, the communists, the parlor pinks of the country.'²⁹ The more widepsread mood, however, recognized the hypocrisy of fighting for freedom abroad while denying it to African Americans at home. Even Frank Dixon, the former governor of Alabama, acknowledged that 'the Huns have wrecked the theory of the master race.'³⁰ As President Truman declared in his message to Congress in February 1948, the 'world position of the United States' now necessitated action in race relations.

Truman's record on civil rights is still much debated. For most historians his actions appeared more symbolic than real, calculated to gain the black vote and yet not alienate the white South. My own view still remains as outlined in chapter 6, that despite their limitations Truman's actions marked important new initiatives which set the agenda for future reform. It could be argued that the failure to turn principles into practice and deliver substantive change added to the frustration which was to 'explode' in the mid-1950s. Certainly any optimistic view of the postwar period has to be qualified. The incidence of racial violence in both North and South should not be ignored: Arnold Hirsch points out, for example, that in Chicago 46 black homes were attacked between 1944 and 1946 and a total of 485 racial incidents were reported to the Chicago Housing Association between 1945 and 1950. But Hirsch also points to a significant change in 'mood and belief' among African Americans in Chicago, and it is clear that the response of both blacks and whites to postwar racial conflict was affected by wartime experiences and America's position in international affairs.[31]

No matter what the reservations, the catalogue of racial progress made during the 1940s, from the Fair Employment Practices Committee through to the beginning of desegregation in the armed forces, the establishing of a civil rights committee, and a series of Supreme Court decisions against discrimination in higher education and housing, coupled with employment gains, encouraged a mood of both optimism and determination among African Americans. While the progressive editor of the *Atlanta Constitution*, Ralph McGill, could write ominously in April 1946, 'There will be no mixing of the races in schools. There will be no social equality measures. Now or later,'[32] it was not until after 1954 that the limits of change became apparent. The response of white Southerners to the *Brown v. Topeka Board of Education* decision made clear the limits of wartime gains and revealed the continuity of racism in American life. As an African American journalist observed to Studs Terkel, 'The war brought some changes for the good. . . . We've come a long way. But racism is just as alive today.'[33]

If World War II should not, then, be seen as turning point, neither was it merely a continuation of earlier developments. Harvard Sitkoff wrote that in the 1930s 'Negro expectations rose, black powerlessness decreased, white hostility diminished,' but 'the basic conditions of life for blacks barely changed.'[34] During the war years the rising black hopes were sustained by real economic progress, by heightened expressions of white support, and by significant shifts in federal policy. Most significant of all, perhaps, was the changing demography of race relations which ultimately helped to make civil rights an issue in both North and South. True, many advances were contested, but if race did not arrive at the center of the domestic stage during the war years, it had moved out of the wings. If there was a turning point it was not to come for almost another twenty years, but like all great moments of change, the uprising of the fifties and sixties would not have been possible without what had gone before.

APPENDIX I

TABLE 1

Percentage distribution of black men and women by major industry group for selected years 1940–52

	1940	1944	1948	1950	1952
Total employed men	100·0	100·0	100·0	100·0	100·0
Agriculture	43·3	31·3	22·4	24·6	19·2
Non-agriculture	56·7	68·7	77·6	75·4	80·8
Mining	1·8	4·1	6·1	2·4	2·7
Construction	4·8	3·7	6·7	7·3	8·8
Manufacturing	16·1	23·6	24·0	21·5	26·4
Transportation, communication and public utilities	6·7	10·0	9·6	7·3	7·5
Trade, finance	11·7	12·3	13·6	17·3	16·2
Domestic and personal service	8·3	6·0	7·6	7·7	7·2
Professional services	2·9	3·2	4·2	4·4	4·4
Government	1·7	3·9	4·2	5·0	4·9
Business, repair services, amusement, recreation	2·7	1·9	2·6	2·5	2·7
Total employed women	100·0	100·0	100·0	100·0	100·0
Agriculture	21·0	10·9	8·7	8·7	6·2
Non-agriculture	79·0	89·1	91·3	91·3	93·8
Mining	0·05	0·05	0·1	0·05	0·05
Construction	0·1	0·05	0·2	0·1	0·05
Manufacturing	3·0	13·0	8·9	7·9	7·0
Transportation, communication, etc.	0·2	1·1	0·5	0·6	0·8
Trade, finance	4·5	11·4	14·1	11·4	12·9
Domestic and personal service	64·6	52·7	55·7	57·6	55·2
Professional services	5·7	7·3	9·4	10·1	13·8
Government	0·6	3·1	1·8	2·5	3·5
Business, repair, etc.	0·4	0·5	0·8	1·0	0·7

Department of Labor, *Negroes in the United States: Their Employment and Economic Status*, Washington, D.C., 1952, 43

TABLE 2

The proportion of blacks to whites in each major occupational group for selected years 1940–52

	1940	1944	1948	1950	1952
Employed black males	8·6	9·8	8·4	8·3	8·9
Professional, technical and kindred workers	2·8	3·3	2·6	2·6	2·5
Managers, officials, proprietors	1·1	2·1	1·8	1·9	1·6
Clerical, sales and kindred workers	1·3	2·8	2·3	2·8	3·4
Craftsmen, foremen and kindred workers	2·6	3·6	3·7	3·9	4·0
Operatives and kindred workers	5·9	10·1	10·1	8·5	10·4
Private household workers	60·2	75·2	53·7	51·3	31·6
Service workers	16·5	21·9	20·7	21·4	21·7
Farmers and farm managers	12·4	11·0	9·8	10·5	10·7
Farm laborers and foremen	21·0	21·1	15·8	19·8	16·2
Laborers, except farm and mine	21·0	27·6	23·6	21·4	26·9
Employed black females	13·8	12·9	11·8	12·0	11·4
Professional, technical and kindred workers	4·5	5·7	5·4	5·2	7·0
Managers, officials, proprietors	2·6	4·8	2·4	2·7	3·1
Clerical, sales and kindred workers	0·7	1·4	2·3	1·9	2·2
Craftsmen, foremen and kindred workers	2·2	5·2	5·4	2·2	4·9
Operatives and kindred workers	4·7	8·3	8·2	7·8	6·8
Private household workers	46·6	60·9	52·4	53·9	53·9
Service workers	12·7	23·9	20·0	19·1	20·0
Farmers and farm managers	30·4	23·8	21·9	20·2	24·1
Farm laborers and foremen	62·0	21·4	15·9	19·2	14·3
Laborers, except farm and mine	13·2	35·6	24·4	42·6	7·8

Department of Labor, *Negroes in the United States, Their Employment and Economic Status*, Washington, D.C., 1952, 45

Note on Appendix I:
These tables, taken together, reveal something of the Afro-American's economic progress during the war and its limitations. From Table I, it is apparent that the numbers of black males and females in domestic or personal service declined. But because there was a decline in the number of whites in this form of employment, proportionately black representation increased. In agriculture the reverse was true. The number of black farmers and farm laborers declined rapidly and so did the proportion of blacks to whites. Apart from farming, gains were made in all forms of employment. However, the greatest progress appears to have been in blue, rather than white, collar jobs. Black representation in professional, clerical or managerial posts was still far below their proportion in the population or in the work force. Moreover, in practically each occupational group blacks suffered a reverse after the war, or at least the rate of progress slowed down. The expectations of the 1940s were not fulfilled in the 1950s.

APPENDIX II

Black and white mortality from selected causes, adjusted for age, per 100,000 population

TABLE 1: *Tuberculosis*

	Black	White
1920	273·7	104·9
1925	230·5	75·3
1930	199·7	60·5
1931	198·8	56·5
1932	180·5	52·0
1933	164·0	49·0
1934	154·8	47·3
1935	150·9	45·7
1936	157·7	45·5
1937	150·8	43·6
1938	142·3	39·1
1939	134·3	37·4
1940	133·1	36·1
1941	128·5	34·7
1942	123·4	33·5
1943	116·6	33·3
1944	109·7	32·7

TABLE 2 : *Diseases of the Heart*

	Black	White
1920	245·8	199·8
1925	310·1	219·6
1930	337·1	244·8
1931	310·3	241·7
1932	298·2	251·9
1933	297·4	252·4
1934	315·1	261·1
1935	307·0	263·2
1936	335·8	280·4
1937	331·2	278·2
1938	327·3	274·2
1939	306·0	277·1
1940	330·3	288·1
1941	326·3	280·6
1942	316·5	281·2
1943	326·9	297·8
1944	320·2	295·5

TABLE 3 : *Pneumonia, all forms*

	Black	White
1935	140·3	77·8
1936	169·2	86·9
1937	158·4	78·7
1938	127·0	61·9
1939	106·5	54·3
1940	99·7	49·9
1941	85·5	41·9
1942	80·0	41·1
1943	91·3	46·5
1944	82·3	41·5

TABLE 4 : *Syphilis, all forms*

	Black	White
1935	61·3	11·2
1936	64·5	11·6
1937	65·8	11·4
1938	66·1	11·0
1939	62·5	10·3
1940	61·6	9·7
1941	54·2	9·0
1942	48·5	8·2
1943	45·8	8·1
1944	43·1	7·4

TABLE 5: *Life expectancy at birth, males*

	Black	White
1930–39	50·06	60·62
1939–41	52·26	62·81
1942	54·28	63·65
1943	54·66	63·16
1944	55·30	63·55

TABLE 6: *Infant mortality per 1000 births, 1940 and 1943*

	Black	White
1940	72·9	43·2
1943	61·5	37·5

Tables from: Mary Gover, 'Negro Mortality: Course of Mortality from Specific Causes, 1920–1944,' *Public Health Reports* Vol. 63, 7, February 13, 1948; Jessie P. Guzman, *Negro Year Book: A Review of Events Affecting Negro Life, 1941–46*, Tuskegee, Alabama, 1947, 323; Florence Murray, *Negro Handbook, 1946–47*, New York 1947, 71

Note on Appendix II

These tables show that, statistically, the health of Afro-Americans continued to improve during the war years. But while the rate of improvement was greater for blacks than for whites (because there was more room for improvement), the huge gap between the races remained. Although the difference between them was closing, a projection based on the figures here shows that the number of deaths among Afro-Americans due to TB would not meet that of whites until 1959 or 1960. Similar predictions could be made based on the other tables, with one exception, that of mortality due to diseases of the heart. In this category, the racial distinctions were not so pronounced, and rather than falling, the number of deaths due to this cause seemed to be rising among both races. Why this should be is not really understood. It may have been because more deaths were recognized as being due to heart disorders. It may also have been a symptom of generally rising standards. Diseases of the heart seem to increase as people live, eat and drink better and work in the more sedentary white-collar occupations. If this were so, these figures would, on the face of it, indicate that blacks were better off than whites. Of course this was not so, and the higher death rate was due to poorer medical care and hospitalization. Notice that the deaths due to syphilis among blacks had been high until 1938 but declined markedly from 1941 on. This could well have been due to the provision of education and prophylactics to men in the armed services and to the medical care given to servicemen unfortunate enough to catch the disease.

Notes

Abbreviations

FDRL	Franklin D. Roosevelt Library
FEPC	Fair Employment Practices Committee
HHFA	Housing and Home Finance Agency
NARG	National Archives Record Group
OASW	Office of the Assistant Secretary of War
OE	Office of Education
OFF	Office of Facts and Figures
OPA	Office of Price Administration
OWI	Office of War Information
WD	War Department

Chapter 1: War, Society and the Afro-American

1. Lingeman, *Don't You Know There's A War On? The American Home Front 1941–1945*, New York, 1970; Polenberg, *War and Society: The United States 1941–45*, New York, 1972; Perrett, *Days of Sadness, Years of Triumph: The American People 1939–1945*, New York, 1973; Nelson, *The Impact of War on American Life*, New York, 1971; de Bedts, *Recent American History: 1933 Through World War II*, Homewood, Ill., 1973; Kirkendall, *The United States, 1919–1945*, New York, 1974.
2. Dalfiume, 'The "Forgotten Years" of the Negro Revolution,' *Journal of American History*, LV, 1, June 1968; Harvard Sitkoff, 'Racial Militancy and Interracial Violence in the Second World War,' *Journal of American History*, LVIII, 3, December 1971; Lee Finkle, 'The Conservative Aims of Militant Rhetoric: Black Protest during World War II,' *Journal of American History*, LX, 3, December 1973.
3. Marwick, *War and Social Change in the Twentieth Century*, London, 1974, 6–14.
4. Marwick, *Britain in the Century of Total War: War, Peace and Social Change*, London, 1968, 12.
5. Quoted in John Hope Franklin, *From Slavery to Freedom: A History of Negro Americans*, New York, 1969, 133.
6. Black participation in the Civil War is dealt with in Dudley Cornish, *The Sable Arm: Negro Troops in the Union Army, 1861–65*, New York, 1956; Thomas Wentworth Higginson, *Army Life in a Black Regiment* (1870), New York, 1969 ed.; Lerone Bennett, Jr, *Before the Mayflower: A History of Black America*, Chicago, 1969, 160–83; Robert W. Mullen, *Blacks in America's Wars*, New York, 1973, 19–33; Franklin, *From Slavery to Freedom*, 271–96.
7. Miller, *The Everlasting Stain*, Washington, D.C., 1924, 10; also see Nancy J. Weiss, 'The

Negro and the New Freedom: Fighting Wilsonian Segregation,' *Political Science Quarterly*, LXXXIV, 1, March 1969.

8. Vardaman quoted in J. L. and H. N. Scheiber, 'The Wilson Administration and the Wartime Mobilization of Black Americans, 1917–18,' *Labor History*, X, 3, 1969, 441.

9. Chester D. Heywood, *Negro Combat Troops in the World War: The Story of the 371st Infantry* (1928), New York, 1969 ed., 46; Edward M. Coffman, *The War to End All Wars: The American Military Experience in World War I*, New York, 1968, 70–1; W. E. B. DuBois, 'An Essay Toward a History of the Black Man in the Great War,' *The Crisis*, June 1919, 69–72; A contemporary view of black soldiers is provided in Arthur W. Little's *From Harlem to the Rhine: The Story of New York's Colored Volunteers*; a more up-to-date and general account is provided in Arthur E. Barbeau and Florette Henri, *The Unknown Soldiers: Black American Troops in World War I*, Philadelphia, 1974.

10. French liaison officer quoted in Coffman, *The War to End All Wars*, 231–2; for riots in Britain, see *Chicago Defender*, June 21, 1919.

11. Emmett J. Scott, *Negro Migrations During the War*, New York, 1920, 3; US Dept of Labor, Division of Negro Economics, *Negro Migrations in 1916–17*, Washington, D.C., 1919, 22–30; Allan Spear, *Black Chicago: The Making of a Negro Ghetto, 1890–1920*, Chicago, 1967, ix, 138–41.

12. Nancy J. Weiss, *The National Urban League, 1910–1940*, New York, 1974, 178.

13. *Chicago Defender*, December 29, 1917; 'Letters of Negro Migrants, 1916–1918,' *Journal of Negro History*, IV, 1919, 291–334; Spear, *Black Chicago*, 151–8.

14. St Clair Drake and Horace R. Cayton, *Black Metropolis: A Study of Negro Life in a Northern City* (1944), New York, 1970 ed., 63; The riot in East St Louis is treated in Elliott M. Rudwick, *Race Riot At East St Louis, July 2, 1917*, Carbondale, Ill., 1964; the Chicago riot of 1919 is dealt with in the Chicago Commission on Race Relations, *The Negro in Chicago: A Study of Race Relations and a Race Riot*, Chicago, 1923; and in Carl Sandburg, *The Chicago Race Riots, July 1919*, New York, 1919. Also see Arthur I. Waskow, *From Race Riot to Sit-In: 1919 and the 1960s*, New York, 1967.

15. *Training of Colored Troops*, Signal Corps Films, in the National Archives Film Library, NA 111H–1211–PPSA–1; also see Kingsley Moses, 'The Negro Comes North' and John Richards, 'Some Experiences with Colored Soldiers,' both in David F. Trask, ed., *World War I At Home: Readings on American Life, 1914–1920*, New York, 1970.

16. *Chicago Defender*, April 6, 1917; November 17, 24, 1917; and May 4, 1918.

17. *The Crisis*, May, June, July 1918.

18. Quoted in Jervis Anderson, *A. Philip Randolph: A Biographical Portrait*, New York, 1973, 112.

19. Chicago Commission on Race Relations, *The Negro in Chicago*, 483.

20. *Chicago Defender*, February 22, August 2, 1919.

21. *The Crisis*, May 1919; and DuBois quoted in Roi Ottley, *New World A'Coming*, New York, 1943, 318.

22. Polenberg, *War and Society*, 4.

23. John Morton Blum, 'World War II,' in C. Vann Woodward, ed., *A Comparative Approach to American History*, Washington, D.C., 1969, 348–9.

24. Perrett, *Days of Sadness, Years of Triumph*, 353–5.

25. Davis R. B. Ross, *Preparing for Ulysses: Politics and Veterans during World War II*, New York, 1969, 34–5.

26. Ross, *Preparing for Ulysses*, 124.

27. Perrett, *Days of Sadness*, 339.

28. Lingeman, *Don't You Know There's A War On?*, 69–71.

29. Polenberg, *War and Society*, 131–50; a detailed, contemporary account of wartime social problems is Francis E. Merrill, *Social Problems on the Home Front: A Study of Wartime Influences*, New York and London, 1948.

30. William H. Chafe, *The American Woman: Her Changing Social, Economic, and Political Roles*, New York, 1972, 135.
31. Margaret Mead, 'The Women in the War,' in Jack Goodman, ed., *While You Were Gone: A Report on Wartime Life in the United States*, New York, 1946, 274–81.
32. Chafe, *The American Woman*, 180–3.
33. Morton Grodzins, *Americans Betrayed: Politics and the Japanese Evacuation*, Chicago, 1949; Harry H. L. Kitano, *Japanese Americans*, Englewood Cliffs, N.J., 1969; Roger Daniels, *Concentration Camps USA: Japanese-Americans and World War II*, New York, 1971.
34. Office of Co-ordinator of Inter-American Affairs, *Spanish Speaking Americans in the War*, n.d., n.p., in files of Fair Employment Practices Committee, National Archives Record Group 228. Stan Steiner, *La Raza: Mexican Americans*, New York, 1969; Manuel P. Servin, ed., *The Mexican Americans: An Awakening Minority*, Beverly Hills, Cal., 1970; John H. Burma, ed., *Mexican Americans in the United States*, Cambridge, Mass., 1970.
35. William T. Hagan, *American Indians*, Chicago, 1961, 158–60.
36. Florence Murray, ed., *The Negro Handbook, 1942*, New York, 1942, 201; Langston Hughes, *Fight For Freedom: The Story of the NAACP*, New York, 1962, 197–8.
37. Chester Himes, 'Now Is The Time! Here Is The Place!,' *Opportunity*, XX, 9, September 1942, 271.

Chapter 2: The Test of War: Afro-Americans and the Armed Forces, 1940–45

1. Paul C. Davis, 'The Negro in the Armed Forces,' *Virginia Quarterly Review*, XXIV, 4, 1948, 499.
2. Lee Nichols, *Breakthrough on the Color Front*, New York, 1954; Ulysses G. Lee, *The Employment of Negro Troops*, US Army in World War II, Special Studies 8, Washington, D.C., 1966; Richard J. Stillman, *Integration of the Negro in the US Armed Forces*, New York, 1968; Richard M. Dalfiume, *Desegregation of the US Armed Forces: Fighting on Two Fronts, 1939–1953*, Columbia, Miss., 1969.
3. Lee, *The Employment of Negro Troops*, 29–38; Dalfiume, *Desegregation of the US Armed Forces*, 21–4; John W. Davis, 'The Negro in the United States Navy, Marine Corps, and Coastguard', *Journal of Negro Education*, XII, 3, Summer 1943.
4. *Pittsburgh Courier*, December 14, 1940.
5. Selective Service System, *Special Groups: Special Monograph No. 10*, Washington, D.C., 1953, 41–4; Lee, *The Employment of Negro Troops*, 72–3.
6. Memo. on the basis of conference, Official File 93, box 4, Franklin D. Roosevelt Library (hereafter 93:4 FDRL). Also see Walter White, *A Man Called White*, New York, 1948, 186–7.
7. The full text was published in *The Crisis*, November 1940.
8. Press release October 9, 1940, 93:4 FDRL.
9. *The Crisis*, November 1940; *Chicago Defender*, October 19, 1940; White to Early, October 21, 1940, 93:4 FDRL.
10. F.D.R. to White, Hill and Randolph, October 25, 1940, 93:4 FDRL; Dalfiume, *Desegregation of the US Armed Forces*, 41–2; Lee, *The Employment of Negro Troops*, 79.
11. Lee, *The Employment of Negro Troops*, 88; Dalfiume, *Desegregation of the US Armed Forces*, 88.
12. Remarks of Col. E. R. Householder at the Conference of Negro Newspaper Representatives, Munitions Building, Washington, D.C., December 8, 1941, OASW 273, NARG 107.
13. *Chicago Defender*, December 13, 1941; *Pittsburgh Courier*, December 13, 1941; *Opportunity* XX, 1, January 1942.
14. *Pittsburgh Courier*, April 18, 1942.
15. *Pittsburgh Courier*, January 11, 1941.

16. *Pittsburgh Courier*, January 18, 1941; *Chicago Defender*, January 18, 1941.

17. *Baltimore Afro-American*, October 10, 1942.

18. *Baltimore Afro-American*, October 31, November 7, 1942; Florence Murray, 'The Negro and Civil Liberties during World War II,' *Social Forces*, December 1945.

19. Florence Murray, ed., *The Negro Handbook, 1946–47*, New York, 1947, 359–60.

20. *Chicago Defender*, March 4, 1944; A. Meier and E. Rudwick, *CORE: A Study in the Civil Rights Movement, 1942–1968*, New York, 1973, 4–6, 19.

21. *Chicago Defender*, January 24, 1942; *Selective Service in Wartime: Second Report*, Washington, D.C., 1943, 292.

22. *Baltimore Afro-American*, December 5, 1942, January 2, 1943; Murray, ed., *The Negro Handbook, 1944*, New York, 1944, 131–2; Selective Service System, *Special Groups*, 49–50.

23. Press release, National Committee for Winfred Lynn, and 'The Story of Winfred Lynn', Lynn file, Schomburg Collection; US ex rel Lynn vs Downer, *US Supreme Court Reports*, Law Ed., 88, 1585.

24. Murray, *Negro Handbook, 1946–47*, 359.

25. *The Nation*, July 1, 1944, 13; release, National Committee for Winfred Lynn, June 1, 1944; *Special Groups*, 50.

26. Dalfiume, *Desegregation of the US Armed Forces*, 83–4.

27. Dalfiume, *Desegregation of the US Armed Forces*, 83; letter of resignation, Hastie to Stimson, January 5, 1943, OASW 243, NARG 107; also black newspapers February 6, 1943.

28. Patterson to White, September 18, 1941, OASW 221, NARG 107; also see Jean Byers, *A Study of the Negro in Military Service*, Dept of Defense, Washington, D.C., 1947, mimeographed in Moorland Collection, Howard University, 64–8; Ruth Danenhower Wilson, *Jim Crow Joins Up: A Study of Negroes in the Armed Forces of the United States*, New York, 1944.

29. Private Charles F. Wilson to F.D.R., May 9, 1944, in OASW 230, NARG 107; there are literally hundreds of such letters in 93:12 and 93:9 FDRL, in OASW files 221, 230, NARG 107, and in NAACP files, box 279, Library of Congress.

30. Private John S. Banks to NAACP, July 28, 1943, forwarded to Truman Gibson; and Gibson to Milton Konvitz, Special Counsel for NAACP, OASW 221, NARG 107.

31. Jessie Parkhurst Guzman, *Negro Year Book: A Review of Events Affecting Negro Life, 1941–1946*, Tuskegee, Ala., 1947, 151.

32. War Department, Special Service Division, Research Branch, *What the Soldier Thinks*, No. 2, August 1943, 14–15, 58–9, in War Department files, NARG 330.

33. Samuel A. Stouffer et al., *The American Soldier*, Princeton, 1949, Vol. I, 506.

34. Stouffer, *The American Soldier*, 504, 508, 514.

35. Private Bert B. Barbero to Gibson, February 13, 1944, OASW 230, NARG 107. Also see Howard Long, 'The Negro in the Army of the United States,' *Journal of Negro Education*, XII, 1, 1943; and Grant Reynolds, 'What the Negro Thinks of This War,' *The Crisis*, September 1944.

36. *The Crisis*, February 1944, 51, October 1944, 322, and February 1945, 53.

37. George B. Nesbitt, 'The Negro Soldier Speaks,' *Opportunity* XXII, 3, July–September 1944; Lucille B. Milner, 'Jim Crow in the Army,' *New Republic*, Vol. 110, 11, March 13, 1944.

38. *Chicago Defender*, June 19, 1943; *Pittsburgh Courier*, June 26, 1943; Harvard Sitkoff, 'Racial Militancy and Interracial Violence in the Second World War,' *Journal of American History*, LVIII, 3, December 1971; 'The Pattern of Race Riots Involving Negro Soldiers,' *Race Relations: A Monthly Summary of Events and Trends*, II, 1–2, August–September 1944.

39. Unheaded memo. on black attitudes, OASW 230, NARG 107.

40. Gibson to Asst Secretary of War Patterson, August 23, 1943, OASW 39, NARG 107.

41. Memo. J. S. Leonard, Secretary, Negro Troops Policy Committee, to Patterson, December 17, 1943, OASW 39, NARG 107.

42. Armed Forces Manual, MS, *Leadership and the Negro Soldier*, October 1944, War Department, Planning Survey, NARG 330; Lee, *The Employment of Negro Troops*, 315–24, 397; *Chicago Defender*, June 3, August 12, 1944.

43. Military Policy Implications of Report by Research Branch, Special Service Division, on 'Attitudes of the Negro Soldier,' July 31, 1943, OASW 230, NARG 107.

44. *The Negro Soldier*, Signal Corps Film, 1944, National Archives NA 1110F–51; War Dept, Morale Services Division, Report No. B–102 'Reactions of Negro and White Soldiers to the Film "The Negro Soldier",' War Department, NARG 330.

45. Florence Murray, ed., *The Negro Handbook, 1946–47*, 265.

46. Joe Louis, *My Life Story*, London, 1947, 145–74.

47. Lee, *The Employment of Negro Troops*, 428–9; Dalfiume, *Desegregation of the US Armed Forces*, 92.

48. Fish to Stimson, February 1, March 31, 1944, Stimson to Fish, February 19, 1944, OASW 190, NARG 107.

49. Gibson to Claude Barnett, March 20, 1944, OASW 190, NARG 107; *Pittsburgh Courier*, March 11, 18, 1944.

50. Gibson to McCloy Committee, February 29, 1944, OASW 190, NARG 107; Dalfiume, *Desegregation of the US Armed Forces*, 96.

51. Quoted in Roi Ottley, *Black Odyssey: The Story of the Negro in America*, London, 1949, 310.

52. Thomas E. Hachey, 'Jim Crow with a British Accent: Attitudes of London Government Officials Toward American Negro Soldiers in England During World War II,' *Journal of Negro History*, LIX, 1, January 1974, 65–77.

53. St Clair Drake, 'The "Colour Problem" in Britain: A Study in Social Definitions,' *Sociological Review*, Vol. III, 1956, 204–7; Anthony H. Richmond, *Colour Prejudice in Britain: A Study of West Indian Workers in Liverpool, 1941–45*, London, 1954, 16–25; Michael Banton, *White and Coloured: The Behaviour of British People Towards Coloured Immigrants*, London, 1959, 117–19, 138.

54. Norman Longmate, *How We Lived Then: A History of Everyday Life during the Second World War*, London, 1971, 478. Also see *Picture Post*, October 31, 1942, October 16, 1943.

55. Eisenhower quoted in Lee, *The Employment of Negro Troops*, 625; numbers of black soldiers from James C. Evans to Miss Shirley Ender, September 25, 1947, in OASW 248, NARG 107.

56. *Welcome to Britain*, Ministry of Information 1943, in London National Film Archives.

57. 'The Colour Problem as the American Sees It,' *Current Affairs*, December 1942, 13–14.

58. Lee, *The Employment of Negro Troops*, 625.

59. Hachey, 'Jim Crow with a British Accent,' 75; Christopher Thorne, 'Britain and the Black GIs,' *Sunday Times* (London) Supplement, December 1973.

60. Gibson to Asst Secretary of War, December 17, 1943, OASW 204, NARG 107.

61. K. L. Little, *Negroes in Britain: A Study of Race Relations in English Society*, London, 1947, 240; St Clair Drake, 'The "Colour Problem" in Britain,' 207; S. McNeill, *Illegitimate Children of English Mothers and Coloured Americans*, London, 1946; Angus Calder, *The People's War: Britain 1939–45*, London, 1971, 356–7; *Regional Commissioners' Reports*, (July 1942), in Scottish Office, HH 50/133.

62. Provost Marshal to Deputy Theater Commander, July 20, 1944, OASW 204, NARG 107; *Chicago Defender*, July 3, September 25, October 23, 1943, April 1, April 29, May 20, 1944.

63. White, *A Rising Wind*, Garden City, N.Y., 1945, 21.

64. McNutt to Stimson and Knox, February 17, 1943, 93:5 FDRL; Dalfiume, *Desegregation of the US Armed Forces*, 90–1.
65. Byers, *A Study of the Negro in Military Service*, 37.
66. The full text of the appeal is quoted in Lee, *The Employment of Negro Troops*, 689–95; also see Charles C. Moskos, *The American Enlisted Man: The Rank and File in Today's Military*, New York, 1970, 110–11.
67. Byers, *A Study of the Negro in Military Service*, 167–79; Lee, *The Employment of Negro Troops*, 696–702; Arnold Rose, 'Army Policies Toward Negro Soldiers: A Report on a Success and a Failure,' *Journal of Social Issues*, III, 4, 1947.
68. See the *Nation*, September 18 and November 6, 1943, and *Pittsburgh Courier*, September 18, November 20, 1943.
69. War Dept, Special Service Division, Research Branch, Report 18, 'Attitudes of White Enlisted Men Toward Sharing Facilities With Negro Troops,' July 30, 1942; Report 43, 'Attitudes of Enlisted Men Toward Negroes for Air Force Duty,' November 30, 1942; Report 46, 'What the Soldier Thinks,' 1943, all in War Dept 47, NARG 330.
70. War Dept, Troop Information and Education Division, Troop Attitudes Research Branch, Special Memo. 21–309C, July 14, 1947, 'Attitudes of Officers and Enlisted Men Toward Certain Minority Groups'; Dept of Army, Office of Chief of Staff, Attitudes Research Branch, Special Memo. 40–309C, April 14, 1949, 'Supplementary Report on Attitudes of White Enlisted Men Toward Serving with Negro Enlisted Men,' both in War Dept 47, NARG 330.
71. All the information which follows is from War Dept, Troop Information and Education Division, Report B–157, July 3, 1945, 'Opinions About Negro Infantry Platoons in White Companies of 7 Divisions', War Dept 47, NARG 330.
72. Dalfiume, *Desegregation of the US Armed Forces*, 53–5, 101–3; Nichols, *Breakthrough on the Color Front*, 54–9; Laurence D. Reddick, 'The Negro in the Navy in World War II,' *Journal of Negro History*, XXII, April 1947.
73. Dalfiume, *Desegregation of the US Armed Forces*, 101; Nichols, *Breakthrough on the Color Front*, 63; Lester B. Granger, 'Racial Democracy—The Navy Way,' *Common Ground*, Winter 1947.
74. Nichols, *Breakthrough on the Color Front*, 74–7; Dalfiume, *Desegregation of the US Armed Forces*, 177–8.
75. The full text of the Report, War Dept Circular No. 124, April 27, 1946, was quoted in the *Chicago Defender*, March 9, 1946. It is summarized in Paul C. Davis, 'The Negro in the Armed Forces,' *Virginia Quarterly Review*, XXIV, 4, 1948.
76. *Baltimore Afro-American*, March 9, 1946; *Chicago Defender*, March 23, 1946.

Chapter 3: Participation: The Impact of World War II on the Employment and Economic Situation of the Afro-American

1. *Negro Labor: A National Problem*, New York, 1946, 236.
2. E. Franklin Frazier, *The Negro in the United States*, New York, 1969 ed., 599; Richard Sterner, *The Negro's Share: A Study of Income, Consumption, Housing and Public Assistance*, New York, 1943, 39–45.
3. Franklin, *From Slavery to Freedom*, 496; Myrdal, *An American Dilemma*, 300.
4. Raymond Wolters, *Negroes and the Great Depression: The Problems of Economic Recovery*, Westport, Conn., 1970, 213.
5. Wolters, *Negroes and the Great Depression*, 78–9; John A. Salmond, 'The Civilian Conservation Corps and the Negro,' in Sternsher, *The Negro in Depression and War*, 78–93.
6. Frazier, *The Negro in the United States*, 606; Social Security Agency, *Negro Workers and the*

National Defense Program, Washington, D.C., September 1941; President's Committee on Fair Employment Practice, *Minorities in Defense*, Washington D.C., 1941.

7. *Negro Workers and the National Defense Program*, 14.

8. Letter to Eric Seberite, April 1, 1941, War Manpower Commission, NARG 211; 'Eliminating Employer Discriminatory Hiring Practices,' Chapter IX of the unpublished and incomplete *History of the Mobilization of Labor for War Production*, prepared by William J. Schuck, 1946, Manuscript in War Manpower Commission, NARG 211.

9. Memo., John W. Studebaker, Commissioner of Office of Education, to Paul V. McNutt, Chairman, War Manpower Commission, September 1942, and copy of Fair Employment Practices Committee hearings on discrimination in defense training, April 13, 1942, both in Office of Education, file 40, NARG 12.

10. Murray, *Negro Handbook, 1942*, 88.

11. Weaver to Truman, June 23, 1941, Special Committee of the Senate to Investigate the National Defense Program, 876, NARG 46.

12. W. Gerard Tuttle to National Negro Congress, August 2, 1940, in Special Committee of the Senate to Investigate the National Defense Program, 876, NARG 46.

13. FEPC hearings, Los Angeles, October 20–1, 1941, FEPC 408, NARG 228; Weaver, *Negro Labor*, 109–18; Council for Democracy, *The Negro and Defense: A Test of Democracy*, New York, 1941, 7–10.

14. Quoted in Earl Brown and George R. Leighton, *The Negro and the War*, Public Affairs Committee, Pamphlet 71, New York, 1942, 9; President's Committee on Fair Employment Practice, *First Report, July 1943–December 1944*, Washington, D.C., 1945, 89.

15. Selective Service System, *Selective Service in Peace Time: First Report of the Director of Selective Service, 1940–41*, Washington, D.C., 1942, 258.

16. 'For Manhood in National Defense,' *The Crisis*, December 1940.

17. SR 75, February 13, 1941, in Special Senate Committee to Investigate the National Defense Program, 1941–8, file 875, NARG 46.

18. Memo. April 30, 1941 and July 2, 1941, Special Senate Committee, 875. Also letter Walter White to Senator Thomas, April 29, 1941, file 876; and White, *A Man Called White*, 189.

19. Preliminary Conference on Racial Discrimination, June 25, 1941, Special Committee of the Senate, 875, NARG 46.

20. Fuller treatment of Randolph's history is provided in Jervis Anderson, *A. Philip Randolph: A Biographical Portrait*; New York, 1973; also articles in *Ebony*, Vol. 13, November 1958, *The United Teacher*, May 4, 1969 and *Glass Horizons*, June 1960. I am also grateful for information provided by the A. Philip Randolph Institute, New York.

21. A. Mitchell Palmer, *Radicalism and Sedition among Negroes as Reflected in their Publications*, Exhibit 10, *Senate Documents*, Vol. 12, 66th Congress, 1st Session, 1919, Washington, D.C., 1919, 172.

22. *Black Worker* (the official organ of the BSCP), May 1940, and Brailsford R. Brazeal, *The Brotherhood of Sleeping Car Porters: its Origins and Development*, New York and London, 1946.

23. The history of the March on Washington Movement is detailed in Herbert Garfinkel, *When Negroes March: The March on Washington Movement in the Organizational Politics for FEPC*, Glencoe, Ill., 1959, reprinted with a preface by Lewis M. Killian, New York, 1969.

24. *Black Worker*, January 1941.

25. *Pittsburgh Courier*, January 25, 1941.

26. White to F.D.R., March 31, 1941, 93:4 FDRL; *Pittsburgh Courier*, March 22, 1941.

27. Edwin M. Watson to White, April 8, 1941, 93:4 FDRL.

28. 'Call to Negro America,' *Black Worker*, May 1941; *Courier*, May 17, 1941.

29. Hillman to all holders of defense contracts, April 11, 1941, quoted in FEPC, *Minorities in Defense*, 11.

30. *Black Worker*, March 1941.

31. Proceedings of MOWM Conference, Detroit, September 26–7, 1942 in Schomburg Collection; and Charles Radford Lawrence, 'Negro Organizations in Crisis: Depression, New Deal, World War II,' unpublished PhD dissertation, Columbia University, 1952, 300.

32. Randolph to Eleanor Roosevelt, June 3, 1941, OASW 215, NARG 107; White, *A Man Called White*, 189; *Pittsburgh Courier*, May 31, 1941; and Randolph to F.D.R., May 29, 1941, 93:4 FDRL.

33. Memo. from F.D.R., June 7, 1941, 93:5 FDRL; Memo. Early to F.D.R., June 6, 1941. Details of the meeting are in White, *A Man Called White*, 189–90.

34. Roosevelt to Hillman and Knudsen, June 12, 1941, quoted in *Minorities in Defense*, 14. For the black reaction see *Black Worker*, June 1941 and *Chicago Defender*, June 21, 1941.

35. White, *A Man Called White*, 192.

36. Memo., Patterson and Forrestal to F.D.R., June 24, 1941, 93:5 FDRL.

37. Executive Order 8802, June 25, 1941.

38. Dalfiume, *Desegregation of the US Armed Forces*, 117–22.

39. *Black Worker*, August 1941.

40. *Chicago Defender*, July 12, 1941; and Bethune to F.D.R., June 26, 1941, 93:5 FDRL.

41. Lewis to F.D.R., June 28, 1941, 93:5 FDRL.

42. *The Crisis*, August 1941.

43. *Pittsburgh Courier*, July 26, 1941; Telegram, Randolph to F.D.R., July 22, 1941. Earlier Randolph had suggested LaGuardia, Wendell Willkie, and Homer Brown as well as Sarnoff and Webster for membership, telegram July 14, 1941, both in 93:5 FDRL.

44. Citation in James Weldon Johnson Collection, Beinecke Library, Yale. See also, Garfinkel, *When Negroes March*, 62.

45. *Chicago Defender*, July 26, 1941.

46. *Pittsburgh Courier*, August 1, 1942; *Baltimore Afro-American*, September 26, 1942; and Randolph, 'Why Should We March?,' *Survey Graphic*, XXXI, 11, November 1942.

47. Dalfiume, *Desegregation of the US Armed Forces*, 121; and Garfinkel, *When Negroes March*, 60, 62.

48. Memo. Hastie to Secretary of War Stimson, OASW 215, NARG 107.

49. *Pittsburgh Courier*, June 27, July 4, 1942; *Baltimore Afro-American*, July 4, 1942; Garfinkel, *When Negroes March*, 95, 98.

50. *Pittsburgh Courier*, January 23, 1943.

51. *Pittsburgh Courier*, October 17, 1942 and April 24, 1943.

52. *Chicago Defender*, July 3, 1943.

53. *Baltimore Afro-American*, July 10, 1943; Helen Buckler, 'The CORE Way,' *Survey Graphic*, XXXV, 2, February 1946; George M. Houser, *Erasing the Color Line*, New York, 1945; August Meier and Elliott Rudwick, 'How CORE Began,' *Social Science Quarterly*, Vol. 49, 4, March 1969; Proceedings of MOWM Conference, Detroit, September 26–7, 1942, in Schomburg Collection, and *Chicago Defender*, January 9, 1943; August Meier and Elliott M. Rudwick, *CORE: A Study in the Civil Rights Movement, 1942–1968*, New York, 1973, 3–40.

54. Ruchames, *Race, Jobs and Politics: The Story of FEPC*, New York, 1953, 4, 156.

55. President's Committee on Fair Employment Practice, *FEPC: How it Operates*, Washington, D.C., 1944, 7.

56. President's Committee on Fair Employment Practice, *Final Report, June 28, 1946*, Washington, D.C., 1947, ix.

57. 'Important Dates in FEPC History,' April 1, 1944, FEPC 407, NARG 228; Ruchames,

Race, Jobs and Politics, 27; and Louis C. Kesselman, *The Social Politics of FEPC: A Study in Reform Pressure Movements*, Chapel Hill, N.C., 1948, 23.

58. Hearings, Los Angeles, October 20–1, 1941, FEPC 408, NARG 228; Weaver, *Negro Labor*, 118.

59. Hearings, FEPC 408, NARG 228, War Manpower Commission, NARG 211, and OASW 190, NARG 107.

60. Quoted in Ruchames, *Race, Jobs and Politics*, 28–30; letter, Congressman W. R. Poage of Texas to Fowler W. Harper, Deputy Chairman, WMC, January 11, 1943, WMC, NARG 211. Other examples are quoted in Kesselman, *The Social Politics of FEPC*, 167.

61. *Baltimore Afro-American*, August 8, 1942; *Pittsburgh Courier*, August 15, 1942; *Black Worker*, September 1942; *Race, Jobs and Politics*, 46. Also see Garfinkel, *When Negroes March*, 102, and Kesselman, *The Social Politics of FEPC*, 19.

62. Roosevelt to McNutt, July 30, 1942 and White House press release, August 17, 1942, WMC, NARG 211.

63. Schuck, 'Eliminating Employer Discriminatory Hiring Practices,' 37–40, 48–9, and letters in WMC, NARG 211.

64. Schuck, 'Eliminating Employer Discriminatory Hiring Practices,' 52, and Kesselman, *The Social Politics of FEPC*, 17–18.

65. *Chicago Defender* and *Pittsburgh Courier*, January 23, 1943; and *Black Worker*, December 1942.

66. Schuck, 'Eliminating Employer Discriminatory Hiring Practices,' 51. This argument was accepted in the *Chicago Defender*, February 26, 1943. Kesselman, *The Social Politics of FEPC*, 21.

67. 'Important Dates in FEPC History,' April 1, 1944, FEPC 407, NARG 228, and Schuck, 'Eliminating Employer Discriminatory Hiring Practices,' 34.

68. *Baltimore Afro-American* and *Pittsburgh Courier*, June 5, 1943; Ruchames, *Race, Jobs and Politics*, 58; and Harvard Sitkoff, 'Racial Militancy and Interracial Violence in the Second World War.' *Journal of American History*, LVIII, 3, 1971, 672.

69. 'Important Dates in FEPC History,' FEPC 407; C. L. Golightly, 'FEPC and the Railroads,' May 8, 1945, FEPC 412, NARG 228; Ruchames, *Race, Jobs and Politics*, 59–68; and *Black Worker*, September and October 1943.

70. December 13, 1943, Golightly, 'FEPC and the Railroads'; and Ruchames, *Race, Jobs and Politics*, 68.

71. Golightly, 'FEPC and the Railroads'; President's Committee on Fair Employment Practice, *Final Report, June 28, 1946*, Washington, D.C., 1947, ix.

72. See for example, Hearings, Portland, Ore., November 15–16, 1943, and Los Angeles, November 19–20, 1943, FEPC 408, NARG 228.

73. The history of the Afro-American in the trade union movement is dealt with in: Abram L. Harris and Sterling D. Spero, *The Black Worker*, New York, 1931; Julius Jacobson ed., *The Negro and the American Labor Movement*, Garden City, N.Y., 1968; Ray Marshall, *The Negro and Organized Labor*, New York, 1965; Herbert R. Northrup, *Organized Labor and the Negro*, New York, 1944.

74. Schuck, 'Eliminating Employer Discriminatory Hiring Practices,' 6; and President's Committee on Fair Employment Practice, *Minorities in Defense*, 11

75. *Reports of Proceedings, AFL Conventions*, New Orleans 1940, Seattle 1941, and Toronto 1942. Also Brazeal, *The Brotherhood of Sleeping Car Porters*, 157–68.

76. *Proceedings, AFL Convention*, Boston, 1943, 442–5; Herbert R. Northrup, 'Organized Labor and Negro Workers,' *Journal of Political Economy*, LI, 3, June 1943.

77. *Proceedings, AFL Convention*, New Orleans, 1944, 557–8.

78. Brazeal, *Brotherhood of Sleeping Car Porters*, 168; Kesselman, *The Social Politics of FEPC*, 148.

79. *Baltimore Afro-American*, November 7, 1942, April 1, 1944; *Chicago Defender*, September 12, 1942, November 25, 1944.

80. *Proceedings of Constitutional Convention of CIO*, Boston, 1942, Resolution 18, 172.
81. *Proceedings, Constitutional Convention, CIO*, Philadelphia, 1943, Resolution 13, 267–8; *Proceedings, Constitutional Convention, CIO*, Chicago, 1944, 93–4.
82. *Chicago Defender*, June 12, 1943.
83. CIO, *Working and Fighting Together*, Washington, D.C., 1943, 7. Council for Democracy, *The Negro in America: How We Treat Him and How We Should*, New York, 1945, 10.
84. *Baltimore Afro-American*, November 21 and 28, 1942.
85. *Chicago Defender*, March 27, 1943, April 17, 1943; and Weaver, *Negro Labor*, 37.
86. American Council on Race Relations, *Negro Platform Workers*, Chicago 1945, 3–17; and Ruchames, *Race, Jobs and Politics*, 100–20.
87. 'Important Dates in FEPC History,' FEPC 407, NARG 228, American Council on Race Relations, *Negro Platform Workers*, 9.
88. *Baltimore Afro-American*, August 5 and 12, 1944; *The Crisis*, September 1944; film C-5275, 'Army Ends Transport Strike,' 2–7, August 1944, Sherman Grinberg Library; and Allen M. Winkler, 'The Philadelphia Transit Strike of 1944,' *Journal of American History*, Vol. 59, 1972, 73–89.
89. *Negro Platform Workers*, 24, and memo., C. L. Golightly to John A. Davis, May 19, 1945, 'FEPC and the Capital Transit Company of Washington, D.C.,' FEPC 413, NARG 228.
90. Weaver, *Negro Labor*, 71–2; and Marshall, *The Negro and Organized Labor*, 38–40.
91. 'Statement on Work Stoppages,' FEPC 413, NARG 228; President's Committee on Fair Employment Practices, *First Report, July 1943–December 1944*, 79; *Baltimore Afro-American*, May 27, 1944.
92. *Baltimore Afro-American*, March 4, 1944; *Chicago Defender*, November 4, 25, 1944; and Kesselman, *The Social Politics of FEPC*, 147–9.
93. Brazeal, *The Brotherhood of Sleeping Car Porters*, 168.
94. *Chicago Defender*, November 6, 1943 and November 25, 1944.
95. Ruchames, *Race, Jobs and Politics*, 81–6.
96. Ruchames, *Race, Jobs and Politics*, 87–8.
97. Wilma Dykeman and James Stokely, *The Seeds of Southern Change: The Life of Will Alexander*, Chicago, 1962, 257; President's Committee on Fair Employment Practices, *First Report, July 1943–December 1944*, 2.
98. Schuck, 'Eliminating Employer Discriminatory Hiring Practices,' 23; and American Council on Race Relations, March 1949, 'Evaluation of State FEPC: Experiences and Forecasts,' in James Weldon Johnson Collection, Yale University.
99. Schuck, 'Eliminating Employer Discriminatory Hiring Practices,' 60–2; Weaver, *Negro Labor*, 79; President's Committee on Fair Employment Practices, *First Report*, 90; and Myrdal, *An American Dilemma*, 409.
100. President's Committee on Fair Employment Practices, *First Report*, 92; Murray, *Negro Handbook 1946–47*, 99; and National Urban League, 'Changes in the Occupational Status of Negroes, 1940–1950,' New York, 1950, mimeographed, in Schomburg Collection.
101. Social Security Board, *Employment Security Review*, IX, 7, July 1942; Murray, *Negro Handbook, 1942*, 142; FEPC, *First Report*, 90, 94; War Manpower Commission, 'Utilization of Reserve Workers: Recently Reported Placements of Negroes in Skilled Occupations,' Washington, D.C., March 1944, FEPC 407, NARG 228.
102. Weaver, *The Negro Ghetto*, New York, 1948, 80; and New York State War Council, Committee on Discrimination in Employment, *How Management Can Integrate Negroes in War Industries*, New York, 1942, 3; and *The Negro Integrated*, New York, 1945, 24.
103. *Chicago Defender*, September 9, 1944; Chicago Mayor's Commission on Human Relations, *Race Relations in Chicago*, Chicago, 1945, 2.
104. Schuck, 'Eliminating Employer Discriminatory Hiring Practices,' 64; Weaver, 'Racial Employment Trends in National Defense,' *Phylon*, III, 1, 1942; Herbert R. Northrup,

'The Negro in the Aerospace Industry,' in Northrup, et al., *Negro Employment in Basic Industry: A Study of Racial Policies in Six Industries*, Philadelphia, 1970. Also see Weaver, *Negro Labor*, 109–18.

105. 'Employment—Negro Women' FEPC 408, NARG 228; Kathryn Blood, *Negro Women War Workers*, Women's Bureau, Dept of Labor Bulletin 205, Washington, D.C., 1945; and National Urban League, 'Changes in the Occupational Status of Negroes.'

106. National Urban League, 'A Summary Report of the Industrial Relations Laboratory: Performance of Negro Workers in Three Hundred War Plants,' New York, 1944, 4, mimeographed, Howard University Library.

107. Blood, *Negro Women War Workers*, 7, 19; Weaver, *The Negro Ghetto*, 81.

108. Quoted in Schuck, 'Eliminating Employer Discriminatory Hiring Practices,' 15.

109. 'Tables and Summary of Employment of Negroes in the Federal Government,' December 1943, FEPC 407; 'The Employment of Negroes in the Federal Goverment,' March 1943. FEPC 408, NARG 228; and FEPC, *First Report*, 65.

110. 'The Employment of Negroes in Federal Government,' March 1943, FEPC 408, NARG 228; memorandum, June 23, 1945, OPA, D–4, NARG 188; memo., 'Negro Participation in the Work of OPA,' March 13, 1944, OPA, D–4, NARG 188.

111. Krislov, *The Negro in Federal Employment*, 31.

112. Weaver, *Negro Labor*, 78; National Urban League, 'Changes in the Occupational Status of Negroes, 1940–1950'; and War Manpower Commission, 'Utilization of Reserve Workers: Recently Reported Placements of Negroes in Skilled Occupations,' FEPC 407, Narg 228.

113. Dept of Labor, *Negroes in the United States: Their Employment and Economic Status*, Bulletin 1119, Washington, D.C., 1952, 13, 45; and Blood, *Negro Women War Workers*, 16.

114. Murray, *Negro Handbook, 1946–47*, 99; and Dept of Labor, *Negroes in the United States*, 43. See Appendix I, Table 1.

115. Department of Labor, *Negroes in the United States*, 25; and Frazier, *The Negro in the United States*, 615, 620.

116. Dept of Labor, Bureau of Labor Statistics, 'Annual Family and Occupational Earnings of Residents of Two Negro Housing Projects in Atlanta, 1937–44,' *Monthly Labor Review*, Vol. 61, 6, December 1945, 1070.

117. Weaver, 'Negro Labor Since 1929,' *Journal of Negro History*, XXXC, 1, January 1950, 29.

118. Committee on Discrimination in Employment, *The Negro Integrated*, 17.

119. Bernice Anita Reed, 'Accommodation between Negro and White Employees in a West Coast Aircraft Industry, 1942–44,' *Social Forces*, XXIV, 1, October 1947.

120. Jessie Parkhurst Guzman, ed., *Negro Yearbook: A Review of Events Affecting Negro Life, 1941–1946*, Tuskegee, Ala., 1947, 134; Walter White, *How Far the Promised Land?*, New York, 1956, 118; Maurice R. Davie, *Negroes in American Society*, New York, 1949, 128; Northrup, 'In the Unions,' *Survey Graphic* XXXVI, 1, January 1947.

121. National Urban League, 'A Summary Report of the Industrial Relations Laboratory: Performance of Negro Workers in Three Hundred War Plants,' New York, 1944. See too, Burleigh B. Gardener and David G. Moore, *Human Relations in Industry*, Chicago, 1950, 312.

122. Schuck, 'Eliminating Employer Discriminatory Hiring Practices,' 63–4; C. L. Golightly, 'Negro Employment Before the War and Now,' undated, FEPC 409, NARG 228.

123. Dept of Labor, *Negroes in the United States*, 15, 45. See Appendix II, Table 2.

124. Dept of Labor, *Negroes in the United States*, 24–5.

125. John Hope II, 'The Employment of Negroes in the United States by Major Occupation and Status,' *Journal of Negro Education*, XXII, 3, Summer 1953, 321.

126. Schuck, 'Eliminating Employer Discriminatory Hiring Practices,' 64; and Weaver, *Negro Labor*, 79.

127. Carl B. King and Howard W. Risher, Jr, 'The Negro in the Petroleum Industry,' and

Herbert R. Northrup, 'The Negro in the Rubber Tire Industry,' both in Northrup, et al., *Negro Employment in Basic Industry*, 410–12, 534–6.

128. Schuck, 'Eliminating Employer Discriminatory Hiring Practices,' 68–71; Weaver, *Negro Labor*, 92.

129. Northrup, 'The Negro in the Automobile Industry,' in *Negro Employment in Basic Industry*, 63–4.

130. National Urban League, 'Racial Aspects of Reconversion: A Memorandum Prepared for the President of the United States,' New York, August 27, 1945, mimeographed, FEPC 407, NARG 228; President's Committee on Fair Employment Practices, *Final Report*, 41; Lloyd H. Bailer, 'The Negro in the Labor Force of the United States,' *Journal of Negro Education*, XXII, 3, Summer 1953, 297.

131. Council for Democracy, *The Negro in America*, 12; Northrup, 'Will Negroes Get Jobs Now?', Public Affairs Committee, Pamphlet 110, New York, 1945; Walter P. Reuther, 'The Negro's Future,' *Opportunity*, XXIII, 4, Fall 1945.

132. Weaver, *Negro Labor*, 245.

Chapter 4: Wartime Migrations and Urban Conflict: The Disruptive Effects of War

1. Charles S. Johnson, 'The Impact of the War Upon Negro-White Relations in the United States,' 1947, Johnson Papers, 164, F4, Fisk University.

2. Reynolds Farley, 'The Urbanization of Negroes in the United States,' *Journal of Social History*, Vol. I, Spring 1968, 251–3; Gilbert Osofsky, *Harlem: The Making of a Ghetto, Negro New York, 1890–1930*, New York and Evanston, Ill., 1968, 17–24; Franklin, *From Slavery to Freedom*, 399.

3. US Dept of Labor, *Negroes in the United States: Their Employment and Economic Status*, Bulletin 1119, Washington, D.C., 1952, 315; Farley, 'The Urbanization of Negroes in the United States,' 245, 255.

4. Memo. Robert C. Weaver to Robert R. Taylor, Consultant, Defense Housing Co-ordinator, June 6, 1941, Housing and Home Finance Agency box 23, NARG 207. (Hereafter HHFA 23, NARG 207.) Weaver, reporting agents from Buffalo, N.Y. recruiting black steel molders in Chattanooga and Nashville, commented that 'The bidding by Northern plants had become so open that Nashville firms were protesting because their workers were being "lured" away.'

5. Lingeman, *Don't You Know There's A War On?*, 71; Weaver, *The Negro Ghetto*, 83; Dept of Labor, *Negroes in the United States*, 5.

6. Weaver, *The Negro Ghetto*, 84. Also see Morton Grodzins, *The Metropolitan Area as a Racial Problem*, Pittsburgh, 1960, 1–2. Farley, 'The Urbanization of Negroes in the United States,' 245.

7. Florence Murray, et al., *Negro Handbook, 1946–47*, New York, 1947, 25–6; Jessie Parkhurst Guzman, ed., *Negro Year Book: A Review of Events Affecting Negro Life, 1941–1946*, Tuskegee, Ala., 1947, 9. Constance McLaughlin Green, *The Secret City: A History of Race Relations in the Nation's Capital*, Princeton, N.J., 1967, 200.

8. Dept of Labor, *Negroes in the United States*, 5.

9. Wesley C. Calef and Howard J. Nelson, 'Distribution of Negro Population in the United States,' *Geographical Review*, Vol 46, 1, 1956, 95; Farley, 'The Urbanization of Negroes,' 255.

10. Dept of Labor, *Negroes in the United States*, 7.

11. Charles Maboio Barresi, 'Residential Invasion and Succession: A Case Study,' unpublished MA thesis, June 1959, SUNY at Buffalo, N.Y., 2; Weaver, *The Negro Ghetto*, 83.

12. Weaver, *The Negro Ghetto*, 49, 85–7; and Otis Dudley Duncan and Beverly Duncan, *The Negro Population of Chicago: A Study of Residential Succession*, Chicago, 1957, 4, 21.

13. Gunnar Myrdal, *An American Dilemma: The Negro Problem and Modern Democracy*, New York, 1944, 276–8; Richard Sterner, *The Negro's Share: A Study of Income, Consumption, Housing and Public Assistance*, New York, 1943, 166–70, 185–200.

14. Weaver, *The Negro Ghetto*, 4. Prior to the war, Weaver had been Assistant Adviser on Negro Affairs in the Dept of the Interior, then a member of the Public Works Administration, and later worked in the US Housing Authority. During the war he was a member of the War Production Board until 1943 when he joined the Negro Manpower Commission. On the development of segregated housing, see too, Spear and Osofsky, op. cit., and Karl Taeuber and Alma Taeuber, *Negroes in Cities: Residential Segration and Neighborhood Change*, Chicago, 1966, 4.

15. Myrdal, *An American Dilemma*, 622–7; Tom C. Clark and Philip B. Perlman, *Prejudice and Property: An Historic Brief Against Racial Covenants*, Washington, D.C., 1948, 11–13; and Clement E. Vose, *Caucasians Only: The Supreme Court, the NAACP and the Restrictive Covenant Cases*, Berkeley and Los Angeles, 1959, vii.

16. On the effects of segregation in housing see Myrdal, *An American Dilemma*, 375–6; Clark and Perlman, *Prejudice and Property*, 14–15; E. Franklin Frazier, *The Negro in the United States*, revised ed., New York, 1969, 634–6.

17 Myrdal, *An American Dilemma*, 350. The federal housing programs and their application to blacks are dealt with in *An American Dilemma*, 348–52; Sterner, *The Negro's Share*, op. cit.; Weaver, *The Negro Ghetto*, 69–75; and in Nathan Glazer and Davis McEntire, eds., *Studies in Housing and Minority Groups*, Berkeley and Los Angeles, 1960.

18. Housing and Home Finance Agency, *Housing of the Non-white Population: 1940 to 1947*, Washington, D.C., 1948, 1.

19. Quoted in *Baltimore Afro-American*, May 23, 1942.

20. 'Negro Share of Priority War Housing—Private and Public, as of December 31, 1944,' Office of Principal Housing Analyst, May 1, 1945, HHFA 91, NARG 207; and HHFA, *Housing of the Non-white Population*, op. cit.

21. Memo. C. F. Palmer, Office of Emergency Management, Division of Defense Housing Co-ordination, to all personnel, January 28, 1941, HHFA 23, NARG 207.

22. Memo. W. P. Seaver, Assistant Administrator for Development, Federal Works Agency, to all Regional Directors, May 9, 1941, 'Defense Housing,' OASW 199, NARG 107.

23. Davis McEntire, *Residence and Race: Final and Comprehensive Report to the Commission on Race and Housing*, Berkeley and Los Angeles, 1960, 318–20; and Weaver, *The Negro Ghetto*, 141–3.

24. 'Negro Share of Priority War Housing—Private and Public,' op. cit.; and Press Release, Office of Emergency Management, Division of Defense Housing Co-ordination, October 28, 1941, 'Defense Housing,' OASW 199, NARG 107.

25. These figures are from 'Negro Share of Priority War Housing,' and Weaver, *The Negro Ghetto*, 144, 162.

26. Weaver, *The Negro Ghetto*, 180.

27. B. T. McGraw, 'Wartime Employment, Migration, and Housing of Negroes in the United States, 1941–44,' HHFA 91, NARG 207.

28. 'A Crucial Problem in Race Relations—Housing: Negro Housing Conditions in Five Cities of the North, 1940–45,' *Race Relations: A Monthly Summary of Events and Trends*, IV, 4, November 1946, 117; and Weaver, *The Negro Ghetto*, viii.

29. Donald O. Cowgill, 'Trends in Residential Segregation of Non-whites in American Cities, 1940–1950,' *American Sociological Review*, XXI, 1, February 1956; Weaver, 'Non-white Population Movements and Urban Ghettos,' *Phylon*, XX, 3, 1959; HHFA, *Housing of the Non-white Population*, 10–13.

30. Cowgill, 'Trends in Residential Segregation,' 46; Weaver, *Hemmed In: ABCs of Race Restrictive Housing Covenants*, American Council on Race Relations, Chicago, 1945; and Charles Abrams, *Race Bias in Housing*, New York, 1947. Some of the limitations of

Cowgill's findings are pointed out by Wendell Bell, 'Comments on Cowgill's "Trends in Residential Segregation of Non-whites",' *American Sociological Review*, XXII, April 1957, 221–2. The main criticism is in the size of the areas used by Cowgill, and the important conclusion drawn is that there was *more* segregation than Cowgill's figures would have us believe.

31. Weaver, 'The Relative Status of the Housing of Negroes in the United States,' *Journal of Negro Education*, XXII, 3, Summer 1953; and Davis McEntire, *Residence and Race*, 39–40.

32. Joseph James, 'San Francisco,' and Charles Bratt, 'Los Angeles,' both in *Journal of Educational Sociology*, XIX, 3, November 1945.

33. Charles S. Johnson, et al., *The Negro War Worker in San Francisco: A Local Self-survey*, San Francisco, 1944, 18, 80.

34. James, 'San Francisco,' 170; Johnson, *The Negro War Worker in San Francisco*, 20; Clark and Perlman, *Prejudice and Property*, 15. 'Los Angeles Negro Housing,' HHFA 91, NARG 207; Guzman, *Negro Year Book, 1941–1946*, 341; Weaver, *The Negro Ghetto*, 84.

35. 'Housing for Negro Occupancy in Seattle and Portland,' March 21, 1945, HHFA 91, NARG 207; Robert W. O'Brien, 'Seattle,' *Journal of Educational Sociology*, XIX, 3, November 1945; Weaver, *The Negro Ghetto*, 188–9, 198.

36. Johnson, *The Negro War Worker in San Francisco*, 24–7.

37. Dorothy W. Baruch, *Glass House of Prejudice*, New York, 1946, 27–36. Agnes E. Meyer, *Journey Through Chaos*, New York, 1944, 324.

38. National Committee on Segregation in the Nation's Capital, *Segregation in Washington*, Chicago, 1948, 41; Meyer, *Journey Through Chaos*, 330.

39. Buffalo *Courier Express*, August 8, 1940, November 1, 1942, February 14, 1943; Weaver, *Negro Labor*, 111–12.

40. See correspondence in OASW 199, 'Defense Housing,' NARG 107; and William L. Evans, *Race Fear and Housing in a Typical American Community*, National Urban League, New York, 1946.

41. Address before CIC by Robert R. Taylor, December 1, 1941, OASW 199, NARG 107.

42. Granger to Rev. John A. Duffy, Bishop, Diocese of Buffalo, October 22, 1941; William H. Hastie to Professor T. W. Turner, November 24, 1941; memo., Hastie to Taylor, December 3, 1941, all in OASW 199. Also letters in HHFA 23, NARG 207.

43. Evans, 'Federal Housing Brings Residential Segregation to Buffalo,' *Opportunity*, XX, 4, April 1942; Weaver, *The Negro Ghetto*, 95.

44. Weaver, *The Negro Ghetto*, 207.

45. Clark and Perlman, *Prejudice and Property*, 14; Abrams, *Race Bias in Housing*, 12; Weaver, *The Negro Ghetto*, 95; Chicago Mayor's Commission on Human Relations, *Human Relations in Chicago: Report for Year 1946*, Chicago 1946, 61–2.

46. Avarh E. Strickland, *History of the Chicago Urban League*, Urbana, Ill., 1966, 157–8; Mayor's Commission, *Race Relations in Chicago*, 25–6; Guzman, *Negro Yearbook, 1941–46*, 341.

47. *Race Relations in Chicago*, 40.

48. 'The Pattern of Race Riots Involving Negro Soldiers,' *Race Relations: A Summary of Events and Trends*, 1–2, August–September 1944; Harvard Sitkoff, 'Racial Militancy and Interracial Violence in the Second World War,' *Journal of American History*, LVIII, 3, December 1971; Guzman, *Negro Year Book, 1941–46*, Chapter X.

49. 'A Crucial Problem in Race Relations: Negro Housing Conditions in Five Cities of the North, 1940–1945,' *Race Relations: A Monthly Summary*, 4, November 1946; Earl Louis Brown, *Why Race Riots? Lessons from Detroit*, Public Affairs Pamphlet 87, New York, 1944, 14–16; Louis E. Martin, 'Detroit,' *Journal of Educational Sociology*, XVII, 5, January 1944; memo. C. E. Rhetts to Attorney General Biddle, July 12, 1943, 93:12 FDRL.

50. Bucklin Moon, *The High Cost of Prejudice*, New York, 1947, 43–5; Weaver, *The Negro*

Ghetto, 92–4; Walter White and Thurgood Marshall, 'What Caused the Detroit Riots?' in Thomas R. Frazier ed., *Afro-American History: Primary Sources*, New York, 1971, 173–81.

51. Brown, *Why Race Riots?*, 19; Joseph D. Keenan, Vice Chairman, Labor Production (WPB) to J. Bron Philipson, Program Supervisor, NHA, August 7, 1943, HHFA 91, NARG 207.

52. Brown, *Why Race Riots?*, 6–8; Walter White, *A Man Called White*, New York, 1948, 224–5; Thomas Sancton, 'The Race Riots,' *New Republic*, July 5, 1943, 130.

53. *Opportunity*, XX, 5, May 1942. Also see Sitkoff, 'The Detroit Race Riot of 1943,' *Michigan History*, LIII, 3, 1969, 188.

54. Detailed accounts of the riot are provided in Alfred McClung Lee and Norman Humphrey, *Race Riot*, New York 1943; Robert Shogan and Tom Craig, *The Detroit Race Riot: A Study in Violence*, New York, 1964.

55. The police were severely criticized by Thurgood Marshall, a black lawyer and representative of the NAACP, in 'The Gestapo in Detroit,' *The Crisis*, August 1943; see too *Pittsburgh Courier*, July 3, 1943.

56. Telegram, Kelly to Roosevelt, June 22, 1943, 93:12 FDRL; Brig. Gen. William E. Guthner to Lt. Col. F. W. Reese, Provost Marshal General's Office, August 2, 1943, 'Detroit Riot,' War Dept, NARG 389. The delay in calling for assistance is dealt with in Sitkoff, 'The Detroit Race Riot,' 191–4, and in White, *A Man Called White*, 226.

57. Military Log, 'Detroit Riot,' War Dept, NARG 389. The War Department had been prepared for such an eventuality for a number of years. A plan existed which stated in detail the action to be taken in case of domestic disorders. For some reason this was known as 'Emergency Plan White.' See, Acting Sec. of War to Roosevelt, August 19, 1943, 93:12 FDRL.

58. Congressman Vito Marcantonio to Roosevelt, June 26, 1943, 93:12 FDRL.

59. LaGuardia to Roosevelt, June 27, 1943, 93:12 FDRL; and White, *A Man Called White*, 230.

60. *Baltimore Afro-American* and *Chicago Defender*, August 7, 1943; *New York Times*, August 2, 1943; and White, *A Man Called White*, 234–5.

61. 'The Ballad of Margie Polite' in *One Way Ticket*, New York, 1949, 75–8. Margie Polite was one of the principal participants in the original scuffle. Also see the editorial in *The Crisis*, September 1943, on the feelings of the riot participants.

62. White, *A Man Called White*, 235; *New York Times*, August 3, 1943.

63. White, *A Man Called White*, 238–9; *New York Times*, August 3, 1943; Langston Hughes, *Fight for Freedom: The Story of the NAACP*, New York, 1962, 97.

64. *New York Times Review*, August 8, 1943; Arthur I. Waskow, *From Race Riot to Sit-in: 1919 and the 1960s*, New York, 1967, 220.

65. *New York Times*, August 3, 1943, 10.

66. Newspaper reports and the findings of the Governor's committee are included in the War Dept files on the riot, NARG 389. See too, Sitkoff, 'The Detroit Race Riot,' 199–204, and Brown, *Why Race Riots?*, 22–3.

67. Telegram, White to Roosevelt, June 21, 1943; Program of Action on Nation-wide Race Riots Adopted by Conference of National Organizations, and many other letters blamed seditionist activity, all in 93:12 FDRL.

68. In a letter to Roosevelt, July 15, 1943, 93:12 FDRL. See also, Sitkoff, 'The Detroit Race Riot,' 204.

69. Roi Ottley, *Black Odyssey: The Story of the Negro in America*, London, 1949, 259; Weaver, *The Negro Ghetto*, 186–7; White, *A Man Called White*, 240; Warren M. Banner, 'New York,' *Journal of Educational Sociology*, XVII, 5, January 1944, 272–9.

70. Coleman Woodbury, NHA, to Jonathan Daniels, Admin. Assistant to the President, August 12, 1943; and Joseph D. Keenan, WPB, to J. Bron Philipson, Program Supervisor, NHA, August 7, 1943, both in HHFA 91, NARG 207.

71. Biddle to Roosevelt, July 15, 1943, following report from C. E. Rhetts to Biddle, July 12, 1943, 93:12 FDRL.
72. Jonathan Daniels was one of four aides appointed to deal with race relations problems and in preference to Biddle's suggestions, Daniels was to correlate all information on race relations. What he was to do afterwards is not clear. See Daniels to John B. Blandford, July 28, 1943, HHFA 91, NARG 207, and letters in 93:12 FDRL. Also Sitkoff, 'The Detroit Race Riot,' 204–5.
73. Allen D. Grimshaw, 'Urban Racial Violence in the United States: Changing Ecological Considerations,' *American Journal of Sociology*, LXVI, 2, September 1968.
74. White, *A Man Called White*, 235.
75. Bernard F. Robinson, 'War and Race Conflicts in the United States,' *Phylon*, IV, 4, 1943; Stanley Lieberson and Arnold R. Silverman, 'The Precipitants and Underlying Conditions of Race Riots,' *American Sociological Review*, XXX, 6, December 1965.
76. Sitkoff, 'Racial Militancy and Interracial Violence,' 670; Brown, *Why Race Riots?*, 6–16. It is worth bearing in mind that both riots began on hot, humid Sundays, and in Detroit started among crowds in a cramped recreational area. It was a situation in which tempers were already frayed.
77. Details of report in War Dept files NARG 389.
78. White and Marshall, 'What Caused the Detroit Riots?,' 178–9.
79. See Sitkoff, 'The Detroit Race Riot,' 189; Lee and Humphrey, *Race Riot*, passim; Lingeman, *Don't You Know There's A War On?*, 350. I should point out that there were cases of white soldiers protecting blacks in Detroit, see photographs in War Dept file, NARG 389.
80. Kenneth B. Clark and James Barker, 'The Zoot Effect in Personality: A Race Riot Participant,' *Journal of Abnormal and Social Psychology*, Vol 40, 1945.
81. Surprisingly, some black commentators disagreed with this view. The *Pittsburgh Courier*, August, 14, 1943, referred to the Harlem riot as 'an orgy of vandalism without reason, without excuse and without defense.' Adam Clayton Powell, Sr called the rioters hoodlums and thieves, in *Riots and Ruins*, New York, 1945, 49–51.
82. Weaver, *The Negro Ghetto*, 90.
83. Myrdal, *An American Dilemma*, 375–6.
84. Mary Gover, 'Negro Mortality: Course of Mortality from Specific Causes, 1920–44,' *Public Health Reports*, Vol 63, 7, February 13, 1948, 212; Murray, *Negro Hand Book, 1946–47*, 71.
85. Dept of Labor, *Negroes in the United States: Their Employment and Economic Status*, Bulletin 1119, Washington, D.C., 1952, 2–3; E. H. Allen, 'Extending Health Horizons Among Negroes,' *Opportunity*, XXIV, 1, January–March, 1946.
86. Dorothy Dickins, 'Food Patterns of White and Negro Families, 1936–1948,' *Social Forces*, XXVII, 4 May 1949; Gover, 'Negro Mortality,' 212; Guzman, *Negro Yearbook, 1952*, 161.
87. Murray, *Negro Hand Book, 1946–47*, 71; Guzman, *Negro Year Book, 1941–46*, 320–2. See Appendix II. Philip F. Williams, 'Maternal Welfare and the Negro,' *Journal of the American Medical Association*, Vol 132, II, November 16, 1946, 611; Murray, *Negro Hand Book, 1946–47*, 71.
88. *Baltimore Afro-American*, March 31, 1945; William Montague Cobb, *Medical Care and the Plight of the Negro*, NAACP, New York 1947, 5.
89. Jean Byers, *A Study of the Negro in Military Service*, Dept of Defense, Washington, D.C., 1947, mimeographed copy in Moorland Collection, Howard University, 14–15. Various letters from Southern congressmen in Selective Service System 220, NARG 147.
90. Guzman, *Negro Yearbook, 1941–46*, 331; Michael M. Davis and Hugh H. Smythe, 'Providing Adequate Health Service to Negroes,' *Journal of Negro Education*, Vol 18, 1949, 308.

91. Cobb, *Medical Care and the Plight of the Negro*, 7, 12–13; Guzman, *Negro Year Book, 1952*, 163.

92. James Worsham Barksdale, *A Comparative Study of Contemporary White and Negro Standards in Health, Education and Welfare, Charlottesville, Virginia*, Phelps-Stokes Fellowship Paper, University of Virginia, 1949, 30; Davis and Smythe, 'Providing Adequate Health Service to Negroes,' 308.

93. Mabel Keaton Staupers, *No Time for Prejudice: A Story of the Integration of Negroes in Nursing in the United States*, New York, 1961, 97; Kathryn Blood, *Negro Women War Workers*, Dept of Labor, Bulletin 205, Washington, D.C., 1945, 13; Myrdal, *An American Dilemma*, 1367.

94. Staupers, *No Time for Prejudice*, 63, 119; Walter White, *How Far The Promised Land?*, New York, 1956, 157.

95. White, *How Far The Promised Land?*, 157.

96. Michael M. Davis, 'What Color is Health?,' *Survey Graphic*, XXXVI, 1, January 1947, 85–6; Davis and Smythe, 'Providing Adequate Health Service to Negroes,' 316.

97. Frazier, *The Negro in the United States*, 425–40; Guzman, *Negro Year Book, 1941–46*, 54–61; Murray, *Negro Handbook, 1942*, 109. The 18 states were Alabama, Arkansas, Delaware, District of Columbia, Florida, Georgia, Kentucky, Louisiana, Maryland, Mississippi, Missouri, N Carolina, Oklahoma, S Carolina, Tennessee, Texas, Virginia, West Virginia.

98. Myrdal, *An American Dilemma*, 343–4. The studies included Doxey A. Wilkerson, *Special Problems of Negro Education*, Washington, D.C., 1939; Advisory Committee on Education, *The Federal Government and Education*, Washington, D.C., 1938; US Office of Education, *National Survey of the Higher Education of Negroes*, Washington, D.C., 1942. See Myrdal, *An American Dilemma*, 1270–1; and Frazier, *The Negro in the United States*, 480–1.

99. Frazier, *The Negro in the United States*, 436–7; Harry S. Ashmore, *The Negro and the Schools*, Chapel Hill, N.C., 1954, 28–9; Virgil A. Clift, et al., *Negro Education in America: Its Adequacy, Problems and Needs*, New York, 1962, 53; Henry Allen Bullock, *A History of Negro Education in the South: From 1619 to the Present*, Cambridge, Mass., 1967, 216–17.

100. Frazier, *The Negro in the United States*, 446; see also Malcolm S. MacLean and R. O'Hara Lanier, 'Negroes, Education and the War,' *Educational Record*, XXIII, 1, January 1942, for comments on the Afro-American as 'a huge and largely untapped resource of manpower, brain power, and service power.'

101. Director of Selective Service, *Selective Service in Wartime: Second Report*, Washington, D.C., 1943, 289.

102. American Teachers' Association, *The Black and White of Rejections for Military Service: A Study of Rejections for Selective Service Registrants by Race, On Account of Educational and Mental Deficiencies*, Montgomery, Ala., 1944, 2–6.

103. American Teachers' Association, *The Black and White of Rejections for Military Service*, 50–1; Caliver, *Postwar Education of Negroes: Educational Implications of Army Data and Experiences of Negro Veterans and War Workers*, Washington, D.C., 1945, 44–55, in Office of Education, 40, NARG 12.

104. Representative Norvell of Arkansas, October 2, 1942, Senator Overton, Louisiana, August 10, 1942, and letter from Edgar Hoover, head of FBI, to Director of Selective Service Hershey, May 28, 1943, all in Selective Service 170, NARG 147. Also see Frazier, *The Negro in the United States*, 447.

105. Byers, *A Study of the Negro in Military Service*, 36–8.

106. Myrdal, *An American Dilemma*, 419; Caliver, *Postwar Education of Negroes*, 2–7.

107. Memo., John W. Studebaker, Commissioner, Office of Education, to Paul V. McNutt, Chairman, War Manpower Commission, September 1942, and Lawrence W. Carmer, Executive Secretary, FEPC, to Studebaker, July 3, 1942, both in Office of Education 40, NARG 12.

108. Weaver to Studebaker, July 18, 1940, OE 40, NARG 12. War Manpower Commission, *Utilization of Reserve Workers: Recently Reported Placements of Negroes in Skilled Occupations*, Washington, D.C., 1944, in FEPC 407, NARG 228; Caliver, 'Office of Education Services for Negroes,' *Education for Victory*, February 20, 1945, in OE 40, NARG 12.

109. Ashmore, *The Negro and the Schools*, 48; Frazier, *The Negro in the United States*, 477; *Negro Colleges in Wartime*, Office of War Information, 1943, National Archives NA 208–7–PPC; Felton G. Clark, 'Negro Higher Education and Some Fundamental Issues Raised by World War II,' *Journal of Negro Education*, XI, 3, July 1942; Ambrose Caliver, 'Certain Significant Developments in the Education of Negroes During the Past Generation,' *Journal of negro History*, XXXV, 2, April 1950.

110. 'Statistics of the Education of Negroes, 1945–46,' Office of Education Statistical Circular, No. 239, March 1948, OE 40, NARG 12; Frazier, *The Negro in the United States*, 447–9.

111. Guzman, *Negro Yearbook, 1941–46*, 71; Dept of Labor, *Negroes in the United States*, 9–10.

112. 'Statistics of the Education of Negroes, 1945–46'; Frazier, *The Negro in the United States*, 447.

113. Papers on Project for Adult Education of Negroes and articles in *School Life*, October 1946, and November 1948, all in OE 40, NARG 12.

114. 'Negro Higher Education and the War', *Journal of Negro Education*, XI, 3, July 1942. This entire volume is devoted to Negro education and the war, and nearly all of the articles concentrate on what will have to be done in the future.

Chapter 5: Blacks in Film, Music and Literature during World War II

1. Lewis Gannet, 'Books,' and Bosley Crowther, 'The Movies,' both in Jack Goodman, ed., *While You Were Gone: A Report on Wartime Life in the United States*, New York, 1946; Richard R. Lingeman, *Don't You Know There's A War On? The American Home Front 1941–1945*, New York, 1970, 175–244.

2. George Noble, 'The Negro in Hollywood,' *Sight and Sound*, Spring 1939, 14.

3. John T. McMann and Louis Kronenberger, 'Motion Pictures, the Theater, and Race Relations,' *Annals of the American Academy of Political and Social Science*, Vol 224, March 1946, 152.

4. Dorothy B. Jones, 'The Hollywood War Film: 1942–1944,' *Hollywood Quarterly*, I, 1, October 1945. Charles Higham and Joel Greenberg, *Hollywood in the Forties*, New York, 1968.

5. Lingeman, *Don't You Know There's A War On?*, 191–2, 201.

6. Walter White, *A Man Called White*, New York 1948, 200–2; *Proceedings of the Writers' Congress, Los Angeles 1943*, Berkeley and Los Angeles, 1944, 14–18, 495–501; *Pittsburgh Courier*, August 8, 1942.

7. *New York Times*, July 24, 1968; Peter Noble, *The Negro in Films*, London, 1949, 147–57.

8. Noble, *The Negro in Films*, 221–2; White, *A Man Called White*, 231–2; Leon H. Hardwick, 'Motion Pictures,' in Florence Murray, ed., *The Negro Handbook, 1946–47*, New York, 1947, 262.

9. Hardwick, 'Negro Stereotypes on the Screen,' *Hollywood Quarterly*, I, 2, January 1946, 234.

10. Noble, *The Negro in Films*, 216–17; *Baltimore Afro-American*, August 29, 1942; *Pittsburgh Courier*, August 29, 1942.

11. John Howard Lawson, *Film: The Creative Process*, New York, 1964, 141–2. Noble, *The Negroes in Films*, 198; Cripps, 'Movies in the Ghetto, BP,' 22; George E. Norford, 'The Future in Films,' *Journal of Negro Education*, XXVI, 3, July–September, 1948, 108.

12. Ethel Waters, *His Eye is on the Sparrow: An Autobiography*, London 1951, 242; Hardwick, 'Negro Stereotypes on the Screen,' 236.

13. V. J. Jerome, *The Negro in Hollywood Films*, New York, 1950, 29–34; Peter Noble, 'Hollywood Thinks Again About the Negro,' *Picture Post*, February 11, 1950, 25; Richard Winnington, 'Negro Films,' *Sight and Sound*, February 1950; Thomas R. Cripps, 'The Death of Rastus: Negroes in American Films Since 1945,' *Phylon*, XXVII, 3, 1967, 270.

14. Jerome, *The Negro in Hollywood Films*, 24; Winnington, 'Negro Films,' 27–31; Noble, 'Hollywood Thinks Again About the Negro,' 24.

15. Cripps, 'The Death of Rastus,' 270; Jerome, *The Negro in Hollywood Films*, 37–9; Ralph Ellison, 'Shadow and Act,' *The Reporter*, December 6, 1949, included in the collection of essays, *Shadow and Act*, New York, 1966 ed., 264–71.

16. *Time*, July 18, 1949; Jerome, *The Negro in Hollywood Films*, 42–3.

17. Ellison, 'Shadow and Act,' in *Shadow and Act*, 267.

18. Hardwick, 'Negro Stereotypes on the Screen,' 235; Noble, *The Negro in Films*, 193; Cripps, 'The Death of Rastus,' 272; George E. Norford, 'The Future in Films,' *Journal of Negro Education*, XXVI, 3, July–September 1948, 109.

19. Noble, *The Negro in Films*, 191–2; McMann and Kronenberger, 'Motion Pictures, the Theater and Race Relations,' 154; Herbert Margolis, 'The Hollywood Scene: The American Minority Problem,' *The Penguin Film Review*, 5, 1948, 84.

20. *The Negro Soldier*, War Dept, 1944, NA 111-OF-51, National Archives; Dorothy Newman, 'A World to Live in "The Negro Soldier",' *New York Post*, 1944.

21. *Baltimore Afro-American*, January 29, 1946; *Ebony*, July 1946. Material and information provided by Professor Dan Leab.

22. *Teamwork*, War Dept, Orientation film 14, 1946, NA 111-OF-14, National Archives.

23. *Negro Colleges in Wartime*, Office of War Information 1943, NA 208-7-PPC, National Archives.

24. *Henry Browne, Farmer*, Dept of Agriculture-United Films 1943, NA 59. 53, National Archives.

25. 'Engineers Stop That Tank,' Paramount, Sherman Grinberg Film Library, Can C.3536; 'Uncle Sam Gets Negro Fliers,' Hearst Metrotrone News, Can 1622; 'Commissioning US Sub Chaser PC 1264,' National Archives NA 1-1421; 'Harlem Riots,' 20th Century Fox Movietone News Library.

26. *One Tenth of Our Nation*, American Film Center, 1940, in film department Museum of Modern Art, New York.

27. William J. Sloan, 'The Documentary Film and the Negro: the Evolution of the Integration Film,' *Journal of the Society of Cinematologists*, Vol 5, 1965, 66–9.

28. For the musical background to the blues see Samuel B. Charters, *The Country Blues*, London, 1960; Charles Keil, *Urban Blues*, Chicago and London, 1966; Leroi Jones, *Blues People: Negro Music in White America*, New York, 1963 (1970 edition quoted in text); Richard Middleton, *Pop Music and the Blues: A Study of the Relationship and Its Significance*, London, 1972; Paul Oliver, *Savannah Syncopators: African Retentions in the Blues*, London, 1970.

29. Paul Oliver, *The Story of the Blues*, London, 1969, 106; Jones, *Blues People*, 120.

30. Paul Oliver, *Blues Fell This Morning*, London, 1960, 43, 249–57; Mike Leadbitter and Neil Slaven, *Blues Records, January 1943 to December 1966*, London, 1968, 21, 82, 360.

31. 'Pearl Harbor Blues' quoted in Oliver, *Blues Fell This Morning*, 250; 'Are You Ready' quoted in Jones, *Blues People*, 178.

32. Eileen Southern, *The Music of Black Americans: A History*, New York, 1971, 459.

33. 'Defense Factory Blues' and 'Uncle Sam Says' quoted in Marjorie E. Greene, 'Josh White Starts Them Listening,' *Opportunity*, XXII, 3, July–September 1944, 114.

34. 'Black, Brown and White,' quoted in William Broonzy and Yannick Bruynoghe, *Big Bill Blues; William Broonzy's Story*, London, 1955, 56–7. 'Baby Remember Me,' quoted in Oliver, *Blues Fell This Morning*, 254–5.

35. Don Heckman, 'Black Music and White America,' in John F. Szwed, ed., *Black America*,

New York and London, 1970, 168; Charlie Gillet, *The Sound of the City: the Rise of Rock and Roll*, London, 1970, 4, 135–7; Lingeman, *Don't You Know There's A War On?*, 223.

36. Oliver, *The Story of the Blues*, 141; Gillet, *The Sound of the City*, 135–7, 91–104; Southern, *The Music of Black Americans*, 497.

37. Jones, *Blues People*, 171.

38. Jones, *Blues People*, 188–99; A. B. Spellman, 'Revolution in Sound' in *Ebony, The Black Revolution*, Chicago, 1970, 86–7; Heckman, 'Black Music and White America,' 168; Frank Kofsky, 'The Jazz Tradition: Black Music and Its White Critics,' *Journal of Black Studies*, I, 4, 1971, 417–29.

39. *The Autobiography of Malcolm X*, Harmondsworth, Middlesex, 1968 ed., 135; Jones, *Blues People*, 190–1. Also see photograph in Richard Wright, *12 Million Black Voices: A Folk History of the Negro in the United States*, New York, 1941, 129.

40. *Autobiography of Malcolm X*, 140; Gillet, *The Sound of the City*, 183–4.

41. Kenneth B. Clark and James Barker, 'The Zoot Effect in Personality: A Race Riot Participant,' *Journal of Abnormal and Social Psychology*, Vol. 40, 1945.

42. Richard Wright, *White Man, Listen!*, New York, 1964 ed., 103.

43. Robert Bone, *The Negro Novel in America*, New Haven, Conn., 1966, 156–7; Carl Milton Hughes, *The Negro Novelist: A Discussion of the Writings of American Negro Novelists, 1940–1950*, New York, 1970 ed., 20; Margaret Just Butcher, *The Negro in American Culture*, New York, 1956, 176–81.

44. James Baldwin, 'Everybody's Protest Novel' (1949) and 'Many Thousands Gone' (1951), both included in *Notes of a Native Son*, London, 1965. Also see 'Alas, Poor Richard' in *Nobody Knows My Name*, London, 1965.

45. Ira Dea Reid, 'The Literature of Race and Culture,' *Phylon*, V, 4, 1944.

46. The literature of the 1920s and 1930s is dealt with in Nathan Irvin Huggins, *Harlem Renaissance*, New York, 1971; Hugh M. Gloster, *Negro Voices in American Fiction*, New York, 1965; Butcher, *The Negro in American Culture*; Nick Aaron Ford, *The Contemporary Negro Novel*, Boston, Mass., 1936. On Hughes, see James A. Emanuel, *Langston Hughes*, New York, 1967.

47. Gloster, *Negro Voices in American Fiction*, 208.

48. Richard Wright, *Uncle Tom's Children* (originally published individually 1936, 1937, 1938), New York, 1940; *Native Son*, New York, 1940. See Robert Bone, *Richard Wright*, University of Minnesota Pamphlets on American Writers, No. 74, Minneapolis, 1969.

49. 'The Way It Is', originally in *New Masses*, October 20, 1942, included in *Shadow and Act*, 272–81. The riot in *Invisible Man*, Harmondsworth, Mdx, 1972 ed., 430–56, is said to be the one in 1943, although it could equally well be that of 1935.

50. 'Harlem is Nowhere' (1948), in *Shadow and Act*, 283.

51. 'Notes of a Native Son,' *Harper's Magazine*, November 1955, included in *Notes of a Native Son*, London, 1965 ed., 82, 84. See too Fern Major Eckman, *The Furious Passage of James Baldwin*, London, 1968, 94–5.

52. Ann Petry, 'In Darkness and Confusion,' in Edwin Seaver, ed., *Cross Section 1947: A Collection of New American Writing*, New York, 1947.

53. Baldwin, 'Notes of a Native Son,' 92.

54. Alexander Saxton, *Bright Web in the Darkness*, Berlin, 1959, 263.

55. Chester Himes, *If He Hollers Let Him Go*, Garden City, N.Y., 1945. Hughes, *The Negro Novelist*, 206–11.

56. *If He Hollers Let Him Go*, 45–6.

57. *If He Hollers Let Him Go*, 139.

58. Chester Himes, 'So Softly Smiling,' *The Crisis*, October 1943. His 'Two Soldiers' in *The Crisis*, January 1943 had a more purely racial theme.

59. William Gardner Smith, *The Last of the Conquerors*, London 1949. Alain Locke, 'Dawn Patrol: A Review of the Literature of the Negro for 1948,' *Phylon* X, 1, 1949, and Hughes, *The Negro Novelist*, 230–2.

60. Avery E. Kolb, *Jigger Witchet's War*, New York, 1959.
61. Nevil Shute, *The Chequer Board*, London 1947, 66; Walter White, *A Rising Wind*, Garden City, N.Y., 1945, 11.
62. John Oliver Killens, *And Then We Heard The Thunder*, New York, 1962, 1971 edition quoted in text; Franklin, *From Slavery to Freedom*, 516. For a less favorable opinion see Charles E. Silberman, *Crisis in Black and White*, London, 1965, 61–3.
62. *And Then We Heard The Thunder*, 497.
64. *And Then We Heard The Thunder*, 46, 68.
65. *The Foxes of Harrow*, New York, 1946; and *The Vixens*, New York, 1948.
66. *Knock on Any Door*, New York, 1947.
67. Butcher, *The Negro in American Culture*, 176; Petry, *The Street*, Boston, Mass., 1946.
68. *Country Place*, Boston, Mass., 1947.
69. Butcher, *The Negro in American Culture*, 176.
70. Howard Fast, *Freedom Road*, London, 1946.
71. Hodding Carter, *The Winds of Fear*, London, 1945, 14, 71.
72. James Gould Cozzens, *Guard of Honour*, London, 1949, 337.
73. Ross Macdonald, *Trouble Follows Me*, New York, 1972 ed., 52.
74. Lillian Smith, *Strange Fruit*, New York, 1944, 302; Lingeman, *Don't You Know There's A War On?*, 273; Gannet, 'Books,' in Goodman, ed., *While You Were Gone*, 458.
75. Mabel Roane, 'The Broadway Theater,' in Murray, ed., *Negro Handbook, 1946–47*, 251; John Lovell, Jr, 'Roundup: The Negro in the American Theater, 1940–47,' *The Crisis*, July 1947; Miles M. Jefferson, 'The Negro on Broadway, 1945–46,' *Phylon*, VIII, 2, 1946; Doris E. Abramson, *Negro Playwrights in the American Theater, 1925–1959*, New York, 1969, 91–5.
76. Witter Bynner, 'Defeat,' in *Take Away the Darkness*, New York, 1947, 12.
77. 'Draftee's Prayer,' *Baltimore Afro-American*, January 16, 1943.
78. Owen Dodson, 'The Decision,' in *Powerful Long Ladder*, New York, 1947, 96. Also see 'Open Letter' and 'Conversation on V,' 103, 91.
79. Alfred A. Duckett, 'Sonnet,' in Langston Hughes and Arna Bontemps, eds., *The Poetry of the Negro, 1746–1949*, Garden City, N.Y., 1951, 202; Allen E. Woodall, 'Questions,' *Phylon*, V, 4, 1944, 315.
80. Myron O'Higgins, 'Sunset Horn,' in *The Poetry of the Negro*, 175.
81. Katie Robinson, 'The Colored Boy,' *Black Worker*, July 1943.
82. 'How About It Dixie?,' *New Masses*, Vol 45, 3, October 20, 1942; 'Roland Hayes Beaten,' in *One Way Ticket*, New York, 1949, 86. See Emanuel, *Langston Hughes*, 40–1.
83. 'World War II' and 'Casualty' in Hughes, *Selected Poems*, New York, 1957, 255, 259.
84. 'Peace,' in Hughes, *The Panther and the Lash: Poems of Our Times*, New York, 1971, 51–60.
85. Butcher, *The Negro in American Culture*, 138.
86. Jones, *Blues People*, 210.

Chapter 6: The Psychological Impact of War: Black Attitudes and the White Response

1. *Chicago Defender*, February 28, 1942 and March 14, 1942; *Pittsburgh Courier*, February 7, 1942 and April 18, 1942; Ralph N. Davis, 'The Negro Newspapers and the War,' *Sociology and Social Research*, XXVII, May–June 1943; and Lester M. Jones, 'The Editorial Policy of Negro Newspapers of 1917–18 as Compared with that of 1941–42,' *Journal of Negro History*, XXIX, January 1944.
2. *Pittsburgh Courier*, March 28, 1942, August 8, 1942; Ottley, *New World A'Coming*, New York, 1969 ed., 287.
3. *Pittsburgh Courier*, December 13, 1941. *The Crisis*, January 1942. See too, *Opportunity*, XX, 1, January 1942 for the view of the more conservative National Urban League.

4. Lee Finkle, 'The Conservative Aims of Black Rhetoric: Black Protest During World War II,' *Journal of American History*, LX, 3, December 1973.

5. R. A. Schermerhorn, *These Our People*, Boston, Mass., 1949, 167; *Pittsburgh Courier*, October 24, 1942. Among the other black writers who spoke of a new militancy were Ellen Tarry, *The Third Door*, London, 1956, 176; H. C. Brearley, 'The Negro's New Belligerency,' *Phylon*, V, 4, 1944; Horace R. Cayton, 'The Negro's Challenge,' *The Nation*, July 3, 1943; Kenneth B. Clark, 'Morale of the Negro on the Home Front: World Wars I and II,' *Journal of Negro Education*, XII, 3, Summer 1943.

6. Office of Facts and Figures, *The Negro Looks at the War: Attitudes of New York Negroes Toward Discrimination Against Negroes and a Comparison of Negro and Poor White Attitudes Toward War-related Issues*, n.p., 1942, in Schomburg Collection.

7. Office of War Information, Survey of Intelligence Materials, Supplement to Survey No. 25, 'Negroes in a Democracy at War,' 1942, OASW 226, NARG 107.

8. Cayton and Drake, *Black Metropolis*, 748.

9. *Opportunity*, XXI, 2, April 1943.

10. A. Philip Randolph, 'Why Should We March?' *Survey Graphic*, XXXI, 11, November 1942, 489.

11. *Chicago Defender*, March 28, 1942 and July 19, 1941.

12. *Pittsburgh Courier*, August 8, 1942. See too issues for February 7, July 11, 1942.

13. *Pittsburgh Courier*, January 1, 1944. The same point was made in the editorial, *Pittsburgh Courier*, June 10, 1944.

14. *Afro-American*, May 20, 1944.

15. Dwight Holmes, *Baltimore Afro-American*, July 8, 1944.

16. Office of Facts and Figures, *The Negro Looks at the War*, III. Other indications of black expectations are apparent in *Chicago Defender*, February 27, 1943; *Pittsburgh Courier*, December 4, 1943; Spencer Logan, *A Negro's Faith in America*, New York, 1946, 72. See Sitkoff, 'Racial Militancy,' 661.

17. Weaver, *Negro Labor*, vii.

18. Myrdal, *An American Dilemma*, xliii; Bibbs, *Pittsburgh Courier*, October 10, 1942. Schuyler in *Courier*, September 14, 1940 and *The Crisis*, November 1943.

19. Mays, 'The Negro and the Present War,' *The Crisis*, May 1942; Quarles, 'Will a Long War Aid the Negro?,' *The Crisis*, September 1943.

20. Office of Facts and Figures, *The Negro Looks at the War*, III; Supplement to Survey No. 25, 'Negroes in a Democracy at War.'

21. Cayton, *The Nation*, September 26, 1942; Ottley, *Common Ground*, Spring 1942; Powell, *Common Sense*, April 1942. The epitaph is quoted by Myrdal, *An American Dilemma*, 1006–7.

22. Selective Service System, *Selective Service in Peace Time: First Report of the Director of Selective Service*, Washington, D.C., 1942, 259; Selective Service System, *Special Groups: Special Monograph No. 10*, 83, and press release, Dept of Justice in FEPC file 413, NARG 228.

23. Randolph quoted in *Pittsburgh Courier*, December 20, 1941, from 'The Negro and the War,' *The Black Worker*, November 1941; *Negroes and the War*, Washington, D.C., nd.

24. *Daily Worker*, May 16, 1941; J. R. Johnson, *Why Negroes Should Oppose the War*, New York, 1939 (?); John Henry Williams, *A Negro Looks at War*, New York, 1940; and Wilson Record, *Race and Radicalism: The NAACP and the Communist Party in Conflict*, New York, 1964, 118–33.

25. Letter, Wright to MacLeish, December 21, 1941, Office of Facts and Figures, National Archives Record Group 208; William A. Nolan, *Communism vs the Negro*, Chicago, 1951, 143. Other examples of this change in tune are James W. Ford, *The War and the Negro People*, New York, 1942, and Pettis Perry, *The Negro Stake in this War*, San Francisco, 1942 (?); memo. from Milton Starr to Ulric Bell, Asst Director, Office of Facts and Figures, February 12, 1942, NARG 208.

26. Joseph D. Bibbs, *Pittsburgh Courier*, October 3, 1942; Louis Martin, 'Fifth Column Among Negroes', *Opportunity*, December 1942; and Murray, 'The Negro and Civil Liberties during World War II,' *Social Forces*, December 1945; A. Philip Randolph, 'Pro-Japanese Activities Among Negroes,' *The Black Worker*, September 1942.

27. *Baltimore Afro-American*, September 26, 1942; *Chicago Defender*, October 3, 1942; C. Eric Lincoln, *The Black Muslims in America*, Boston, Mass., 1969, 188.

28. *Defender*, October 10, 1942.

29. *Chicago Defender*, December 5, 1942; and Ottley, *New World A'Coming*, 332.

30. *Baltimore Afro-American*, May 23, 1942.

31. *Baltimore Afro-American*, September 26, 1942; Murray, *Negro Handbook, 1944*, 133; E. David Cronon, *Black Moses: The Story of Marcus Garvey*, Madison, Wis., 1969, 166; Harry Haywood, *Negro Liberation*, New York, 1948, 203.

32. *Baltimore Afro-American* and *Chicago Defender*, September 19, 1942; *Chicago Defender*, January 16, 1943, *New York Times*, January 15, 1943; Murray, *Negro Handbook, 1944*, 134.

33. *New York Times*, January 15, 1943; *Chicago Defender*, January 23, 1943.

34. *Chicago Defender*, March 14, 1942; Haywood, *Negro Liberation*, 203 and E. U. Essien-Udom, *Black Nationalism: The Rise of the Black Muslims in the USA*, Harmondsworth, Mdx, 1966, 56; Murray, *Negro Handbook, 1944*, 134.

35. *New York Times*, January 14, 1943; *Baltimore Afro-American*, January 23, 1943.

36. *Chicago Defender*, August 23, 1941, November 7, 1942; *Baltimore Afro-American*, January 2, 1943; Ottley, *New World A'Coming*, 333, 334.

37. Randolph in *Chicago Defender*, October 3, 1942; Ottley, *New World A'Coming*, 327–43.

38. *Chicago Defender*, October 3, 1942; American Civil Liberties Union quoted in Murray, 'The Negro and Civil Liberties,' 211.

39. Office of Facts and Figures, *The Negro Looks at the War*, and Supplement to Survey No. 25, 'Negroes in a Democracy at War.'

40. 'How "Bigger" was Born,' *The Saturday Review of Literature*, June 1, 1940, included as an introduction to *Native Son*, New York, 1966 ed., xiv.

41. Rayford W. Logan, ed., *What the Negro Wants*, Chapel Hill, N. Carolina, 1944, ix, 7, 14, 65, 71, 103, 163, 193ff.

42. Bucklin Moon, ed., *Primer for White Folks*, New York, 1945.

43. *This Is Our Way*, Baltimore, Md, 1945, see *Afro-American*, March 10, 1945; Arthur Furr, *Democracy's Negroes*, Boston, Mass., 1947; also Florence Murray, ed., *The Negro Handbook, 1946–47*, New York, 1947; Guzman, ed., *The Negro Year Book, 1941–46*, Tuskegee. Ala, 1947.

44. Letter in *Pittsburgh Courier*, May 19, 1945; *Baltimore Afro-American*, May 12, 1945.

45. Dennis I. Imbert, *The Negro After The War*, New Orleans, 1943.

46. W. Stegner and the Editors of *Look, One Nation*, Boston, 1945; Buell G. Gallagher, *Color and Conscience: The Irrepressible Conflict*, New York, 1946; John D. Silvera, *The Negro in World War II*, New York, 1946; Carey McWilliams, *Brothers Under the Skin*, Boston, 1943.

47. Helen Gahagan Douglas, 'The Negro Soldier: A Partial Record of Negro Devotion and Heroism in the Cause of Freedom Gathered from the Files of the War and Navy Departments,' a copy of her speech in the House of Representatives, February 1, 1946, in Moorland Collection, Howard University.

48. *Baltimore Afro-American*, August 15, 1942, and resolution to the war policy session of the Republican National Committee, April 20, 1942, quoted in *Afro-American*, April 25, 1942.

49. Willkie, *One World*, London 1943, 148–56. See Donald Bruce Johnson, *The Republican Party and Wendell Willkie*, Urbana, Ill., 1960, 287, 304; Walter White, *A Man Called White*, New York, 1948, 198–204.

50. Carey McWilliams, 'What We Did About Racial Minorities' in Jack Goodman, ed.,

While You Were Gone: A Report on Wartime Life in the United States, New York, 1946, 95; *Chicago Defender*, October 14, 1944; *Pittsburgh Courier*, October 14, 1944; *Baltimore Afro-American*, October 14, 21, 1944.

51. *New York Times*, November 15, 1941.
52. 'A Letter to Colored Americans', *Opportunity*, XX, 3, March 1942.
53. Office of War Information, Bureau of Special Services, Division of Research, Report No. C-12, 'Opinions About Inter-Racial Tension,' August 25, 1943, in OASW 230, NARG 107.
54. National Opinion Research Center, June 20, 1942 and May 1944, in Hadley Cantril, *Public Opinion, 1935–1946*, Princeton, N.J., 1951, 988–9.
55. Guzman, *Negro Year Book, 1941–46*, 226; American Council on Race Relations, *Directory of Agencies in Intergroup Relations: National Regional, State and Local, 1948–49*, Chicago, 1949; 'Programs of Action on the Democratic Front', *Race Relations: A Monthly Summary of Events and Trends*, II, 1–2, August–September 1944.
56. Goodwin Watson, *Action for Unity*, New York, 1947, 5.
57. *Chicago Defender*, March 30, 1946; *Baltimore Afro-American*, May 13, 1944; Robert C. Weaver, 'Whither Northern Race Relations Committees?', *Phylon*, V, 3, 1944; A. A. Liveright, 'The Community and Race Relations', *Annals of the American Academy of Political and Social Science*, Vol 244, March 1946.
58. 'War and Race Relations: Student Opinion,' *The Crisis*, September 1943; Cantril, *Public Opinion, 1935–1946*, 477.
59. NORC polls, May 1944, Cantril *Public Opinion, 1935–1946*, 509–10, 988–9; and in *Pittsburgh Courier*, August 19, October 28, 1944.
60. American Institute of Public Opinion, June 12, 1945, Cantril, 477–8.
61. Quoted in Sterling A. Brown, 'Count Us In,' in Logan, ed., *What the Negro Wants*, 322; Gallagher, *Color and Conscience*, 1; see Brown, 'Count Us In,' 318.
62. Charles S. Johnson, 'The Present Status of Race Relations in the South,' *Social Forces*, XXIII, 1, October 1944; John Samuel Ezell, *The South Since 1865*, New York, 1963, 417; Thomas D. Clark and Albert D. Kirwan, *The South Since Appomattox*, New York, 1967, 286.
63. Howard Washington Odum, *Race and Rumors of Race: Challenge to American Crisis*, Chapel Hill, N. Carolina, 1943. Also see the manuscript by Odum, 'On Trying to Analyze Southern Race Tensions with Special Reference to the War Situation and to the Total National Picture,' Winter 1943, in Yale University Library: Joseph P. Lash, *Eleanor and Franklin: The Story of their Relationship*, New York, 1971, 672–4, and letter to F.D.R. complaining of his wife's supposed activities, September 1942, 93:7 FDRL.
64. Odum, *Race and Rumors of Race*, 105; letters in Selective Service System files, 170, NARG 147 quoted above, 172, 178; *Pittsburgh Courier*, September 26, 1944.
65. Ina Corinne Brown, *Race Relations in a Democracy*, New York, 1949, 143–5; Charles S. Johnson, *Into the Mainstream: A Survey of Best Practices in Race Relations in the South*, Chapel Hill, N. Carolina, 1947, 5–7.
66. Southern Regional Council, *Changing Problems in the New South*, Atlanta, 1955; *The Southern Frontier*, III, 11, November 1942, IV, 1, January 1943, IV, 8, August 1943.
67. 'Virginians Speak on Jim Crow,' *The Crisis*, February 1944.
68. Graves, 'The Southern Negro and the War Crisis,' *Virginia Quarterly Review*, XVIII, 4, 1942; Dabney, 'Nearer and Nearer the Precipice,' *Atlantic*, January 1943, also in NAACP 279, Library of Congress.
69. V. O. Key, *Southern Politics in State and Nation*, New York, 1949, 351–2, 371–2, 345–82.
70. Richard R. Polenberg, *War and Society: The United States, 1941–1945*, New York, 1972, 187–92. *Pittsburgh Courier*, July 22, 1944; *Chicago Defender*, July 29, 1944.
71. Office of Facts and Figures, *The Negro Looks at the War: Attitudes of New York Negroes Toward Discrimination Against Negroes and a Comparison of Negro and Poor White Attitudes Toward War Related Issues*, n.p., in Schomburg Collection; Office of War Information,

Supplement to Survey No. 25, 'Negroes in a Democracy at War', July 14, 1942, in OASW 226, NARG 107; Analysis Branch, News Division, Bureau of Public Relations, 'Reports on Trends in the Negro Press,' in OASW 223, NARG 107.

72. 'Statement of Negro War Aims,' undated, FDRL 93:9; Correspondence in Office of Facts and Figures, 40, and Office of War Information 1050, both NARG 208; Walter White, *A Man Called White*, 207–9; Roi Ottley, *New World A'Coming*, 269; *Pittsburgh Courier*, February 12, 1944.

73. Extracts from propaganda programs in OFF 40, NARG 208.

74. Office of Facts and Figures, *Report to the Nation: The American Preparation for War*, Washington, D.C., 1942; Office of War Information, *Negroes and the War*, Washington, D.C., n.d.

75. F.D.R. to Edwin R. Embree, March 16, 1942 in reply to letter of February 3, FDRL 93:5. Also telegram, A. Philip Randolph to F.D.R., August 2, 1942, and reply, August 6, FDRL 93:5.

76. Ottley, *New World A'Coming*, 320; letter of address, September 7, 1943, in National Urban League, 'Victory Through Unity: Annual Conference of the National Urban League,' September 28–October 3, 1943, in Schomburg Collection.

77. Message to the Nation, October 5, 1944, in Samuel I. Rosenman, ed., *Public Papers and Addresses of Franklin D. Roosevelt: Victory and the Threshold of Peace, 1944–45*, New York, 1950, 317–21.

78. *Chicago Defender*, December 9, 1944.

79. *Baltimore Afro-American*, July 18, 1942; Lash, *Eleanor and Franklin*, 673–4.

80. White to F.D.R., October 5; F.D.R. to White, October 14, 1944, FDRL 93:10. Subsequently, however, meetings were held between White and General Hines of the Veterans Administration to discuss racial policies, see White to F.D.R., October 23, 1944, FDRL 93:10.

81. Ross, *Preparing for Ulysses*, 34–5; for expression of such fears see *Pittsburgh Courier*, August 25, 1945; *Chicago Defender*, September 9, 1944; *Baltimore Afro-American*, August 25, September 1, 1945; National Urban League, 'Racial Aspects of Reconversion: A Memorandum Prepared for the President of the United States,' August 27, 1945, in FEPC 417, NARG 228.

82. Clarence M. Mitchell, Asst Director of Field Operations to Malcolm Ross, FEPC chairman, March 22, 1944, in FEPC 407; and Malcolm Ross to John A. Davis, 'Significant Facts about the Negro in Postwar Employment,' July 28, 1944, in FEPC 410, NARG 228.

83. FEPC, *Final Report, June 28, 1946*, Washington, D.C., 1947, 41–5; Davis McEntire and Julia Tarnopol, 'Postwar Status of Negro Workers in San Francisco Area,' *Monthly Labor Review*, 70, 6, June 1950; Herman D. Bloch, *The Circle of Discrimination: An Economic and Social Study of the Black Man in New York*, New York and London, 1969, 64.

84. Robert C. Weaver, 'The Negro Veteran,' *Annals of the American Academy of Political and Social Science*, 238, March 1945, 130; National Urban League, Dept of Industrial Relations, 'Occupational Adjustment for Negro Veterans; A Memorandum on the Problem of Counselling Negro Veterans'; July 27, 1944 in OASW 225, NARG 107.

85. The history and details of the GI Bill are dealt with in Ross, *Preparing for Ulysses*, 90–124. See too NAACP, *Veterans Handbook*, New York, n.d.

86. War Dept Report, B-133, 'Postwar Educational Plans of Soldiers,' March 14, 1945, in Selective Service System, *Special Groups: Special Monograph 10*, Washington, D.C., 1953, 174–5; Ambrose Caliver, 'Post-war Educational Implications of Army Data and Experiences of Negro Veterans and War Workers,' Office of Education, 1945, in OE 40, NARG 12; Robert C. Weaver, 'Negro Veterans Return,' *Race Relations*, III, 1–2, 1945.

87. War Dept Report, B-128, 'Postwar Migration Plans of Soldiers,' 1944, in *Special Monograph*, 170–1; Weaver, 'Negro Veterans Return'; Charles G. Bolte and Louis

Harris, *Our Negro Veterans*, New York Public Affairs Committee Pamphlet 128, New York, 1947, 4.

88. Weaver, 'Negro Veterans Return,' 14–15; Bolte and Harris, *Our Negro Veterans*, 18.

89. Weaver, 'Negro Veterans Return,' 15–16; B. T. McGraw, 'Minority Group Participation in the Veteran's Emergency Housing Program,' February 19, 1946, HHFA 91, NARG 207.

90. National Urban League, Dept of Industrial Relations, 'Adjustment of Negro Veterans: A Report of Negro Veterans in 50 Cities,' 1946, in War Manpower Commission, NARG 211; American Council on Race Relations, 'Survey of Community Veteran Information Centers,' March 29, 1946, in Schomburg Collection; Bolte and Harris, *Our Negro Veterans*, 11; Howard Johnson, 'The Negro Veteran Fights for Freedom,' *Political Affairs*, Vol 26, May 1947, 429–31; Donald R. McCoy and Richard T. Ruetten, *Quest and Response: Minority Rights and the Truman Administration*, Kansas, 1973, 38–9.

91. Telegrams and letters concerning the Hotels Theresa and Pershing in New York and Chicago, and Stimson's comments to F.D.R., September 20, 1944, in FDRL 93:12.

92. Charles G. Bolte, 'He Fought For Freedom,' *Survey Graphic*, XXXVI, 1, January 1947, 117.

93. *Baltimore Afro-American*, March 9, August 17, 1946; *New York Times*, December 11, 1946; Langston Hughes, *Fight for Freedom: The Story of the NAACP*, New York 1962, 102–4; Arvarh E. Strickland, *History of the Chicago Urban League*, Urbana, Ill., 1966, 159–60.

94. *Baltimore Afro-American*, June 22, August 3, 1946; Hughes, *Fight for Freedom*, 112–13.

95. *Chicago Defender*, February 2, 1946; and *Pittsburgh Courier*, December 8, 1945.

96. White, *A Man Called White*, 325–30; *Baltimore Afro-American*, June 22, August 3, 1946; William C. Berman, *The Politics of Civil Rights in the Truman Administration*, Columbus, Ohio, 1970, 50.

97. Berman, *The Politics of Civil Rights*, 8–19; *Pittsburgh Courier*, July 22, 1944, April 21, 1945; *Baltimore Afro-American*, April 21, 1945.

98. White, *A Man Called White*, 330–1; *Pittsburgh Courier*, September 28, 1946; Berman, *The Politics of Civil Rights*, 50–1; McCoy and Ruetten, *Quest and Response*, 47–52.

99. Executive Order 9808, President's Committee on Civil Rights, *To Secure These Rights*, Washington, D.C., 1947, vii; *New York Times*, December 5, 1946; Berman, *The Politics of Civil Rights*, 53–6.

100. July 5, 1947, Paramount News, National Archive Film Library, NA 200 PN 6.89; White, *A Man Called White*, 347–9; State of the Union Message, January 6, 1947, Economic Message, January 8, 1947, in *Public Papers of the Presidents: Harry S. Truman, 1947*, Washington, D.C., 1962, 31–2.

101. 'Our Civil Rights Become a World Issue,' *New York Times Magazine*, January 11, 1948; Berman, *The Politics of Civil Rights*, 65–6; Dalfiume, *Desegregation of the US Armed Forces*, 139.

102. *To Secure These Rights*, 8, 40–1, 162.

103. *To Secure These Rights*, 63–5, 81–2, 139–73, 151–9.

104. *Public Papers of the Presidents: Harry S. Truman, 1948*, 125–6.

105. McCoy and Ruetten, *Quest and Response*, 105; Berman, *The Politics of Civil Rights*, 80–2, 238–40. For a more realistic appraisal see Dalfiume, *Desegregation of the US Armed Forces*, 139–40, and Harry S. Truman, *Memoirs: Years of Trial and Hope, 1946–1953*, London, 1956, 191–4.

106. *New York Times*, July 14, 15, 1948; *Pittsburgh Courier*, July 24, 1948; Key, *Southern Politics*, 329–38; Berman, *The Politics of Civil Rights*, 108–12; Kirk H. Porter and Donald B. Johnson, *National Party Platforms, 1840–1964*, London, 1966, 467–8.

107. President's Committee on Civil Rights, *To Secure These Rights*, Washington, D.C., 1947, 41.

108. *Pittsburgh Courier*, April 10, 1948; *The Crisis*, May 1948; *New York Times*, March 23, 1948.
109. *New York Times*, April 27, 1948.
110. Berman, *The Politics of Civil Rights*, 124–32; Clark and Kirwan, *The South Since Appomattox*, 295.
111. Walter White, *How Far the Promised Land?*, New York, 1956, 208; Berman, *The Politics of Civil Rights*, 179–80.
112. President's Commission on Higher Education, *Higher Education for American Democracy*, New York 1948, 34–8; John T. Hubbell, 'The Desegregation of the University of Oklahoma,' *Journal of Negro History*, LVII, 4, 1972; Monroe Berger, *Equality by Statute*, New York, 1952.
113. Tom C. Clark and Philip B. Perlman, *Prejudice and Property: An Historic Brief Against Racial Covenants*, Washington, D.C., 1948; Berman, *The Politics of Civil Rights*, 74–5.
114. White, *How Far the Promised Land?*, Davis McEntire, *Residence and Race: Final and Comprehensive Report to the Commission on Race and Housing*, Berkeley and Los Angeles, 1960, 294–334; Richard O. Davies, *Housing Reform During the Truman Administration*, Columbia, Mo., 1966.
115. 'Postwar Trends in Negro Employment,' *Monthly Labor Review*, 65, 6, 1947; National Urban League, 'Changes in the Occupational Status of Negroes, 1940–50,' New York, 1950, in Schomburg Collection.
116. O. Douglas Weeks, 'The White Primary, 1944–1948,' and Donald S. Strong, 'The Rise of Negro Voting in Texas,' both in *American Political Science Review*, XLII, 3, 1948; 'Race and Suffrage Today,' in *New South, Changing Patterns in the New South*, 12–15; Joseph P. Frank, 'Legal Developments in Race Relations, 1945–1962,' in Sindler, *Change in the Contemporary South*, 67–81; Davis M. Chalmers, *Hooded Americanism: The First Century of the Ku Klux Klan, 1865–1965*, New York, 1965, 325–7.
117. Bennett, *Confrontation: Black and White*, Baltimore, Md., 1965, 168; also see Richard M. Dalfiume, 'The "Forgotten" Years of the Negro Revolution,' *Journal of American History*, LV, 1, June 1968.

Chapter 7: The Postwar Years: World War II in Perspective

1. Malcolm X, *The Autobiography of Malcolm X*, Harmondsworth, Mdx, 1968, 344.
2. Walter White, *How Far the Promised Land?*, New York, 1956, 96.
3. White, *How Far the Promised Land?*, 117–20; William C. Berman, *The Politics of Civil Rights in the Truman Administration*, Columbus, Ohio, 1970, 185; Donald R. McCoy and Richard T. Ruetten, *Quest and Response: Minority Rights and the Truman Administration*, Kansas, 1973, 350.
4. White, *How Far the Promised Land?*, 82, 117–20; US Information Service, *The People Take the Lead: Civil Rights, 1948–1956*, Washington, D.C., 1956; Constance McLaughlin Green, *The Secret City: A History of Race Relations in the Nation's Capital*, Princeton, N.J., 1967, 274–300.
5. H. H. Hyman and P. B. Sheatsley, 'Attitudes on Desegregation,' *Scientific American*, 195, 6, December 1956, 36–40; Monroe Berger, *Equality by Statute*, New York, 1952, 72–109; McCoy and Ruetten, *Quest and Response*, 292–5.
6. Berman, *The Politics of Civil Rights*, 196, 230–1.
7. Lerone Bennett, Jr, *Confrontation: Black and White*, Baltimore 1965, 189–90; John Hope Franklin, *From Slavery to Freedom: A History of Negro Americans*, New York, 1969, 614–20.
8. Anthony Lewis, *The Second American Revolution: A Firsthand Account of the Struggle for Civil Rights*, London 1966, xiv; Lerone Bennett, Jr, *Before the Mayflower: A History of Black America*, Chicago, 1969, 311–24, 421–33.
9. Louis Lomax, *The Negro Revolt*, London, 1963, 81.
10. Baldwin quoted in Lomax, *The Negro Revolt*, 77; also see Rupert Emerson and Martin

Kilson, 'The American Dilemma in a Changing World: The Rise of Africa and the Negro American,' *Daedalus*, 94, 4, Fall 1965.

11. August Meier and Elliott M. Rudwick, *From Plantation to Ghetto: An Interpretive History of American Negroes*, New York, 1966, 248–51; Charles C. Moskos, Jr, *The American Enlisted Man: The Rank and File in Today's Military*, New York, 1970, 131.

12. Reynolds Farley, 'The Urbanization of Negroes in the United States,' *Journal of Social History*, I, Spring 1968.

13. Charles Abrams, *The City is the Frontier*, New York, 1965, 54–71.

14. Harry A. Ploski and Ernest Kaiser, *The Negro Almanac*, New York, 1971, 407–20.

15. Louis A. Ferman, ed., *Poverty in America: A Book of Readings*, Ann Arbor, Mich., 1965, xix; Dept of Commerce, Bureau of Census, *Trends in the Income of Families and Persons in the United States: 1947–1960*, Washington, D.C., 1963, 7, 18–23.

16. Moskos, 'The Negro and the Draft,' in Roger W. Little, ed., *Selective Service and American Society*, New York, 1969, 161; McCoy and Ruetten, *Quest and Response*, 228–48.

17. American Broadcasting Companies, 'The Vietnam War: Black and White,' *Scope* part 63, 1967, Library of Congress Film Division, FBA 5852; King, *Chaos or Community*, Harmondsworth, Mdx, 1969, 41, 87–8, 174.

18. *New York Times Magazine*, July 24, 1966; Leo Bogart, ed., *Social Research and the Desegregation of the US Army*, Chicago, 1969, 1–2.

19. *New York Times Magazine*, July 24, 1966; Wallace Terry, 'Bringing the War Home,' *Black Scholar*, November 1970.

20. Robin M. Williams, Jr, 'Social Change and Social Conflict: Race Relations in the United States, 1944–1964,' *Sociological Inquiry*, XXXV, 1, 1965, 17.

21. Maurice R. Davie, *Negroes in American Society*, New York, 1949, 314.

Epilogue

1. See for example, A. Russell Buchanan, *Black Americans in World War II*, New York, 1977; Richard M. Dalfiume, *Desegregation of the U.S. Armed Forces: Fighting on Two Fronts, 1939–1953*, Columbia, Mo., 1969; Lee Finkle, *Forum for Protest: The Black Press During World War II*, Rutherford, N.J., 1975; Harvard Sitkoff, 'Racial Militancy and Interracial Violence in the Second World War,' *Journal of American History*, LVIII, June 1971; see chapters in John Morton Blum, *V Was For Victory: Politics and American Culture During World War II*, New York and London, 1976; Richard Polenberg, *War and Society: The United States, 1941–1945*, Philadelphia and New York, 1972.

2. Richard Dalfiume, 'The "Forgotten Years" of the Negro Revolution,' *Journal of American History*, LV, June 1968; Buchanan, *Black Americans in World War II*, 132; Polenberg, *War and Society*, 99, 130; William H. Chafe, *The Unfinished Journey: America since World War II*, New York and Oxford, 1986, 17, 18; Steven F. Lawson, *Running for Freedom: Civil Rights and Black Politics in America since 1941*, New York, 1991, 9–14.

3. Myrdal, *An American Dilemma*, 997; Murray, quoted in Blum, *V Was For Victory*, 218; Charles S. Johnson, 'The Impact of the War upon Negro-White Relations in the United States', 1947, Johnson Papers, 164, F4, Fisk University.

4. *Chicago Defender*, December 13, 1941; Josh White, 'Defense Factory Blues', *Opportunity*, July–September 1944.

5. August Meier and Elliott Rudwick, 'The Origins of Nonviolent Direct Action in Afro-American Protest: A Note on Historical Discontinuities,' in *Along the Color Line: Explorations in the Black Experience*, Urbana, Ill., Chicago, and London, 1976, 345.

6. See Meier and Rudwick, 'The Origins of Nonviolent Direct Action'; also Harvard Sitkoff, *A New Deal for Blacks: The Emergence of Civil Rights as a National Issue*, New York, 1978, and *The Struggle for Black Equality, 1954–1980*, New York, 1981, 9–13; John B. Kirby, *Black Americans in the Roosevelt Era*, Knoxville, Tenn., 180.

7. Lee Finkle, 'The Conservative Aims of Militant Rhetoric: Black Protest During World War II,' *Journal of American History*, LX, 3, December 1973.
8. Patrick S. Washburn, *A Question of Sedition: The Federal Government's Investigation of the Black Press During World War II*, New York and London, 1986. Also see Dominic J. Capeci, Jr., *The Harlem Riot of 1943*, Philadelphia, 1977, 92–93, 152.
9. Sitkoff, 'Racial Militancy and Interracial Violence,' 679.
10. *Pittsburgh Courier*, March 4 and 11, 1944; Truman Gibson to Assistant Secretary of War, December 20, 1943, OASW, NARG 107, Box 190.
11. Alexander Allen, in Mark J. Harris, Franklin D. Mitchell, and Steven J. Schecter, eds., *The Home Front: America During World War II*, New York, 1984, 88.
12. William H. Harris, *The Harder We Run: Black Workers Since the Civil War*, New York and Oxford, 1982, 96.
13. Sybil Lewis, in Harris et al., *The Home Front*, 251.
14. Karen T. Anderson, 'Last Hired, First Fired: Black Women Workers during World War II,' *Journal of American History*, LXIX, 1, June 1982; also see Chester W. Gregory, *Women in Defense Work During World War II*, New York, 1974; Maureen Honey, *Creating Rosie the Riveter: Class, Gender and Propaganda during World War II*, Amherst, Mass., 1984; Susan Hartman, *The Home Front and Beyond: American Women in the 1940s*, Boston, 1982; Sherna Berger Gluck, *Rosie the Riveter Revisited: Women, the War and Social Change*, New York, 1987.
15. Ibid., p. 24; D'Ann Campbell, *Women at War with America: Private Lives in a Patriotic Era*, Cambridge, Mass., and London, 1984, 173–74; Studs Terkel, *"The Good War": An Oral History of World War II*, London, 1985, 334.
16. Anderson, 'Last Hired, First Fired,' 97; and see William H. Chafe, *The American Woman: Her Changing Social, Economic, and Political Roles*, New York, 1972, for the more positive view.
17. Sarah Killingsworth in Terkel, *"The Good War,"* 116; Sybil Lewis, quoted by Allen, in Harris et al., *The Home Front*, 251.
18. Pete Daniel, 'Going Among Strangers: Southern Reactions to World War II,' *Journal of American History*, LXXVII, December 1990; see also Jack M. Bloom, *Class, Race and the Civil Rights Movement*, Bloomington and Indianapolis, 1987, 66–73. Nicholas Lemann in *The Promised Land: The Great Black Migration and How It Changed America*, New York, 1991, 4–7, points to the significance of the war in encouraging the mechanization of cotton picking, which transformed Southern agriculture and displaced black workers.
19. Jo Ann Robinson in Henry Hampton and Steven Fayer, eds., *Voices of Freedom: An Oral History of the Civil Rights Movement from the 1950s through the 1980s*, New York, 1990, 22.
20. See Steven F. Lawson, *Running for Freedom*, especially 17–28.
21. George Q. Flynn, 'Selective Service and American Blacks During World War II,' *Journal of Negro History*, LXIX, 1, Winter 1984, 19.
22. Private Bert Barbero to Truman Gibson, February 13, 1944, OASW, NARG 107, Box 230, 'Attitudes of Negro Soldiers.'
23. John Modell, Marc Goulden, and Sigurder Magnusson, 'World War II in the Lives of Black Americans: Some Findings and an Interpretation,' *Journal of American History*, LXXVI, 3, December 1989, 845.
24. *Afro-American*, May 20, 1944.
25. Modell et al., 'World War II in the Lives of Black Americans,' 838.
26. Charles A. Gates in Terkel, *"The Good War,"* 270.
27. Daniel, 'Going Among Strangers: Southern Reactions to World War II,' 905–8.
28. Ethridge quoted in David Southern, 'Beyond Jim Crow Liberalism,' *Journal of Negro History*, LXVI, 3, Fall 1981, 211; also see Walter White, *A Man Called White*, New York, 1948, 268.
29. Richard Polenberg, *One Nation Divisible: Class, Race, and Ethnicity in the United States since 1938*, Harmondsworth, Middlesex, 1980, 108–10.

30. Quoted ibid., 71.
31. Arnold R. Hirsch, *Making the Second Ghetto: Race and Housing in Chicago, 1940–1960*, Cambridge and London, 1983, 52–53.
32. Quoted in Southern, 'Beyond Jim Crow Liberalism', 211.
33. Alfred Duckett in Terkel, *"The Good War,"* 372.
34. Sitkoff, *A New Deal for Blacks*, 330.

Bibliography

1. *Manuscript Collections*

Fair Employment Practices Committee, National Archives, Record Group 228. (Contains records of FEPC hearings, papers and reports on economic developments, and a collection of relevant pamphlets and articles.)

Housing and Home Finance Agency, National Archives, Record Group 207. (Has a great deal of material on defense housing and employment.)

Charles Spurgeon Johnson Collection, Fisk University. (Includes two important unpublished essays by Johnson on the impact of the war on the Afro-American and race relations.)

James Weldon Johnson Collection, Beinecke Library, Yale University. (Useful mainly for newspaper clippings and papers on FEPC and Randolph but also has correspondence with various black writers.)

National Association for the Advancement of Colored People, Library of Congress. (The records for the post-1939 period have yet to be processed and catalogued and the previous arrangement of material has been disturbed, making it impossible to trace important files. Material quoted in text, on soldiers' attitudes, was found at random.)

Office of the Assistant Secretary of War, National Archives, Record Group 107. (Contains files and records on every aspect of black life, housing, employment, and of course, service in the Army. Also letters from black soldiers and civilians, and the responses of military officials.)

Office of Education, National Archives, Record Group 12. (Information relevant purely to education, largely the papers and records of the indefatigable Ambrose Caliver.)

Office of Facts and Figures, later Office of War Information, National Archives, Record Group 208. (Records of plans to be used to mobilize the black population and boost black morale, revealing the importance race relations had achieved as a result of the war emergency.)

Office of Price Administration, National Archives, Record Group 188. (Details of rationing and price controls as they affected Afro-Americans, and also details of the employment of blacks within the OPA itself.)

Franklin Delano Roosevelt Papers, Hyde Park, New York. (Files containing a wealth of material on race relations, correspondence to Roosevelt from blacks and white federal officials and the President's replies.)

Schomburg Collection, Harlem Branch New York Public Library. (Files of unpublished material on the Lynn Committee and the National Citizens' Committee for Winfred Lynn, Veterans, Education, and the March on Washington Movement.)

Selective Service System, National Archives, Record Group 147. (Surprisingly, very little on Selective Service and Afro-Americans, but some interesting correspondence from white Southerners concerning the 'favorable' consideration blacks were thought to be getting in the draft.)

Special Committee of the Senate to Investigate the National Defense Program, 1941–48 (Truman Committee), National Archives, Record Group 46. (Includes correspondence from individuals and organizations concerning discrimination in industry, and details of the campaign for an anti-discrimination bill, Senate Resolution 75.)

War Department, National Archives, Record Groups 330, 389. (Contains reports and surveys on the attitudes of black and white soldiers toward integration and the Army records of the Detroit riot of 1943.)

War Manpower Commission, National Archives, Record Group 211. (Information on the employment situation and discrimination in industry. Also includes an extremely valuable unpublished (and incomplete) 'History of the Mobilization of Labor for War Production During World War II' with a lengthy chapter on discrimination.)

Walter White Papers, in James Weldon Johnson Collection, Yale University. (Although these are largely the papers and letters relating to the post-war period, they do reveal the close relationship White had with the Roosevelts, particularly Eleanor. There is also some correspondence with the President concerning White's tour of the overseas military bases.)

2. Other Unpublished Materials

American Council on Race Relations, 'Survey of Community Veteran Information Centers,' 1946, in Schomburg Collection.

American Council on Race Relations, 'Evaluation of State FEPC: Experiences and Forecasts,' 1949, in Yale University Library.

Byers, Jean, 'A Study of the Negro in Military Service,' Department of Defense, Washington, D.C., 1947, in Moorland-Spingarn Collection, Howard University.

Fisk University, Social Science Institute, 'Racial Attitudes: Interviews Revealing Attitudes of Northern and Southern White Persons, of a Wide Range of Occupational and Educational Levels, Toward Negroes,' Nashville, Tenn., 1946.

March on Washington Movement, 'Proceedings of Conference Held in Detroit, September 26–27, 1942,' 1942, in Schomburg Collection.

National Urban League, 'Changes in the Occupational Status of Negroes, 1940–1950,' New York, 1950, in Schomburg Collection.

National Urban League, 'A Summary Report of the Industrial Relations Laboratory: Performance of Negro Workers in Three Hundred War Plants,' New York, 1944, in Moorland-Spingarn Collection.

Odum, Howard Washington, 'On Trying to Analyze Southern Race Tensions with Special Reference to the War Situation and to the Total National Picture,' 1943, in Yale University Library.

Office of Facts and Figures, 'The Negro Looks At The War: Attitudes of New York Negroes Toward Discrimination Against Negroes and a Comparison of Negro and Poor White Attitudes Toward War-Related Issues,' 1942, in Schomburg Collection.

Wirth, Louis, 'The Effect of War on American Minorities: A Research Memorandum,' New York, 1943, in Schomburg Collection.

3. *Government Publications*

Advisory Committee on Education, *The Federal Government and Education*, Washington, D.C., 1938.

Blood, Kathryn, *Negro Women War Workers*, Department of Labor, Women's Bureau, Bulletin 205, Washington, D.C., 1945.

Bureau of Employment Security, *Employment Security Review*, IX, 7, July 1942.

Caliver, Ambrose, *Postwar Education of Negroes: Educational Implications of Army Data and Experiences of Negro Veterans and War Workers*, Office of Education, Washington, D.C., 1945.

Congressional Record, Vol 94, No. 66, 80th Congress, Second Session, Senate, April 12, 1948.

Department of Commerce, Bureau of the Census, *Negroes in the United States 1920–1932*, Washington, D.C., 1935.

Department of Commerce, Bureau of the Census, *Trends in the Income of Families and Persons in the United States, 1947 to 1960*, Technical Paper 8, Washington, D.C., 1963.

Department of Labor, *Negroes in the United States: Their Employment and Economic Status*, Bulletin 1119, Washington, D.C., 1952.

Department of Labor, 'Annual family and occupational earnings of residents of two Negro housing projects in Atlanta, 1937–1944,' *Monthly Labor Review*, Vol 61, No. 6, December 1945.

Department of Labor, 'Postwar Trends in Negro Employment,' *Monthly Labor Review*, Vol 65, No. 6, December 1947.

Department of Labor, 'Postwar Status of Negro Workers in San Francisco,' *Monthly Labor Review*, Vol 70, No. 6, June 1950.

Department of Labor, 'A Century of Change: Negroes in the US Economy, 1860–1960,' *Monthly Labor Review*, Vol 85, No. 12, December 1962.

Department of Labor, Division of Negro Economics, *Negro Migrations in 1916–17*, Washington, D.C., 1919.

Federal Security Agency, Social Security Board, *Negroes and the National Defense Program*, Washington, D.C., September 1941.

Housing and Home Finance Agency, *Negro Share of Priority War Housing—Private and Public as of December 31, 1944*, Office of Principal Housing Analyst, Washington, D.C., 1945.

Housing and Home Finance Agency, *Housing of the Non-white Population, 1940 to 1947*, Washington, D.C., 1948.

Housing and Home Finance Agency, *Housing of the Non-white Population, 1940 to 1950*, Washington, D.C., 1952.

Lee, Ulysses G., *The Employment of Negro Troops*, US Army in World War II, Special Studies 8, Washington, D.C., 1966.

National Resources Planning Board, *Report for 1942, Part I: Post-war Plan and Program*, Washington, D.C., 1943.

Office of Education, *National Survey of the Higher Education of Negroes*, Washington, D.C., 1942.

Office of Facts and Figures, *Report to the Nation: The American Preparation for War*, Washington, D.C., 1942.

Office of War Information, *Negroes and the War*, Washington, D.C., n.d.

Palmer, A. Mitchell, *Radicalism and Sedition Among the Negroes as Reflected in their Publications*, Exhibit No. 10, Senate Documents, Vol 12, 66th Congress, 1st Session, 1919, Washington, D.C., 1919.

President's Commission on Higher Education, *Higher Education For American Democracy*, New York, 1948.

President's Committee on Civil Rights, *To Secure These Rights*, Washington, D.C., 1947.

President's Committee on Equality of Treatment and Opportunity in the Armed Services, *Freedom to Serve*, Washington, D.C., 1950.

President's Committee on Fair Employment Practice, *Minorities in Defense*, Washington, D.C., 1941.

President's Committee on Fair Employment Practice, *FEPC: How it Operates*, Washington, D.C., 1944.

President's Committee on Fair Employment Practice, *First Report: July 1943–December 1944*, Washington, D.C., 1945.

President's Committee on Fair Employment Practice, *Final Report: June 28, 1946*, Washington, D.C., 1947.

Public Papers of the Presidents: Harry S. Truman, 1945, 1946, 1947, 1948, Washington, D.C., 1961, 1962.

Selective Service System, *Selective Service in Peace Time: First Report of the Director of Selective Service, 1940–41*, Washington, D.C., 1942.

Selective Service System, *Selective Service in Wartime: Second Report . . . 1941–42*, Washington, D.C., 1943.

Selective Service System, *Selective Services as the Tide of War Turns: Third Report . . . 1943–44*, Washington, D.C., 1945.

Selective Service System, *Selective Service and Victory: Fourth Report. . . .* Washington, D.C., 1948.

Selective Service System, *Special Groups: Special Monograph No. 10*, Volume 11, Washington, D.C., 1953.

US Information Service, *The People Take The Lead: A Record of Progress in Civil Rights, 1948 to 1956*, Washington, D.C., 1956.

War Manpower Commission, *Man Power: One Tenth of a Nation*, Washington, D.C., n.d.

Wilkerson, Doxey A., *Special Problems of Negro Education*, Washington, D.C., 1939.

4. *Newspapers, Magazines, and Journals*

Baltimore Afro-American, 1942–6.
Black Worker: The Official Organ of the Brotherhood of Sleeping Car Porters, 1940–5.
Chicago Defender, 1917–20, 1941–6.
Congress Vue (National Negro Congress), 1943–6.
The Crisis (NAACP), 1918–20, 1940–8.
Journal of Negro Education, 1941–6.
New York Times, 1941–50.
Opportunity: Journal of Negro Life (NUL), 1941–6.
Pittsburgh Courier, 1940–8.
Phylon Quarterly: A Review of Race and Culture, 1941–50.
Race Relations: A Monthly Summary of Events and Trends, 1943–7.
The Southern Frontier (Commission on Interracial Co-operation), 1941/5.

5. *Other Contemporary Published Materials*

A. *Pamphlets, Reports and Papers*
Abrams, Charles, *Race Bias in Housing*, New York, 1947.

American Council on Race Relations, *Negro Platform Workers*, Chicago, 1945.

American Council on Race Relations, *Directory of Agencies in Intergroup Relations: National, Regional, State and Local, 1948–49*, Chicago, 1949.

American Federation of Labor, *Proceedings of Annual Conventions*, New Orleans 1940, Seattle 1941, Toronto 1942, Boston 1943, New Orleans 1944.

American Teachers Association, *The Black and White of Rejections for Military Service*, Montgomery, Ala., 1944.

Barksdale, James Worsham, *A Comparative Study of Contemporary White and Negro Standards in Health, Education, and Welfare, Charlottesville, Virginia*, Phelps-Stokes Fellowship Paper 20, Virginia, 1949.

Bolte, Charles G. and Louis Harris, *Our Negro Veterans*, New York Public Affairs Committee Pamphlet 128, New York, 1947.

Brown, Earl Louis, *Why Race Riots? Lessons from Detroit*, New York Public Affairs Committee Pamphlet 87, New York, 1944.

Brown, Earl Louis and George R. Leighton, *The Negro and the War*, New York Public Affairs Committee Pamphlet 71, New York, 1942.

Chicago Commission on Race Relations, *The Negro in Chicago: A Study of Race Relations and a Race Riot*, Chicago, 1923.

Chicago Mayor's Commission on Human Relations, *Race Relations in Chicago: Report for 1945*, Chicago, 1945.

Chicago Mayor's Commission on Human Relations, *Human Relations in Chicago: Report for 1946*, Chicago, 1946.

Chicago Mayor's Committee on Race Relations, *Negroes in Chicago*, Chicago, 1944.

Cobb, William Montague, *Medical Care and the Plight of the Negro*, NAACP, New York, 1947.

Cobb, William Montague, *Progress and Portents for the Negro in Medicine*, NAACP, New York, 1948.

Commission to Study the Organization of Peace, *Toward Greater Freedom: Problems of War and Peace*, New York, 1942.

Congress of Industrial Organizations, *Proceedings of Annual Constitutional Conventions*, Boston 1942, Philadelphia 1943, Chicago 1944.

Congress of Industrial Organizations: Committee to Abolish Racial Discrimination, *Working and Fighting Together*, Washington, D.C., 1943.

Council for Democracy, *The Negro and Defense: A Test of Democracy*, New York, 1941.

Council for Democracy, *The Negro in America: How We Treat Him and How We Should*, New York, 1945.

DeAngelis, Gabriel, *Nobody Knows . . .*, Committee Against Jim Crow in Military Service and Training, New York, 1949.

Douglas, Helen Gahagan, *The Negro Soldier: A Partial Record of Negro Devotion and Heroism in the Cause of Freedom, Gathered from the Files of the War and Navy Departments*, Washington, D.C., 1946.

Evans, William L., *Race Fear and Housing In a Typical American Community*, National Urban League, New York, 1946.

Ford, James W., *The War and the Negro People*, New York, 1942.

Hewes, Laurence I., Jr, and William Y. Bell, *Intergroup Relations in San Diego: Some Aspects of Community Life in San Diego Which Particularly Affect Minority Groups*, American Council on Race Relations, San Francisco, 1946.

Houser, George M., *Erasing the Color Line*, New York, 1945.

Imbert, Dennis I., *The Negro After the War*, New Orleans, 1943.

International Union, United Automobile, Aircraft and Agricultural Implement Workers of America, *To Unite . . . Regardless*, Detroit, n.d.

Johnson, Charles S., et al., *The Negro War Worker in San Francisco: A Local Self-Survey*, San Francisco, 1944.

Johnson, J. R., *Why Negroes Should Oppose the War*, New York, 1939 (?).

MacDonald, Dwight and Nancy MacDonald, *The War's Greatest Scandal: The Story of Jim Crow in Uniform*, MOWM, New York, n.d.

McWilliams, Carey, *Race Discrimination—and the Law*, National Federation for Constitutional Liberties, n.p., n.d.

National Association for the Advancement of Colored People, *Veterans Handbook*, New York, n.d.

National Committee on Segregation in the Nation's Capital, *Segregation in Washington*, Chicago, 1948.

National Negro Congress, *Negro Workers After the War*, New York, 1945.

National Urban League, *Victory Through Unity: Annual Conference, September 28–October 3, 1943*, Chicago, 1943.

National Urban League, *Racial Conflict: A Home Front Danger: Lessons of the Detroit Riot*, New York, 1943.

New York State War Council, Committee on Discrimination in Employment, *How Management Can Integrate Negroes in War Industries*, New York, 1942.

New York State War Council, Committee on Discrimination in Employment, *The Negro Integrated*, New York, 1945.

New York State Commission Against Discrimination, *The State of the Community*, New York, 1949.

Northrup, Herbert R., *Will Negroes Get Jobs Now?*, New York Public Affairs Committee Pamphlet 110, New York, 1945.

Perry, Pettis, *The Negro's Stake in This War*, San Francisco, 1942.

Randolph, A. Philip and Norman Thomas, *Victory's Victims: The Negro's Future*, New York 1943.

Rosenwald Fund, *Directory of Agencies in Race Relations: National, State, and Local*, Chicago, 1945.

Saunders, John and Albert Parker, *The Struggle For Negro Equality*, New York, 1943.

Stewart Maxwell, *The Negro in America*, New York Public Affairs Committee Pamphlet 95, New York, 1944.

Weaver, Robert C., *Hemmed In: ABCs of Race Restrictive Housing Covenants*, Chicago, 1945.

Weckler, J. E., and Theo E. Hall, *The Police and Minority Groups: A Program to Prevent Disorder and to Improve Relations between Different Racial Religions and National Groups*, Chicago, 1944.

Williams, John Henry, *A Negro Looks At War*, New York, 1940.

Wilson, Ruth Danenhower, *Jim Crow Joins Up: A Study of Negroes in the Armed Forces of the United States*, New York, 1944.

Wright, Richard R., *What the Negro Needs: A Post-war Plan to Integrate the Negro's Activities and Build Toward Full Social and Economical Security*, New York, 194– (?).

B. *Books*

Baruch, Dorothy W., *Glass House of Prejudice*, New York, 1946.

Bontemps, Arna and Jack Conroy, *They Seek a City*, Garden City, N.Y., 1945.

Brameld, Theodore, *Minority Problems in the Public Schools: A Study of Administrative Policies and Practices in Seven School Systems*, New York, 1946.

Brazeal, Brailsford R., *The Brotherhood of Sleeping Car Porters: its Origin and Development*, New York and London, 1946.

Brown, Ina Corinne, *Race Relations in a Democracy*, New York, 1949.

Chase, Stuart, *For This We Fought: Guide Lines to America's Future as Reported to the Twentieth Century Fund*, New York, 1946.

Clark, Evans, ed., *Wartime Facts and Postwar Problems: A Study and Discussion Manual*, Twentieth Century Fund, New York, 1943.

Clark, Tom C. and Philip B. Perlman, *Prejudice and Property: An Historic Brief Against Racial Covenants*, Washington, D.C., 1948.

Conrad, Earl, *Jim Crow America*, New York, 1947.

Davie, Maurice R., *Negroes in American Society*, New York, 1949.

Drake, St Clair and Horace R. Cayton, *Black Metropolis: A Study of Negro Life in a Northern City*, New York, 1944.

Embree, Edwin R. and Julia Waxman, *Investment in the People: The Story of the Julius Rosenwald Fund*, New York, 1949.

Embree, Edwin R., *Thirteen Against the Odds*, New York, 1944.

Embree, Edwin R., *Brown Americans: The Story of a Tenth of the Nation*, New York, 1944.

Ford, Nick Aaron, *The Contemporary Negro Novel: A Study in Race Relations*, Boston, 1936.

Furr, Arthur, *Democracy's Negroes*, Boston, 1947.

Gallagher, Buell G., *Color and Conscience: The Irrepressible Conflict*, New York and London, 1946.

Gardner, Burleigh B., *Human Relations in Industry*, Chicago, 1946.

Gloster, Hugh M., *Negro Voices in American Fiction*, New York, 1948.

Goodman, Jack, ed., *While You Were Gone: A Report on Wartime Life in the United States*, New York, 1946.

Grodzins, Morton, *Americans Betrayed: Politics and the Japanese Evacuation*, Chicago, 1949.

Guzman, Jessie Parkhurst, ed., *Negro Year Book: A Review of Events Affecting Negro Life, 1941–46*, Tuskegee, Ala., 1947.

Guzman, Jessie Parkhurst, ed., *Negro Year Book 1952: A Review of Events Affecting Negro Life*, New York, 1952.

Halsey, Margaret, *Some of My Best Friends*, Sydney, 1946.

Harris, Abram L., and Sterling D. Spero, *The Black Worker*, New York, 1931.

Haywood, Harry, *Negro Liberation*, New York, 1948.

Heywood, Chester D., *Negro Combat Troops in the World War: The Story of the 371st Infantry*, New York, 1928.

Johnson, Charles S., *Patterns of Negro Segregation*, London, 1944.

Johnson, Charles S., and associates, *Into the Mainstream: A Survey of Best Practices in Race Relations in the South*, Chapel Hill, N. Carolina, 1947.

Kesselman, Louis Coleridge, *The Social Politics of FEPC: A Study in Reform Pressure Movements*, Chapel Hill, N. Carolina, 1948.

Key, V. O., Jr, *Southern Politics in State and Nation*, New York, 1949.

Konvitz, Milton R., *The Constitution and Civil Rights*, New York, 1947.

Lee, Alfred McClung and Norman Humphrey, *Race Riot*, New York, 1943.

Little, Arthur W., *From Harlem to the Rhine: The Story of New York's Colored Volunteers*, New York, 1936.

Little, K. L., *Negroes in Britain: A Study of Race Relations in English Society*, London, 1947.

Logan, Rayford W., ed., *What the Negro Wants*, Chapel Hill, N. Carolina, 1944.

Logan, Rayford W., *The Negro and the Post-war World—A Primer*, Washington, D.C., 1945.

Logan, Spencer, *A Negro's Faith in America*, New York, 1946.

Long, Herman H. and Charles S. Johnson *People vs Property: Race Restrictive Covenants in Housing*, Nashville, Tenn., 1947.

McWilliams, Carey, *Brothers Under the Skin*, Boston, 1943.

Merrill, Francis E., *Social Problems in the Home Front: A Study of Wartime Influence*, New York and London, 1948.

Meyer, Agnes E., *Journey Through Chaos*, New York, 1944.

Moon, Bucklin, ed., *Primer for White Folks*, New York, 1945.

Moon, Bucklin, *The High Cost of Prejudice*, New York, 1947.

Moon, Henry Lee, *Balance of Power: The Negro Vote*, New York, 1949.

Murray, Florence, ed., *The Negro Handbook; 1942*, New York, 1942.

Murray, Florence, ed., *The Negro Handbook; 1944*, New York, 1944.

Murray, Florence, ed., *The Negro Handbook; 1946–47*, New York, 1947.

Myrdal, Gunnar, *An American Dilemma: The Negro Problem and Modern Democracy*, New York, 1944.

Noble, Peter, *The Negro in Films*, London, 1949.

Northrup, Herbert R., *Organized Labor and the Negro*, New York and London, 1944.

Odum, Howard Washington, *Race and Rumors of Race: Challenge to American Crisis*, Chapel Hill, N. Carolina, 1943.

Ogburn, William Fielding, ed., *American Society in Wartime*, Chicago, 1943.

Ottley, Roi, *New World A'Coming*, New York, 1943.

Ottley, Roi, *Black Odyssey: The Story of the Negro in America*, London, 1949.

Parker, Albert, *Negroes in the Post-war World*, New York, 1944.

Porter, James A., *Modern Negro Art*, New York, 1943.

Powell, Adam Clayton, Sr, *Riots and Ruins*, New York, 1945.

Powell, Adam Clayton, Jr, *Marching Blacks: An Interpretive History of the Rise of the Black Common Man*, New York, 1945.

Proceedings of the Writers Congress, Los Angeles 1943, Berkeley and Los Angeles, 1944.

Rose, Arnold M., *The Negro's Morale: Group Identification and Protest*, Minnesota, 1949.

Sandburg, Carl, *The Chicago Race Riots, July 1919*, New York, 1919.

Schermerhorn, R. A., *These Our People*, Boston, 1949.

Schoenfeld, Seymour J., *The Negro in the Armed Forces: His Value and Status—Past, Present and Potential*, Washington, D.C., 1945.

Scott, Emmett J., *Negro Migrations During the War*, New York, 1920.

Seaver, Edwin, ed., *Cross Section 1947: A Collection of New American Writing*, New York, 1947.

Silvera, John D., *The Negro in World War II*, New York, 1946.

Sprigle, Ray, *In the Land of Jim Crow*, New York, 1949.

Stegner, W. and Editors of *Look, One Nation*, Boston, 1945.

Sterner, Richard, *The Negro's Share: A Study of Income, Consumption, Housing and Public Assistance*, New York, 1943.

Stouffer, Samuel A., et al., *The American Soldier*, Princeton, 1949.

Thorp, Margaret Farrand, *America at the Movies*, London, 1946.

Watkins, Sylvestre C., ed., *Anthology of American Negro Literature*, New York, 1944.

Watson, Goodwin, *Action for Unity*, New York, 1947.

Watson, Goodwin, ed., *Civilian Morale*, New York, 1942.

Weaver, Robert C., *Negro Labor: A National Problem*, New York, 1946.

Weaver, Robert C., *The Negro Ghetto*, New York, 1948.

White, Walter Francis, *A Rising Wind*, Garden City, N.Y., 1945.

Willkie, Wendell L., *One World*, London, 1943.

Wright, Richard, *Twelve Million Black Voices: A Folk History of the Negro in the United States of America*, London, 1947.

C. *Articles*

Banner, Warren M., 'New York,' *Journal of Educational Sociology*, XVII, 5, January 1944.

Bolte, Charles G., 'He Fought For Freedom,' *Survey Graphic*, XXXVI, 1, January 1947.

Bond, Horace Mann, 'Should the Negro Care Who Wins the War?,' *Annals of the American Academy of Political and Social Science*, Vol 223, September 1942.

Bratt, Charles, 'Los Angeles,' *Journal of Educational Sociology*, XIX, 3, November 1945.

Brown, Earl, 'American Negroes and the War,' *Harpers*, April 1942.

Brown, Earl, 'The Negro Vote 1944: A Forecast,' *Harpers*, July 1944.

Buckler, Helen, 'The CORE Way,' *Survey Graphic*, XXXV, 2, February 1946.

Cayton, Horace R., 'The Negro's Challenge,' *The Nation*, July 3, 1943.

Cayton, Horace R., 'Fighting for White Folks?,' *The Nation*, September 26, 1942.

Clark, Kenneth B. and James Barker, 'The Zoot Effect in Personality: A Race Riot Participant,' *Journal of Abnormal and Social Psychology*, Vol 45, 1945.

Current Affairs, December 1942, 'The Colour Problem as the American Sees It.'

Dabney, Virginius, 'Nearer and Nearer the Precipice,' *Atlantic*, January 1943.

Davis, Michael M., 'What Color is Health?,' *Survey Graphic*, XXXVI, 2, January 1947.

Davis, Paul C., 'The Negro in the Armed Forces,' *Virginia Quarterly Review*, XXIV, 4, 1948.

Davis, Ralph N., 'The Negro Newspapers and the War,' *Sociology and Social Research*, XXVII, May–June 1943.

Dickins, Dorothy, 'Food Patterns of White and Negro Families, 1936–1948,' *Social Forces*, XXVII, May 1949.

Ford, Nick Aaron, 'What Negroes Are Fighting For,' *Vital Speeches*, IX, 8, February 1, 1943.

Fortune, XXV (entire issue), June 1942, 'The Negro's War.'

Frazier, E. Franklin, 'Ethnic and Minority Groups in Wartime with Special Reference to the Negro,' *American Journal of Sociology*, XLVII, 3, November 1942.

Gover, Mary, 'Negro Mortality: Course of Mortality from Specific Causes, 1920–1944,' *Public Health Reports*, Vol 63, 7, February 13, 1948.

Granger, Lester B., 'Racial Democracy—The Navy Way,' *Common Ground*, Winter 1947.

Graves, John Temple, 'The Southern Negro and the War Crisis,' *Virginia Quarterly Review*, XVIII, 4, Autumn 1942.

Hall, E. T., Jr, 'Race Prejudice and Negro-White Relations in the Army,' *American Journal of Sociology*, LII, 5, March 1947.

Hardwick, Leon H., 'Negro Stereotypes on the Screen,' *Hollywood Quarterly*, I, 2, January 1946.

Hastie, William H., 'The Negro in the Army Today,' *Annals of American Academy of Political and Social Science*, Vol 223, September 1942.

Haynes, George Edmund, 'Effects of War Conditions on Negro Labor,' *Proceedings of Academy of Political Science*, Vol 8, February 1919.

James, Joseph, 'San Francisco,' *Journal of Educational Sociology*, XIX, 3, November 1945.

Johnson, Charles S., 'The Negro,' *American Journal of Sociology*, Vol. 47, 6, May 1942.

Johnson, Charles S., 'The Present Status of Race Relations in the South,' *Social Forces*, XXIII, 1, 1944.

Johnson, Charles S., 'Social Changes and Their Effects on Race Relations in the South,' *Social Forces*, XXIII, 3, 1945.

Johnson, Howard, 'The Negro Veteran Fights for Freedom,' *Political Affairs,* Vol 26, May 1947.

Jones, Dorothy B., 'The Hollywood War Film: 1942–1944,' *Hollywood Quarterly*, I, 1, October 1945.

Jones, Lester M., 'The Editorial Policy of the Negro Newspapers of 1917–18 as compared with that of 1941–42,'*Journal of Negro History*, XXIX, 1, January 1944.

Liveright, A. A., 'The Community and Race Relations,' *Annals of American Academy of Political and Social Science*, Vol 244, March 1946.

MacDonald, Dwight, 'The Novel Case of Winfred Lynn,' *The Nation*, February 20, 1943.

MacLean, Malcolm S. and R. O'Hara Lanier, 'Negroes, Education, and the War,' *Educational Record*, XXIII, 1, January 1942.

McCann, John T. and Louis Kronenberger, 'Motion Pictures, the Theater, and Race Relations,' *Annals of American Academy of Political and Social Science*, Vol 224, March 1946.

Margolis, Herbert, 'The Hollywood Scene: The American Minority Problem,' *Penguin Film Review*, 5, 1948.

Martin, Louis E., 'Detroit,'*Journal of Educational Sociology*, XVII, 5, January 1944.

Milner, Lucille B., 'Jim Crow in the Army,' *New Republic*, Vol 110, 11, March 1944.

Murray, Florence, 'The Negro and Civil Liberties During World War II,' *Social Forces*, XXIV, 2, December 1945.

New Republic, October 18, 1943, 'The Negro: His Future in America' (entire issue).

Noble, Georg, 'The Negro in Hollywood,' *Sight and Sound*, Spring 1939.

Northrup, Herbert R., 'Organized Labor and Negro Workers,' *Journal of Political Economy*, LI, 3, June 1943.

Northrup, Herbert R., 'In the Unions,' *Survey Graphic*, XXXVI, 1, January 1947.

O'Brien, Robert W., 'Seattle,'*Journal of Educational Sociology*, XIX, 3, November 1945.

Powell, Adam Clayton, 'Is This A "White Man's War"?,' *Common Sense*, XI, 4, April 1942.

Randolph, A. Philip, 'Why Should We March?,' *Survey Graphic*, XXXI, 11, November 1942.

Reddick, Laurence D., ed., 'The Negro in the North During Wartime,'*Journal of Educational Sociology*, XVII, 5, 1944.

Reddick, Laurence D., ed., 'Race Relations on the Pacific Coast,' *Journal of Educational Sociology*, XIX, 3, 1945.

Reddick, Laurence D., 'The Negro in the US Navy in World War II,'*Journal of Negro History*, XXXII, April 1947.

Reed, Bernice Anita, 'Accommodation Between Negro and White Employees in a West Coast Aircraft Industry, 1942–44,' *Social Forces*, XXVI, 1, October 1947.

Rose, Arnold M., 'Army Policies Toward Negro Soldiers: A Report on a Success and a Failure,'*Journal of Social Issues*, III, 4, Fall 1947.

Sancton, Thomas, 'The Race Riots,' *New Republic*, July 5, 1943.

Sancton, Thomas, 'Something's Happened to the Negro,' *New Republic*, February 8, 1943.

Social Service Review, XVIII, 3, September 1944, 'The Winfred Lynn Case Again: Segregation In The Armed Forces.'

Survey Graphic, XXXI, 11, November 1942, 'Color: Unfinished Business of Democracy' (entire issue).

Survey Graphic, XXXVI, 1, January 1947, 'Segregation' (entire issue).

Weaver, Robert C., 'The Negro Veteran,' *Annals of the American Academy of Political and Social Science*, Vol 238, March 1945.

Williams, Philip F., 'Maternal Welfare and the Negro,' *Journal of the American Medical Association*, Vol 132, 11, November 16, 1946.

Wirth, Louis, 'Morale and Minority Groups,' *American Journal of Sociology*, Vol 47, 3, November 1941.

6. *Film Material*

'Army Ends Segregation: Korea,' Hearst Metrotone News 1951, Hearst Metrotone Library.

The Black Soldier, CBS 'Of America Series' 1968, Library of Congress.

'Brown Bomber on Tour Overseas,' Hearst Metrotone News 1944, Hearst Metrotone.

'Fighting Liberators Hailed,' Newsreel 1944, Sherman Grinberg.

Negro Colleges in Wartime, Office of War Information 1943, National Archives.

The Negro Soldier, War Department 1945, National Archives.

'Negro Troops in Clark's Army Rout Nazis in Italian Front,' Hearst metrotone News 1944, Hearst Metrotone.

One Tenth of Our Nation, American Film Center 1940, Museum of Modern Art.

Teamwork, War Department 1946, National Archives.

'The Twentieth Century: Integration in the Military,' CBS 1966, Library of Congress.

'Truman Urges New Action on Civil Rights,' Paramount News 1947, National Archives.

'The Vietnam War: Black and White,' ABC 'Scope' part 63, 1967, Library of Congress.

7. *Autobiographies and Reminiscences*

Anderson, Marian, *My Lord, What A Morning*, London, 1957.

Broonzy, William and Yannick Bruynoghe, *Big Bill Blues: William Broonzy's Story*, London, 1955.

Horne, Lena and Richard Schickel, *Lena*, London, 1966.

Louis, Joe, *My Life Story*, London, 1947.

Malcolm X, *Autobiography of Malcolm X*, New York, 1965.

Schuyler, George, *Black and Conservative: Autobiography of George S. Schuyler*, New Rochelle, N.Y., 1966.

Tarry, Ellen, *The Third Door: The Autobiography of an American Negro Woman*, London, 1956.

Truman, Harry S., *The Memoirs of Harry S. Truman*, two vols., London, 1955, 1956.

Waters, Ethel, *His Eye is on the Sparrow: An Autobiography*, London, 1951.

White, Walter, *A Man Called White: The Autobiography of Walter White*, New York, 1948.

Wright, Richard, *Black Boy: A Record of Childhood and Youth*, New York, 1945.

8. *Novels and Poetry*

Bynner, Witter, *Take Away the Darkness*, New York, 1947.

Carter, Hodding, *The Winds of Fear*, London, 1945.

Cozzens, James Gould, *Guard of Honour*, London, 1949.

Dodson, Owen, *Powerful Long Ladder*, New York, 1947.

Ellison, Ralph, *Invisible Man*, New York, 1952.

Fast, Howard, *Freedom Road*, London, 1945.

Himes, Chester, *If He Hollers Let Him Go*, Garden City, N.Y., 1945.

Hughes, Langston, *Fields of Wonder*, New York, 1947.

Hughes, Langston, *One-Way Ticket*, New York, 1949.

Hughes, Langston, *Selected Poems*, New York, 1957.

Hughes, Langston, *The Panther and the Lash: Poems of Our Times*, New York, 1971.

Killens, John Oliver, *And Then We Heard The Thunder*, London, 1964.

Kolb, Avery E., *Jigger Witchet's War*, New York, 1959.

Motley, Willard, *Knock On Any Door*, New York, 1947.

Petry, Ann, *The Street*, Boston, 1946.

Petry, Ann, *Country Place*, Boston, 1947.

Saxton, Alexander, *Bright Web in the Darkness*, Berlin, 1959.

Shute, Nevil, *The Chequer Board*, London, 1947.

Smith, Lillian, *Strange Fruit*, New York, 1944.

Smith, William Gardner, *The Last of the Conquerors*, London, 1949.

Williams, John, *Captain Blackman*, New York, 1972.

Wright, Richard, *Uncle Tom's Children*, New York, 1940.

Wright, Richard, *Native Son*, New York, 1940.

Yerby, Frank, *The Foxes of Harrow*, New York, 1946.

Yerby, Frank, *The Vixens*, New York, 1948.

9. *Selected Secondary Sources*

A. *Books*

Anderson, Jervis, *A. Philip Randolph: A Biographical Portrait*, New York, 1973.

Andreski, Stanislav, *Military Organization and Society*, London, 1954.

Ashmore, Harry S., *The Negro and the Schools*, Chapel Hill, N. Carolina, 1954.

Barbeau, Arthur E. and Florette Henri, *The Unknown Soldiers: Black American Troops in World War I*, Philadelphia 1974.

Becker, Gary S., *The Economics of Discrimination*, Chicago, 1957.

Berger, Monroe, *Equality by Statute: Legal Controls Over Group Discrimination*, New York, 1952.

Berman, William C., *The Politics of Civil Rights in the Truman Administration*, Columbus, Ohio, 1970.

Bloch, Herman D., *The Circle of Discrimination: An Economic and Social Study of the Black Man in New York*, New York and London, 1969.

Bogart, Leo, ed., *Social Research and the Desegregation of the US Army*, Chicago, 1969.

Bone, Robert, *The Negro Novel in America*, New Haven, Conn., 1966.

Bullock, Henry Allen, *A History of Negro Education in the South: From 1916 to the Present*, Cambridge, Mass., 1967.

Burns, W. Haywood, *The Voices of Negro Protest in America*, New York, 1963.

Butcher, Margaret Just, *The Negro in American Culture*, New York, 1956.

Cantril, Hadley, *Public Opinion, 1935–1946*, Princeton, N.J., 1951.

Chambers, M. M., *The Colleges and the Courts 1946–50: Judicial Decisions Regarding Higher Education in the United States*, New York, 1952.

Charters, Samuel B., *The Country Blues*, London, 1960.

Clark, Thomas D. and Albert D. Kirwan, *The South since Appomattox: A Century of Regional Change*, New York, 1967.

Coffman, Edward M., *The War To End All Wars: The American Military Experience in World War I*, New York, 1968.

Dalfiume, Richard M., *Desegregation of the US Armed Forces: Fighting on Two Fronts, 1939–1953*, Columbia, Mo., 1969.

Davies, Richard O., *Housing Reform During the Truman Administration*, Columbia, Mo., 1966.

Duncan, Otis Dudley and Beverly Duncan, *The Negro Population of Chicago: A Study of Residential Succession*, Chicago, 1957.

Ellison, Ralph, *Shadow and Act*, New York, 1964.

Emanuel, James A., *Langston Hughes*, New York, 1967.

Ferman, Louis A., *The Negro and Equal Employment Opportunities: A Review of Management Experiences in Twenty Companies*, New York, 1968.

Franklin, John Hope, *From Slavery to Freedom: A History of Negro Americans*, New York, 3rd ed. 1969.

Garfinkel, Herbert, *When Negroes March: The March on Washington Movement in the Organizational Politics of FEPC*, New York, 1969 ed.

Glazer, Nathan and Davis McEntire, eds., *Studies in Housing and Minority Groups*, Berkeley and Los Angeles, 1960.

Green, Constance McLaughlin, *The Secret City: A History of Race Relations in the Nation's Capital*, Princeton, N.J., 1967.

Grodzins, Morton, *The Metropolitan Area as a Racial Problem*, Pittsburgh, 1960.

Hughes, Carl Milton, *The Negro Novelist: A Discussion of the Writings of American Negro Novelists, 1940–1950*, New York, 1970 ed.

Hughes, Langston, *Fight For Freedom: The Story of the NAACP*, New York, 1962.

Isaacs, Harold, *The New World of Negro Americans*, London, 1964.

Jacobson, Julius, ed., *The Negro and the American Labor Movement*, Garden City, N.Y., 1968.

Jerome, V. J., *The Negro in Hollywood Films*, New York, 1950.

Jones, Leroi, *Blues People: Negro Music in White America*, London, 1965.

Keil, Charles, *Urban Blues*, Chicago and London, 1966.

Kirkendall, R. S., *The United States, 1919–1945*, New York, 1974.

Krislov, Samuel, *The Negro in Federal Employment: The Quest for Equal Employment*, Minneapolis, 1967.

Leadbitter, Mike and Neil Slaven, *Blues Records, January 1943 to December 1966*, London, 1968.

Lewis, Anthony, *The Second American Revolution: A First-hand Account of the Struggle for Civil Rights*, London, 1966.

Lingeman, Richard R., *Don't You Know There's A War On? The American Home Front, 1941–1945*, New York, 1970.

Little, Roger W., ed., *Selective Service and American Society*, New York, 1969.

Lomax, Louis, *The Negro Revolt*, London, 1963.

McCoy, Donald R. and Richard T. Ruetten, *Quest and Response: Minority Rights and the Truman Administration*, Kansas, 1973.

McEntire, Davis, *Residence and Race: Final and Comprehensive Report to the Commission on Race and Housing*, Berkeley and Los Angeles, 1960.

Mandelbaum, David G., *Soldier Groups and Negro Soldiers*, London, 1952.

Marshall, Ray, *The Negro and Organized Labor*, New York, 1965.

Marwick, Arthur, *War and Social Change in the Twentieth Century*, London, 1974.

Meier, August and Elliott Rudwick, *CORE: A Study in the Civil Rights Movement 1942–1968*, New York, 1973.

Mullen, Robert W., *Blacks in America's Wars*, New York, 1973.

Nelson, Keith L., *The Impact of War on American Life: The Twentieth Century Experience*, New York, 1971.

Nichols, Lee, *Breakthrough on the Color Front*, New York, 1954.

Norgren, Paul H. and Samuel E. Hill, *Toward Fair Employment,* New York and London, 1964.

Northrup, Herbert R., et al., *Negro Employment in Basic Industry: A Study of Racial Practices in Six Industries,* Philadelphia, 1970.

Oliver, Paul, *Blues Fell This Morning*, London, 1960.

Perrett, Geoffrey, *Days of Sadness, Years of Triumph: The American People, 1939–1945*, New York, 1973.

Polenberg, Richard, ed., *America at War: The Home Front 1941–1945*, Englewood Cliffs, N.J., 1968.

Polenberg, Richard, *War and Society: The United States, 1941–1945*, New York, 1972,

Record, Wilson, *Race and Radicalism: The NAACP and the Communist Party*, New York, 1964.

Reitzes, Dietrich C., *Negroes and Medicine*, Cambridge, Mass., 1958.

Ross, Davis R. B., *Preparing for Ulysses: Politics and Veterans During World War II*, New York and London, 1969.

Ruchames, Louis, *Race, Jobs, and Politics: The Story of FEPC*, New York and London, 1969.

Schwartz, Mildred A., *Trends in White Attitudes Toward Negroes*, Chicago, 1967.

Shogan, Robert and Tom Craig, *The Detroit Race Riot: A Study in Violence*, New York, 1964.

Sindler, Allan P., ed., *Change in the Contemporary South*, Durham, N. Carolina, 1963.

Southern, Eileen, *The Music of Black Americans: A History*, New York, 1971.

Staupers, Mabel Keaton, *No Time For Prejudice: A Story of Integration of Negroes in Nursing in the United States*, New York, 1961.

Sternsher, Bernard, ed., *The Negro in Depression and War: Prelude to Revolution, 1930–1945*, Chicago, 1969.

Taeuber, Karl E. and Alma F. Taeuber, *Negroes in Cities: Residential Segregation and Neighborhood Change*, Chicago, 1966.

Vose, Clement E., *Caucasians Only: The Supreme Court, the NAACP, and the Restrictive Covenant Cases*, Berkeley and Los Angeles, 1959.

Waskow, Arthur I., *From Race Riot to Sit-In: 1919 and the 1960s*, New York, 1967.

Weiss, Nancy J., *The National Urban League 1910–1940*, New York, 1974.

White, Walter, *How Far the Promised Land?*, New York, 1956.

Wolters, Raymond, *Negroes and the Great Depression: The Problem of Economic Recovery*, Westport, Conn., 1970.

B. *Articles*

Billington, Monroe, 'Freedom to Serve: The President's Committee on Equality of Treatment and Opportunity in the Armed Forces, 1949–1950,' *Journal of Negro History*, LI, 4, October 1966.

Cowgill, Donald O., 'Trends in Residential Segregation of Non-whites in American Cities, 1940–50,' *American Sociological Review*, XXI, 1, February 1956.

Cripps, Thomas R., 'The Death of Rastus: Negroes in American Films Since 1945,' *Phylon*, XXVIII, 3, 1967.

Cripps, Thomas R., 'Movies in the Ghetto, BP (Before Poitier),' *Negro Digest*, XVIII, 4, February 1969.

Dalfiume, Richard M., 'The Fahy Committee and Desegregation of the Armed Forces,' *The Historian*, XXXI, 1, November 1968.

Dalfiume, Richard M., 'The "Forgotten Years" of the Negro Revolution,' *Journal of American History*, LV, 1, June 1968.

Drake, St Clair, 'The "Colour Problem" in Britain: A Study in Social Definitions,' *Sociological Review*, 3, 1956.

Farley, Reynolds, 'The Urbanization of Negroes in the United States,' *Journal of Social History*, I, Spring 1968.

Finkle, Lee, 'The Conservative Aims of Militant Rhetoric: Black Protest During World War II,' *Journal of American History*, LX, 3, December 1973.

Hachey, Thomas E., 'Jim Crow With A British Accent: Attitudes of London Government Officials Toward American Negro Soldiers in England During World War II.' *Journal of Negro History*, LIX, 1, January 1974.

Lieberson, Stanley and Arnold R. Silverman, 'The Precipitants and Underlying Conditions of Race Riots,' *American Sociological Review*, XXX, 6, December 1965.

Meier, August and Elliott Rudwick, 'How CORE Began,' *Social Science Quarterly*, Vol 49, 4, March 1969.

Moskos, Charles C., 'Racial Integration in the Armed Forces.' *American Journal of Sociology*, Vol 72, 2, September 1966.

Scheiber, Jane Lang and Harry N. Scheiber, 'The Wilson Administration and the Wartime Mobilization of Black Americans, 1917–18,' *Labor History*, X, 3, 1969.

Sitkoff, Harvard, 'The Detroit Race Riot of 1943,' *Michigan History*, LIII, 3, 1969.

Sitkoff, Harvard, 'Racial Militancy and Interracial Violence in the Second World War,' *Journal of American History*, LVIII, 3, December 1971.

Smith, T. Lynn, 'The Redistribution of the Negro Population of the United States, 1910–1960,' *Journal of Negro History*, LI, 3, July 1966.

Weaver, Robert C., 'Negro Labor Since 1929,' *Journal of Negro History*, XXXV, 1, January 1950.

Weaver, Robert C., 'Non-white Population Movements and Urban Ghettos,' *Phylon*, XX, 3, 1959.

Williams, Robin M., 'Social Change and Social Conflict: Race Relations in the United States, 1944–1964,' *Sociological Inquiry*, XXXV, 1, 1965.

Winkler, Allen M., 'The Philadelphia Transit Strike of 1944,' *Journal of American History*, LIX, 2, 1972.

Wynn, Neil A., 'The Impact of the Second World War on the American Negro,' *Journal of Contemporary History*, VI, 2, 1971.

Wynn, Neil A., 'Black Attitudes Toward Participation in the American War Effort, 1941–1945,' *Afro-American Studies*, III, 1, June 1972.

C. *Unpublished Theses and Essays*

Barresi, Charles Maboio, 'Residential Invasion and Succession: A Case Study,' MA thesis, SUNY at Buffalo, 1959.

Lawrence, Charles Radford, 'Negro Organizations in Crisis: Depression, New Deal, World War II,' PhD dissertation, Columbia University, 1952.

Pines, Jim, 'Blacks in the Cinema: The Changing Image,' Education Department, British Film Institute, June 1971.

Wynn, Neil A., 'The Afro-American and the Second World War,' PhD dissertation, The Open University, England, 1973.

Index